FAITH FOR THE FUTURE

You are unique

There has never been anyone the same as
you... and there never will be again.
Each individual's finger print, ear print, DNA,
is theirs alone. It is not shared by
anyone else.
Although distinct and different, we share a
common bond with every other human
being.
The common bond that unites
us is that we are made in
the image of God.

FAITH FOR THE FUTURE

An illustrated catechism
of Catholic belief in words and
pictures

A REDEMPTORIST PUBLICATION

FAITH FOR THE FUTURE

Published by
Redemptorist Publications

Text by Mares Walter
Additional material Rosemary Gallagher, Steve Givens, John Trenchard, Timothy Buckley.
Design: Roger Smith   Cover: Wayne Theisinger

First Published   September 1997
Fourth Printing   November 2001 (26th thousand)

ISBN 0 85231 167 2

Nihil Obstat:
Canon Cyril Murtagh, M.A., S.T.L.
Censor Deputatus

Imprimatur: + Crispian Hollis
Episcopus Portus Magni
Portus Magni August 1997

Photographs:The Image Bank: Cover. Pages: 4, 5, 10, 11, 18, 20, 21, 22, 23, 25, 28, 30, 34, 37, 42, 43, 47, 53, 55, 56, 60, 61, 62, 63, 64, 65, 70, 71, 76, 77, 96, 97, 98, 107, 110, 111, 130, 131, 132, 133, 134, 135, 138, 139, 146, 149, 151, 152, 153, 158, 159, 160, 161, 168, 169, 174. Zefa/Stockmarket: Pages 14, 16, 17, 32, 33, 40, 86, 87, 101, 106, 109, 112, 113, 114, 140, 141. Britstock: Page 42. Robert Harding: Pages 36, 115, 126, 127, 150, 166, 167. Superstock: Pages: 4, 5, 6, 8, 14, 15, 18, 19, 24, 25, 33, 36, 39, 41, 44, 45, 52, 53, 54, 55, 58, 59, 60, 61, 82, 83, 92, 106, 107, 124, 125, 128, 129, 156, 157. Photographers Library: Page:119. National Gallery: Pages 48, 49. Science Photo Library: Pages 46, 47. David Toase: Pages 35, 43, 57, 63, 69, 78, 85, 88, 94, 95, 100, 102, 104, 106, 108, 110, 120, 121, 136, 137, 144, 147, 148, 154, 159, 176, 177, 190, 192, 197, 198. Jesus Mafa: Page 68. Alex Gillespie: Pages: 77, 164 David Alexander: Pages: 79, 145, 157. Ron Gregory: Pages: 81, 155. Viktor Laszlo: Pages: 85, 166. Ymson: Page 91, 186. Michael Henesy: Pages: 9, 93, 99, 119. John Howard: Pages: 131,170. S.A.Rotheray: Page 165. Photodiscs: Pages 5, 16, 17, 19, 33, 38, 40, 58, 61, 72, 73, 90, 91, 116, 118, 119, 120, 161, 179, 182. British Museum: Pages 26, 28. Joan Brown SND: Pages 185.

Printed in the United States by R R Donnelley.

Redemptorist
P U B L I C A T I O N S
Alphonsus House Chawton Hampshire GU34 3HQ
Telephone 01420 88222   Fax 01420 88805
email: rp@redempt.org   web: http://www.redempt.org

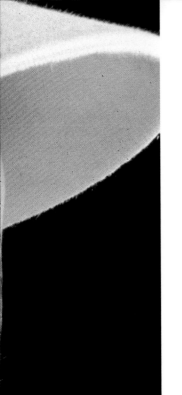

What does that mean for you ... for each of us today? Where did I come from? What am I doing here? Where am I going?

A baby stares. It seems to have eyes only for the outside world, upon which it fixes its gaze.

It is not long, of course, before baby is told that "it is rude to stare". But that is not really the reason why the baby stops staring. The truth is that as children begin to take in the outside world they become more aware, too, of themselves. Eyes which used to be wide open and blank become alive with personality. A deepening consciousness of the world around leads to deeper consciousness of self.

The experiences which each of us take in vary so much. They are mirrored in our different interests and concerns. But the *ultimate* reflection remains the same: it is the reflection that we see written in every pair of eyes that are alive and seeing. It is the reflection that every one of us makes at some moment in life, although more intensely at some moments than others. It is the reflection: "Who am I?"

We want to know. The questions are almost instinctive: "Where did I come from?… What am I doing?… Where am I going?…" But although every sane person who ever lived has asked these questions in some form, the answers seem elusive. Still, men and women wonder.

All the great religions of the past grew out of these questions. Hinduism, for example, sees life as a search for salvation through "release" from the round of birth, death and re-birth. Like Buddhism and many religions far more ancient than Christianity, it exalts the qualities of wisdom and kindness. But it tries to answer our fundamental questions without looking at the true source of life.

This, however, was not the way of the Jewish Faith. "The eyes of all creatures look to you, O Lord", was the cry of the Hebrew Psalmist. And indeed all the Psalms, which we still pray during every Mass, focus our attention on God. The life of every Jew, like the life of the Jewish nation, was directed to God as the source of fulfilment.

This, we might say, was the difference in the ancient world between the Jews and other peoples. Others tried to answer their deepest questioning by looking at the world around them or at false gods; the Jews were led to realise that it could only be answered by looking at the living God.

In the modern world this remains the difference between Christians and those who ignore God. Some non-Christians achieve astonishing success in their search for answers to men and women's questions. But many flounder. The multiplication of all kinds of strange beliefs prove the correctness of Chesterton's remark that "when people stop believing in God they don't believe in nothing; they believe in anything."

faith for the future **begins with God. For we believe that it is only by looking at God as he has shown himself to us that we can begin to answer our deepest questions: Where did I come from?… What am I doing?… Where am I going?**

Part 1: The faith of the Church

Part 2: Celebrating the presence of Christ

Part 3: Life in Christ

Part 4: Prayer

Part 1
The faith
of the Church

The Church Teaches

"A man was sitting on a bus when he overheard a conversation between a couple of housewives in front of him. They were discussing the horrors of the world and all the terrible things that were happening. After a while one of the women paused, looked out of the window and then turned to the other and said, 'You know, dear, I think the best thing is just to be philosophical and not think about it'."

In contrast to our friend on the bus, the Church has always tried to encourage people to 'think about it', to think about everything that really matters: why we are here, why we believe what we do, why we act the way we do. The Church has also tried its best to 'think about it', and the fruits of centuries of thought are passed down to us in its teachings and traditions. Together with the Church, each individual is invited to 'think along', to join in the excitement of trying to understand the faith that we profess.

"What we have seen and heard we are telling you so that you too may be in union with us, as we are in union with the Father and with his Son Jesus Christ." (1 John 1:3) In his first letter, Saint John focuses our attention on the main concern of the catechesis of the primitive Church: the proclamation of the Word of God. The early catechists were spurred on in their work by the memory of Pentecost Day when the disciples were filled with the Holy Spirit and began to speak in every language of "the wonderful works of God" (Acts 2:11). In the first centuries of the Church's life this same joyful faith was transmitted by a spoken explanation of the Creed, which as the works of the early Fathers of the Church show, was rooted firmly in the Scriptures and enlivened with examples taken from everyday life.

What's in a word – Catechism
The word 'catechism' comes from the Greek word 'catecheo' which simply means to teach or inform. Originally 'catechism' just meant the teaching given to candidates for baptism, but later it took on a wider meaning and included the more general instruction of everyone in the Church.

Martin Luther was the first to use the invention of printing for religious instruction in the form of a catechism. Its appearance in 1529 did much to strengthen the Protestant movement and led in 1530 to a Catholic response in the form of Augsburg Catechism. This was followed by a series of counter-reformation catechisms which proved a major factor in safeguarding the purity of doctrine.

From the Early Church to the present day, many local churches have produced catechisms for their own use — in Britain a very popular one was the 'Penny Catechism' which was first issued in 1898. It was set out as a series of questions and answers and began with '**Who made me?**' Answer: '**God made me.**'

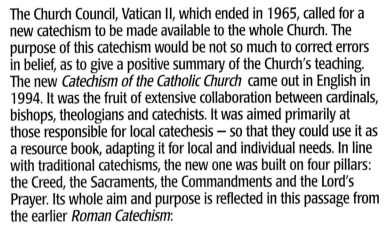

The Church Council, Vatican II, which ended in 1965, called for a new catechism to be made available to the whole Church. The purpose of this catechism would be not so much to correct errors in belief, as to give a positive summary of the Church's teaching. The new *Catechism of the Catholic Church* came out in English in 1994. It was the fruit of extensive collaboration between cardinals, bishops, theologians and catechists. It was aimed primarily at those responsible for local catechesis — so that they could use it as a resource book, adapting it for local and individual needs. In line with traditional catechisms, the new one was built on four pillars: the Creed, the Sacraments, the Commandments and the Lord's Prayer. Its whole aim and purpose is reflected in this passage from the earlier *Roman Catechism*:

The whole concern of doctrine and its teaching must be directed to the love that never ends. Whether something is proposed for belief, for hope or for action, the love of our Lord must always be made accessible, so that anyone can see that all the works of perfect Christian virtue spring from love and have no other objective than to arrive at love.
(Roman Catechism, Preface 10)

Those preparing to enter the Early Church were known as 'catechumens' and their instruction usually lasted about three years. When someone expressed a desire to become a Christian they first had to show that they were sincere and lived a good life. At this point they were known simply as 'audientes' or 'hearers' because they were only allowed to listen to the early part of the Mass and had to leave after the sermon. Even when they moved up the ranks to become proper catechumens, they were still only allowed to attend the liturgy of the word (the readings and the sermon) and were totally excluded from the eucharistic liturgy. They were only included when they were finally baptised two years later on the vigil Mass of Easter Sunday.

Today, a similar process is followed for those wishing to enter the Church. It is known as the Rite of Christian Initiation for Adults (RCIA for short).

Our search for God

(Catechism of the Catholic Church 27-43)

"And this world is in a ferment of seeking God without knowing that there be a God."

Conrad Pepler OP

The world is full of all sorts of different religions and faiths. We may find some of these religions more to our taste than others, but all have one thing in common – all reflect a need or a desire to find some sort of meaning in life. A human being is fundamentally a religious being, with a built-in need for God. Most of the different religions and faiths of the world do, in their own way, express this deep desire for God. Vatican II acknowledged this fact when it spoke of the relationship between the Church and other religions:

Part of the search for God involves asking whether or not he exists in the first place, and if he does, then what is he like? These questions have been debated for centuries by Christians and non-Christians alike. Broadly speaking, there are two main arguments in favour of God's existence.

1 We know that God exists because the world would not exist without something or someone that made it exist. There must have been something that created the universe in the first place. Saint Augustine puts this argument in a much more poetic way:

"Question the beauty of the earth, question the beauty of the sea, question the beauty of the air distending and diffusing itself, question the beauty of the sky...question all these realities. All respond: "See we are beautiful!" Their beauty is a profession. These beauties are subject to change. Who made them if not the Beautiful One who is not subject to change?"

"The Catholic Church rejects nothing of what is true and holy in these religions. She has a high regard for the manner of life and conduct, the precepts and doctrines which, although differing in many ways from her own teaching, nevertheless often reflect a ray of that truth which enlightens all. Yet she proclaims and is in duty bound to proclaim without fail, Christ who is the way, the truth and the life (John 14:6). In him, in whom God reconciled all things to himself (2 Corinthians 5:18-19), we find the fullness of their religious life."
Vatican II Nostra Aetate, 28 October 1965

2 We know that God exists because we can see in ourselves signs of a spiritual awareness. This points to our souls, the 'seeds of eternity' that we bear within us, whose origin lies in God.

These arguments have been discussed for centuries, and have been accepted and rejected by many different philosophers and theologians. In the end they are only aids to faith – the whole of Catholic doctrine does not stand or fall on whether or not we find these arguments convincing. Some may find them helpful, others may not. What they may do is help us to see that our faith need not be opposed to our intellect or our reason. We can still be 'scientific' and believe in God.

Although we can see God in the beauty of creation and in the love and goodness of a human person, we are still hard put to try and describe what God is like. This is not surprising because, while human beings are 'made in the image of God', we cannot say that God is made in our image. God transcends the world so that all of creation is only a pale reflection of what he really is. Because of this it is hard for us to speak accurately about God or describe him clearly. It is like the Chinese philosophers who said, "He who knows Tao does not talk about it. He who talks about it does not know Tao." We cannot with any certainty say what God is like – though we can say clearly what God is not like. God is not evil, God is not unkind. These sorts of things we can say clearly. It is for this reason that the theologian St Thomas Aquinas said, "Concerning God, we cannot grasp what he is, but only what he is not."

God's search for us

(Catechism of the Catholic Church 51-133)

So far we have seen that everyone can come to know God. Most religions and faiths express some sort of an awareness of God. All of us have a capacity for God written into our very being because God has made us for himself and given us a thirsting and a yearning for him. But the story does not end there; sadly the easy intimacy which first existed between God and humanity was shattered by original sin. Sin entered the world and crippled the whole of humanity. Our sight of God is often obscured; our own fears and cares can lead us away from him. We come face to face with God and we do not recognise him, or if we do, we run from his love like the wretch in Francis Thompson's poem, 'The Hound of Heaven':

'I fled Him, down the nights and down the days;
I fled Him, down the arches of the years;
I fled Him, down the labyrinthine ways
Of my own mind; and in the mist of tears
I hid from Him..."

Crippled by sin, we are unable to find our way easily to God. Not only can sin lead us to reject God's love, but it can also blind and confuse us, so that when we search for God, we cannot be completely certain when we have found him. Thankfully, the story does not end there, either, because God comes to find us...

'Revelation' is the word used to describe how God shows himself to us. God can reveal himself to us in a huge variety of ways, but the primary way we can come to know God is through the scriptures and the Church.

St Thomas Aquinas, writing in the twelfth century, gives three reasons why we need revelation:

- So that we can reach a knowledge of God quickly;
- So that those of us who do not have the time or the ability to find God easily can still be sure of finding him;
- So that everyone can come to a knowledge of God free of doubt and uncertainty. If God tells us himself, we can know for sure that it is true, because God cannot lie.

"We can't be sure of anything!"

"Are you sure about that?"

"Of course I'm sure!"

Throughout history various people have had a number of 'private' revelations, some of which have been recognised by the Church. These cannot improve or complete the revelation of Christ, but they can help people to live more fully by it.

Mother Julian was a recluse who lived in Norwich in the fourteenth century. After a serious illness she had a series of sixteen visions which she wrote down in a book called 'Revelations of Divine Love'. Here is an extract from her book:

It was at this time that our Lord showed me spiritually how intimately he loves us. I saw that he is everything that we know to be good and helpful. In his love he clothes us, enfolds and embraces us; that tender love completely surrounds us, never to leave us. As I saw it he is everything that is good.

And he showed me more, a little thing, the size of a hazelnut, on the palm of my hand, round like a ball. I looked at it thoughtfully and wondered, 'What is this?' and the answer came, 'It is all that is made.' I marvelled that it continued to exist and did not suddenly disintegrate; it was so small. And again my mind supplied the answer, 'It exists, both now and for ever, because God loves it.' In short, everything owes its existence to the love of God.

(Julian of Norwich, Revelations of Divine Love, Chapter 5)

God has revealed himself to humanity through the writings of the Old Testament which culminate in the person and mission of Jesus Christ. Because Jesus is God, we can know God fully through knowing Jesus. We can know what God is like by seeing what Jesus is like. Jesus is the full revelation of God – this means that apart from Jesus we do not need any further revelation. Jesus is the most complete revelation of God because he is God. This is why Christianity believes that it is the truest religion, that it has a more perfect way to God: it is a religion based on the words, and guided by the Spirit, of God.

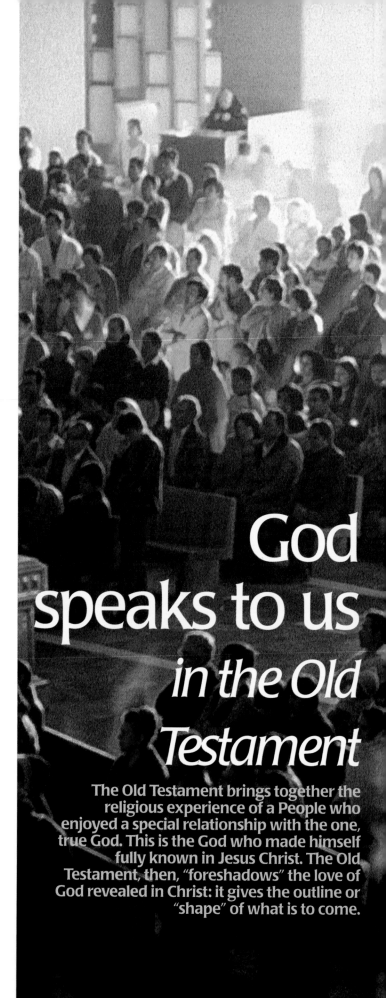

Why do Christians read the Old Testament?
Christians read the Old Testament because it's a record of a people who reflect on their experience of the one true God. Other nations knew the 'gods' of nature. The Jews were led to recognise ever more deeply their unique relationship with God and to express this relationship in every aspect of their national, social and family life. In the first instance, this awareness of God's love was passed on by word of mouth.
What had been passed on by word of mouth came to be recorded in written form, inspired by God, to make up the substance of the Old Testament which existed in the lifetime of Christ and which we know today. These writings reflect every aspect of a People who enjoy a unique relationship with God: their history, their laws, their social customs, their folklore, their poetry and above all their worship.

God reveals himself

If we try to pinpoint one single event in the Old Testament when God most clearly revealed his true character to the Jewish People, we would have to choose the Exodus from slavery in Egypt. However, to isolate this moment in such a way might be misleading. The truth is that the Jewish awareness of God deepened and developed over many centuries as God revealed himself more fully. This revelation is recorded in the Old Testament.

A history of Salvation

It's important, then, to understand what kind of history the Old Testament is. It's the history of a unique relationship between God and his People: something that can never be recorded in the clinical language of the modern historian. The Bible has only one purpose and one alone: it tells us of the deepening relationship between God and men and women – the single most significant process of history since creation itself.
In a word, the Old Testament is a history of salvation.

God speaks to us *in the Old Testament*

The Old Testament brings together the religious experience of a People who enjoyed a special relationship with the one, true God. This is the God who made himself fully known in Jesus Christ. The Old Testament, then, "foreshadows" the love of God revealed in Christ: it gives the outline or "shape" of what is to come.

What are the most important texts of the Old Testament?

The most important texts of the Old Testament are the first five books which make up the Torah or Pentateuch. In our own reading and in the Church's liturgy, this forms the starting point of our look at the Old Testament. The Pentateuch outlines:

1. How God chose Israel to be his own people, beginning with his promise to Abraham to make him the "father of a multitude of nations… and his descendants as many as the stars of heaven".

(Genesis 17:5; 22:17)

2. How God makes a covenant with the Jews to make them the channel of his mercy if they keep the laws he gives them. And so to Moses, the dominant figure of the Pentateuch and the whole Old Testament, God says, "I will adopt you as my own people and I will be your God."

(Exodus 6:7)

3. How God gave the Law to Israel as the most direct revelation of his will. This is symbolised in the tradition that the Ten Commandments were originally inscribed by God on two tablets of stone.

The Book

From the earliest times the Jewish faith revolved around a book. The reading of the Scriptures was the highlight of the synagogue service. This service began by the reciting of the creed of Judaism and some prayers, after which the Rabbi said a few words. But then – and this was why the people came – the Scriptures were read. The Jews are indeed the People of the Book. Wherever they find themselves they take the book of the Scriptures.

An intense awareness of God's presence is usually a once in a lifetime experience. For most of us it probably isn't even that. In this life we are simply not ready to look God in the face – we are safer living in the world of "faith" rather than "visions". This is the world even Christ's closest followers have always lived in. But for three of the Apostles, Peter, James and John, the once in a lifetime experience came after they had been "led up a high mountain" by Jesus. In this most mysterious event, "Jesus was transfigured: his face shone like the sun and his clothes became as white as the light. Suddenly Moses and Elijah appeared to them; they were talking with him." Why should Moses and Elijah appear with Jesus? There are two principal reasons. Firstly, Moses and Elijah represent the two major sections of the Old Testament – the Law and the Prophets. And secondly, Moses and Elijah themselves both enjoyed an intense awareness of God on another mountain – Mount Sinai.

Moses' experience of God's presence is closely linked with his role as "lawgiver". As he came down from Mount Sinai with "the two tablets of the Testimony in his hands… the skin of his face was radiant after speaking with Yahweh" (Exodus 34:29). This could be said to be the central event of the first five books of the Old Testament. And these five books are the centre of the Old Testament.

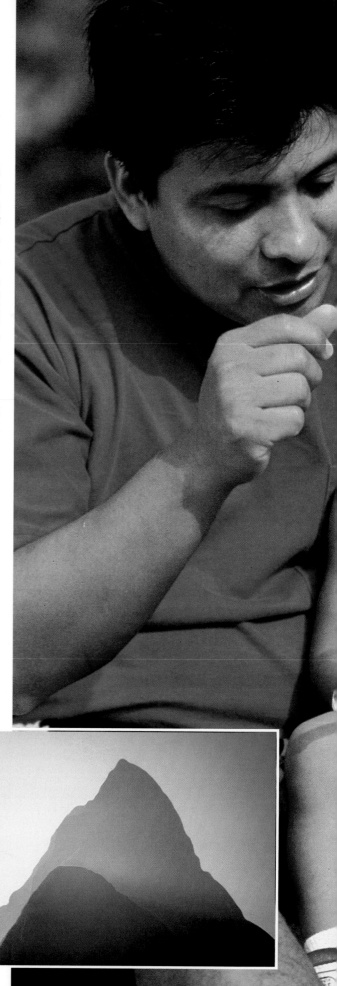

There are several titles for the most important texts of the Old Testament. The principal ones are:

Torah: This Jewish title is best translated as "teaching" or "instruction".

The Law. This title comes from the third century BC Greek translation of the scriptures, known as the *Septuagint.*

Five-fifths of the Law: A title which emphasises its importance in Jewish belief.

Pentateuch: A word which comes from two Greek words meaning five scrolls.

This "centre" of the Jewish religion was, according to tradition, written by Moses himself thirteen hundred years before Christ. Research in more recent times has shown that Moses could only have been responsible for the nucleus of what we now know as the Pentateuch – a single, massive but unified work which probably didn't reach the form in which we know it today until eight or nine hundred years after Moses' death. But this does not in any way diminish his stature. His experience of God became the inspiration for the Jewish People of every generation to come. As the final words of the Pentateuch tell us, since his death, "never has there been such a prophet in Israel as Moses, the man Yahweh knew face to face". (Deuteronomy 34:10)

Moses' talking with God on Mount Sinai and his talking with Jesus Christ at the transfiguration show the closeness of the Old and the New Testaments. As we try to put together the pieces of both Testaments to form an overall picture, we cannot do better in the first instance than concentrate on the faces of Moses for the Old Testament and Jesus for the New. Those faces give us a clear vision of God.

God speaks to us
in Jesus Christ

The face of Jesus shows us God himself. One of his disciples said to Jesus: "Lord, let us see the Father and then we shall be satisfied." And Jesus replied: "To have seen me is to have seen the Father."
(John 14:9)

The words and life of Jesus will be looked at throughout "Faith for the Future". Jesus is the centre of our faith. He is not simply an historical figure. He still lives. God speaks in Jesus Christ today. He does this through his followers formed in the Scriptures and in the tradition of the Church. Jesus left his words and deeds not only in the form of the written tradition of the Gospels and the writings of the New Testament, but also in the oral tradition, the life and faith of the Church which he founded. Both the Scriptures and tradition are inspired by the Holy Spirit. The New Testament writings grew out of the oral traditions of the Church and were interpreted by the Church.

The New Testament

After his death and resurrection the Good News of Jesus Christ wasn't initially recorded in writing at all. It was thirty years or more before the first of the Gospels was written in the form that we know them today. This doesn't mean that the first disciples of Jesus didn't read the Scriptures. The first Christians were Jews. They had been brought up to love and revere the word of God. It was hardly likely, then, that these first disciples would leave the precious Scriptures behind them. And they did not. When the synagogue doors were closed to them, they took the Scriptures with them. Undoubtedly the Old Testament was read at all Christian services – it was the sacred book of the early Church. But there is an important question which needs to be answered. Why did it take thirty-five years before anyone felt the need for a book about Jesus Christ?

The Apostles

One simple reason was this. As long as the Apostles were still alive there was less need of a written book. The Apostles had lived with Christ, they had known him intimately. They had seen him live, die and rise from the dead. As William Barclay graphically puts it in his book, *Introducing the Bible:* "The Apostles and their immediate associates were the living books on which the Christian message was written. They were the eyewitnesses, and so long as they lived, books were not necessary."

There were other reasons, too

1. The age in which the first Christians lived was primarily a non-literary one. Printing was a long way off.
2. A single sheet of papyrus cost more than a man's daily wage.
3. The first Christians were, for the most part, poor and uncultured. They could not read.
4. The Jews, like most of their contemporaries, preferred to commit knowledge to memory rather than write it down.

Birth of the New Testament

How, then, did the New Testament come to be? We do not have to look far beyond our own experience for the answer. The Apostles were only human. Even for those who escaped martyrdom, death had to come. The living books would close forever.

Our Lord had said: "Go, preach the Gospel to all nations." Soon Christians would take the Gospel to Rome, to a cultured people, to a city where books were mass-produced by the sweated labour of thousands of slaves.

These missionaries would also have to face new problems. Even only a few years after the resurrection strange heresies began to appear. Jesus Christ, the Way, the Truth and the Life, must not be betrayed.

The time had come for a clear, definitive statement about the life and teaching of our Lord. The early Church was about to give birth to the New Testament.

The New Testament

The New Testament, in contrast to the Old, came from a Christian setting, though it is still influenced by the Jewish roots of early Christians. It also contains a variety of writings: the four Gospels, Matthew, Mark, Luke and John, which give accounts of the life of Jesus, the Acts of the Apostles, which describes the foundation of the early Church, various letters sent to the early church communities and finally the book of Revelation, written in the style of Jewish apocalyptic literature.

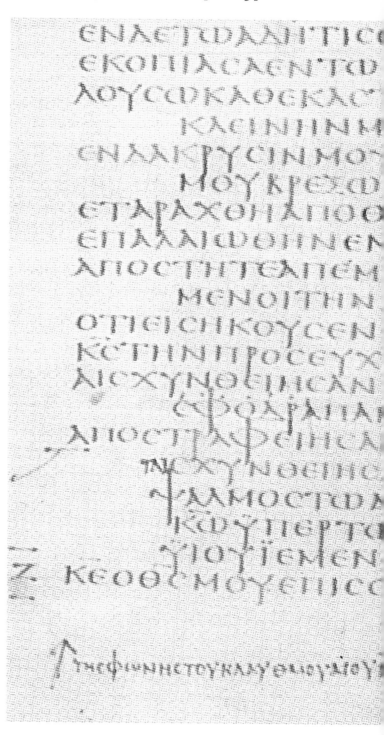

The Living Books

The years of Christ's public ministry. Christ chose twelve Apostles – the special witnesses to his life and mission.	27-30AD
After the Resurrection the Apostles began to preach, proclaiming Christ's message. While the Apostles were alive, written records were not necessary.	

They only came later... Approximate dates of the Gospels:	Mark: 67AD.
	Matthew: 70-80AD.
	Luke: 70-80AD.
	John: 90AD.

What is a Gospel?

We have already examined the various stages in the formation of the Gospels. We need now only list them in order:

1. The preaching of the Apostles passed on by word of mouth.
2. Vivid memories of Jesus also passed on by word of mouth.
3. Possibly a written account of some incidents from our Lord's life.
4. The reflections of the early Church and other material added by the evangelists.

Examine this list carefully and one point becomes immediately obvious. The evangelists did not simply sit down and compose a book out of their heads. A modern author can sit down, choose his own material, and arrange it in any order he wants. The evangelists did not do this and could not. Most of the material they used had already taken shape under the influence of the Apostles – and these were the official witnesses of the life of Jesus. Right from the start then, we see this is no ordinary book. How, then, can we best describe it? Is it a ...

History book?

Yes and no. Much in the Gospels is historically accurate but it is, for example, impossible to construct an accurate timetable of the life of Jesus from a reading of them. Is it a ...

Biography?

Any biography would surely give a description of what our Lord looked like. The Gospels tell us a great deal about our Lord but the absence of an accurate timetable of his life again leads us to answer – yes and no.

So the New Testament is not strictly a history book, neither is it entirely a biography. How, then, can we possibly describe it? St John is very helpful here. He tells us exactly why he wrote his Gospel. "These things are recorded so that you may believe that Jesus is the Christ, the Son of God, and that believing you may have life through his name." (John 20:31).

John wanted his account of the life of Christ to be more than just a list of facts: he wanted it to lead men and women to a deeper knowledge of Christ and to have faith in him.

In his book, *Introducing the Bible,* William Barclay points out there are two ways of telling a story. You can tell it in minute detail, omitting nothing. This provides your listener with a simple timetable of events. Or you can tell a story by simply picking out the most significant incidents. This way your listener not only knows the most important things that happened but can also be given an insight into the meaning of these events. Barclay makes it still clearer by a simple example. Compare a photograph and a portrait. A photograph tells you only what a person looks like; a portrait tells you a great deal about his character – what he is really like deep down. The Gospel is not like a photograph of Christ: it is more like a portrait.

An answer

How, then, can we define a Gospel? We can say a Gospel is a portrait of Christ. By putting before us the preaching of the Church about the public life, death and exaltation of our Lord, a Gospel gives us a true witness and interpretation of his life. But something else – and we will have more to say about this – a Gospel is an inspired book. It is the word of God. It is God speaking to us.

Which version of the New Testament is the right one?

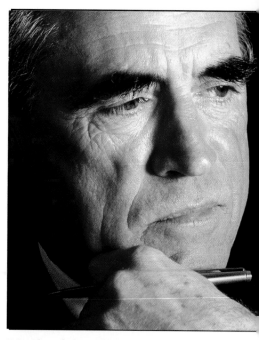

Many different manuscripts of the New Testament have survived. In an age before photocopiers and printing, each manuscript had to be written out laboriously by hand. Scribes copied each text word for word and so it is not surprising that they sometimes made mistakes. Texts were inadvertently changed. For example, if a scribe accidentally left out a word, he would write it in the margin, and the next scribe to copy the manuscript would put it back into the body of the text. This was all well and good, but as notes and comments were also written in the margins, these too often found their way into the main text, making it very difficult for later interpreters to work out what was the original text and what was a note which had been added in. Scribes were also very human, and it is easy to see how a tired scribe may have accidentally changed the text by writing in what he thought the text was saying rather than what it really said.

When faced with a variety of manuscripts saying different things, biblical scholars have to decide which one is closest to the original. Some manuscripts are thought to be more reliable than others, especially if they are older. A general rule of thumb when choosing between two texts that disagree is to choose the shorter of the two, as a text is more likely to have had bits added to it than taken away. Another is to choose the more difficult passage, the one which makes less sense – because someone changing a text would probably change it so that it made more sense. This would mean that the harder reading is probably nearer the original.

Much of the Bible was translated into various languages. The Old Testament was originally written in Hebrew, but very early on it was translated into several languages including Greek, Latin and Aramaic. The New Testament was written in Greek, though it was also translated into Latin and Syriac (a dialect of Aramaic). Jesus would have spoken Aramaic, but by the time most of the Gospels came to be written, Jerusalem had been destroyed by the Romans and the Christian Church was based in the Greek-speaking world.

> Still, the Christian faith is not a 'religion of the book'. Christianity is the religion of the 'Word' of God, 'not a written and mute word, but incarnate and living'.
> *St Bernard*

The Word of God in the Tradition of the Church

The Gospel of Jesus Christ was preached long before it was written. The first disciples who were witnesses to the resurrection of Jesus obeyed his command to teach all nations. They did so eagerly, confident that the Holy Spirit given by Jesus would bring to their minds, and help them to understand, everything he had taught them. In the early Church, then, there was an *oral tradition* which preceded the *written tradition* of the New Testament.

We have already seen that although Christians had access to the Old Testament, Christian writings were not originally considered to be Scripture. The faith of the early Christian communities was focused on the person of Jesus of Nazareth, who was preached about rather than written about. An oral tradition of his words and deeds was carefully passed on and later was written down in the form of the Gospels that we know today. Only gradually did these Christian writings come to have the status of Scripture, and even then the oral tradition remained important.

It was only in the second century that the early Church felt the need to order its writings into some sort of a canon. Not until the fifth century was this canon finalised, excluding some writings which were acknowledged to be 'authoritative' but not 'scriptural', and including the writings that now make up the New Testament.

The word 'canon' comes originally from the Hebrew word *qaneh* which means 'reed'. It was imported into the Greek as *kanon,* a 'measuring stick'.

The Goths were a particularly ferocious bunch of people. They were part of the barbarian hordes which overran the Roman Empire in the fifth century. They were the first barbarians to embrace Christianity and one of their bishops, one Ulfilas by name, became known as the 'apostle to the Goths' because of his heroic efforts to spread Christianity among his countrymen. He managed to translate the whole of the Bible into Gothic – but he left out the book of Kings, an Old Testament book full of stories of war and conquest. He thought that his people were quite violent enough as it was, and this sort of reading would only make them worse! (Incidentally, the word 'barbarian' simply means 'the bearded one'. It comes from the Latin *barba* which means 'beard'. The barbarians were just bearded tribesmen, unlike the smooth-shaven Romans.)

A very early Syriac version of the Gospels was found in the 1880's by a couple of very adventurous Victorian women, Mrs Lewis and Mrs Gibson. When they were both tragically widowed in their forties, they decided to go travelling. They made their way to the Holy Land and ended up in St Catherine's, a monastery on Mount Sinai, where the bemused monks let them look through their library of ancient manuscripts. At breakfast one day, and quite by chance, they discovered the codex Sinaiticus, an early version of the Gospels written in Syriac. The monks had been using the precious document as a butter dish. St Catherine's had a substantial library of ancient documents, many written on stiff leather able to resist the grease of the breakfast butter for a short while. To save on washing up, the breakfast butter was dished up on disposable fragments from the library. Breakfast in the monastery was silent, and there was little for the two women to do but read the butter dish. Each day the butter arrived on a different manuscript, and one day Mrs Lewis noticed that the document carrying the butter was a very ancient Syriac version of the Gospels. Unable to read Syriac, the monks had been completely unaware of its value.

The canon of Scripture...
The complete canon of scripture includes 46 books for the Old Testament and 27 for the New.

The Old Testament:
Genesis, Exodus, Leviticus, Numbers, Deuteronomy, Joshua, Judges, Ruth, 1 and 2 Samuel, 1 and 2 Kings, 1 and 2 Chronicles, Ezra and Nehemiah, Tobit, Judith, Esther, 1 and 2 Maccabees, Job, Psalms, Proverbs, Ecclesiastes, the Song of Songs, the Wisdom of Solomon, Sirach (Ecclesiasticus), Isaiah, Jeremiah, Lamentations, Baruch, Ezekiel, Daniel, Hosea, Joel, Amos, Obadiah, Jonah, Micah, Nahum, Habakkuk, Zephaniah, Haggai, Zechariah and Malachi.

The New Testament:
The Gospels according to Matthew, Mark, Luke and John, the Acts of the Apostles, the Letters of St Paul to the Romans, 1 and 2 Corinthians, Galatians, Ephesians, Philippians, Colossians, 1 and 2 Thessalonians, 1 and 2 Timothy, Titus, Philemon, The Letter to the Hebrews, the Letters of James, 1 and 2 Peter, 1, 2, and 3 John, and Jude, and Revelation (the Apocalypse).

The inspired word of God

Scripture is often spoken of as being 'inspired'. The word 'inspiration' literally means breathed into. It comes from a Latin word *inspiratus*, to breathe upon. Just as in the book of Genesis God is said to have breathed life into the body of the first human being, so God has breathed life into scripture. Inspired scripture is scripture breathed upon by God. In order to reveal himself to us, God speaks to us in human words: indeed the words of God, expressed in human words, are in every way like human language, just as the Word of the eternal Father, when he took on himself the flesh of human weakness, became like us.

Scripture is said to be 'the word of God', but this does not deny the fact that it was written by human beings. When we come to look at scripture it is important to realise that God's word is always mediated through the human world. When reading scripture it is important to understand what the original author was trying to say. For example, if an upper crust English lady tells you she is 'mad about her flat', you would be right in assuming that she was very pleased with her new home. If an American motorist says that he is 'mad about his flat' he is probably upset because his car has a puncture. To understand what being 'mad about my flat' means we need to understand what the person who said it meant. When we are trying to understand what scripture is telling us, it helps to bear in mind what the person who wrote it wanted it to mean. The tradition of the Church is important in guiding the reader as to the intention of the author.

The Bible was not dictated. Every writer has his own purpose and style. Nor were the writers of the Bible inspired as a poet is inspired. God inspired the writer directly so that God became the principal author.

We must always remember that Matthew, Mark, Luke and John wrote their Gospels many years after the Resurrection. The Church was facing new conditions and problems which needed different approaches. But in all four Gospels the message is the same.

The human conditions which influenced the writing of the Gospels were vitally important. But the divine influence was far more so. Indeed, the value of the Gospels rests precisely on the fact that they are the 'inspired word of God.' It is our faith that Scripture is not merely the work of human beings, but principally the work of God.

How did the Holy Spirit and the writers of the Bible work together? This is not an easy question to answer, and many explanations have been proposed over the centuries. Critics of the Gospels have been quick to notice apparent inconsistencies. 'If the Bible is

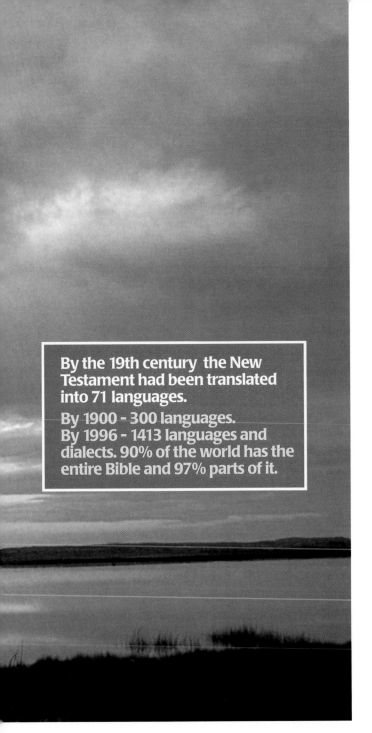

By the 19th century the New Testament had been translated into 71 languages.

By 1900 - 300 languages.
By 1996 - 1413 languages and dialects. 90% of the world has the entire Bible and 97% parts of it.

'Partnership'

In their task, the Holy Spirit so inspired the writers that they accurately wrote down all that God intended, and only what he intended. The mystery of God using men and women to achieve his purpose is not, of course, confined to the writing of the Scriptures. Today, the Holy Spirit inspires people in all walks of life to spread the Gospel. But in the books of the Bible surely we see the marvel of this 'partnership' at its most powerful.

How do we explain it?

When we try to explain how the sacred writers were inspired, we can recognise immediately, then, that they were not 'told' what to write by the Holy Spirit. They were not like the office secretary who writes down, word for word, what is dictated by the boss. The sacred writer knew the plans and the mind of God. For God revealed them, either to the writer personally, or through the apostolic tradition built up in the early Church. But the inspiration of the Holy Spirit did not mean that the writer's own personality became lost. On the contrary, we know that the grace of God within us, far from weakening our individuality, makes us more human. The grace of God makes it possible for us to achieve our true purpose.

The true author

The writers of the Bible fulfilled their true purpose in writing the word of God. Even the exact words used in Scripture are not primarily their own, but are so inspired that God is their true author.

It is important to realise this, for the full significance of his own writing was not always recognised by the Gospel-writer himself. It is the task of the Church, under the inspiration of the same Holy Spirit by whose influence the sacred books were written, to penetrate and explain their meaning more deeply.

The formation of the Gospels was a lengthy process which began with the coming of the Holy Spirit at Pentecost.

The promises of God

The many translations of the New Testament show the missionary spirit of the Christian religion. By the 3rd century there were translations in Coptic, Sahidic, Bohairic and Middle Egyptian. The earliest western translator was Ulfilas (311-381), Bishop of Gothia. He devised the Gothic alphabet and translated most of the Bible.

inspired by God,' they ask, 'how do you explain these contradictions and inaccuracies?'

We have seen that the Gospel writers were not concerned with historical detail in the way we are today. When they composed the four Gospels, 'they made a selection of some of the many things that had been transmitted by word of mouth or in writing. Some of these they related in abbreviated form or explained with due regard for the situation of the Churches. They did this in such a way as always to give us an honest and true account of Jesus'. (cf. Dogmatic Constitution on Divine Revelation, article 19)

Our response to God

(Catechism of the Catholic Church 142-175)

God offers himself to all of humanity, longing for us to be fully human and to enter into eternal life with him. He has revealed himself to us through the Scriptures and through his Son Jesus Christ. Our response is to believe in him and trust him. This is what we call faith.

Faith is a gift of God. Before a car can start, the starter motor has to start the main motor running. In the same way, in order for us to have faith in God, we need the help of the Holy Spirit to move our hearts and allow us to receive God's revelation. Although we need God's Spirit to start the whole process of faith, it does not mean that receiving faith is not a free human act. We cooperate with the grace of God when we choose to believe in him.

God made us to be thinking, rational creatures. It's natural for us to question and try to understand ourselves and the world about us. Having faith doesn't mean that we have to stop thinking and questioning what it is that we believe. On the contrary, faith may well spur us on to try and understand more and more, and ask more and more awkward questions. That's the way God made us. Faith in him isn't just a matter of blind obedience. Nor is it irrational. Saint Anselm spoke of "faith seeking understanding". Our faith is not opposed to our reason.

Having faith in God isn't just a matter of gritting our teeth and blindly believing in him. Faith is about much more than that. Faith is about responding lovingly to God with our whole being – our hearts and bodies and minds and all.

What we personally believe is important, but faith is not a solitary act. No one can believe alone, just as no one can live alone. When we believe we are caught up into the belief of the whole Church. I cannot believe without being carried by the faith of others, and my faith can help to support others.

Faith is free....

In order to give a fully human response to God, we must be free. Nobody should be forced to embrace the faith against their will. Christ invited people to faith and conversion, but he never coerced them. The act of faith is of its very nature a free act.

And after all, the Gospel is always good news. Vincent McNabb OP says:

"We mustn't go out into the world as if the world were our enemy and we had to conquer it. It is like the poor wounded man on the road to Jericho; it is hungry, and we want to give it something to eat; thirsty, and we want to give it something to drink; homeless and we want to open the door and give it a lodging and a home."

Faith is the beginning of eternal life. When we live in faith, we bring the Kingdom of God closer, we live the sort of life that Christ lived, the life of God. Faith gives us a foretaste of eternal life. Having faith in God doesn't mean that we will have a cosy, doubt-free existence. It may mean quite the opposite. The world can often seem a very dark and frightening place, with so much evil and suffering that even the strongest faith can collapse. Sometimes the easiest thing to do is to throw in our lot with those who say 'there is no God!' In some sense our Christian belief is about *not* believing that the suffering and pain we see about us is the whole story. In spite of all the evil in the world, we still want to respond with hope and not despair. We still want to say, 'God is good.'

St Albert the Great lived in the Middle Ages and had a great fascination for all things natural. He saw no contradiction between science and faith and included in his studies the nesting habits of vultures, the laying practices of different types of flies and the noise made by mating fish. He even tried feeding ostriches with bits of metal to see if thy would eat them. When asked if all this was relevant to his theological studies, he smartly replied, "But the whole world is theology for us! The heavens proclaim the glory of God!"

Introduction to the Creeds

(Catechism of the Catholic Church 185-197)

In order to pass on her teaching clearly and simply, the Church has from the beginning expressed and handed on her faith in brief, easily remembered formulae, called 'professions of faith' or 'creeds'. They are called 'creeds' because they started with the words 'I believe' which in Latin was *credo*. The very earliest creeds were quite short. This is one from the middle of the second century AD:

"I believe in the Father Almighty, and in Jesus Christ, our Saviour; and in the Holy Spirit, the Paraclete, in the holy Church, and in the remission of sins."

Creeds have traditionally been divided up into three sections, the first speaking of God the Father, the second of God the Son and the third of God the Holy Spirit. They were also divided into twelve more minor sections or 'articles' symbolising the twelve Apostles.

The Church still recognises the truth of all the different creeds, but acknowledges that some are more appropriate than others for modern needs and tastes. Among all of the creeds produced within the Church, two occupy a special place: *the Apostles' Creed* and the *Nicene Creed*.

The *Apostles' Creed* is a very ancient baptismal profession of faith from the Church of Rome. The *Nicene Creed* came out of the first two great Ecumenical Councils (in 325AD and 381AD) and still remains common to both the Eastern and Western Churches. Both the Apostles' Creed and the Nicene Creed originally began with the words 'I believe', but after Vatican II the Nicene Creed was changed to 'we believe' to express the Church's shared faith.

Through the centuries many Creeds have been composed in response to the needs of different times and places. Some were very involved and complicated – especially when they were created to oppose a particular heresy or to clarify a very obscure point of theological belief. For example, the Athanasian Creed was produced at a time when there were fierce disputes raging about the nature of the Trinity and whether or not Jesus was really divine. (Athanasius was the Bishop of Alexandria from 328-73 AD, though the Athanasian Creed was probably not written by Athanasius, but by a theologian living in Spain. It was only attributed to Athanasius because he was more famous!). Here is a small chunk of the Athanasian Creed:

"Of such a nature as the Father is, so is the Son, so is the Holy Spirit; the Father is uncreated, the Son is uncreated, the Holy Spirit is uncreated; the Father is immense, the Son is immense, the Holy Spirit is immense; the Father is eternal, the Son is eternal, the Holy Spirit is eternal..."

As you can see, the Athanasian Creed leaves nothing to chance!

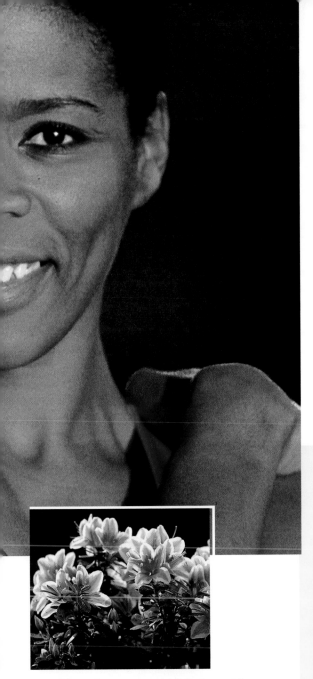

The great split between the Church of Rome and what is now known as the Eastern Orthodox Church took place in the eleventh century. In 1014 Pope Benedict VIII decided to make a slight change in the wording of the Nicene Creed. Where it used to say "We believe in the Holy Spirit, the Lord the giver of life, who proceeds from the Father," the Pope added in "and the Son". The Orthodox were up in arms, arguing that God the Father was the only generative principle of the Trinity. They also thought that the Pope did not have the right to change the wording of the Creed without calling an ecumenical council and consulting the whole Church. The result of this was a split between the Roman Catholic Church and the Eastern Orthodox. This split is still very evident today.

The Nicene Creed that we say each Sunday at Mass seems like a clear-cut and solid expression of Catholic belief — and so it is; but it was created in the mess and tangle of dispute and argument during which the president of an ecumenical council resigned and insulted the remaining participants by telling them that they were children who had no idea what they were talking about!

An old gardener once said that most human institutions were like rhododendron bushes. From the outside they could look lovely, with huge colourful flowers and lush green leaves, but if you climbed inside you were faced with a grotesque mass of tangled branches and dead wood. Those standing on the outside were unaware of the tensions and strains inside, and those inside were unable to see outside, beyond the mass of tangled wood, to the impressive floral display. The Church grows in much the same way. The Creeds that we have today have often come out of a dark and confused time. We see the Creeds as a package presented to us in pristine form, without perhaps being aware of the knotty, gnarled history that went into their making.

The Apostles' Creed
I believe in God, the Father almighty, creator of heaven and earth.

I believe in Jesus Christ, his only Son, our Lord. He was conceived by the power of the Holy Spirit and born of the Virgin Mary. He suffered under Pontius Pilate, was crucified, died and was buried. He descended to the dead. On the third day he rose again. He ascended into heaven and is seated at the right hand of the Father. He will come again to judge the living and the dead.

I believe in the Holy Spirit, the Holy Catholic Church, the communion of saints, the forgiveness of sins, the resurrection of the body, and the life everlasting. Amen.

The Nicene Creed
We believe in one God, the Father, the almighty, maker of heaven and earth, of all that is, seen and unseen.

We believe in one Lord, Jesus Christ, the only Son of God, eternally begotten of the Father, God from God, Light from Light, true God from true God, begotten, not made, of one Being with the Father. Through him all things were made. For us men and for our salvation, he came down from heaven; by the power of the Holy Spirit he became incarnate of the Virgin Mary, and became man. For our sake he was crucified under Pontius Pilate; he suffered death and was buried. On the third day he rose again in accordance with the Scriptures; he ascended into heaven and is seated at the right hand of the Father. He will come again in glory to judge the living and the dead and his kingdom will have no end.

We believe in the Holy Spirit, the Lord, the giver of life, who proceeds from the Father and the Son. With the Father and the Son he is worshipped and glorified. He has spoken through the prophets. We believe in one holy catholic and apostolic church. We acknowledge one baptism for the forgiveness of sins. We look for the resurrection of the dead, and the life of the world to come. Amen.

"I believe in God the Father Almighty, Creator of Heaven and Earth"

(Catechism of the Catholic Church 199-421)

When we tell someone our name we make ourselves more accessible to them and allow ourselves to be known more intimately. In the same way, by revealing his name to us, God has chosen not to remain an anonymous and distant power, but instead has told us who he is and invited us to share a more intimate relationship with him.

Out of respect for the holiness of God, the ancient people of Israel did not say his name — traditionally, the name of God was only uttered once a year by the High Priest in the temple sanctuary. This means that the Old Testament is often quite cryptic when it speaks of God. For example, when God tells Moses his name, we are told:

Moses said to God, 'If I come to the people of Israel and say to them, "The God of your fathers has sent me to you", and they ask me, "What is his name?" what shall I say to them?' God said to Moses, 'I AM WHO I AM.' And he said, 'Say this to the people of Israel, "I AM has sent me to you"...This is my name for ever, and thus I am to be remembered throughout all generations.'

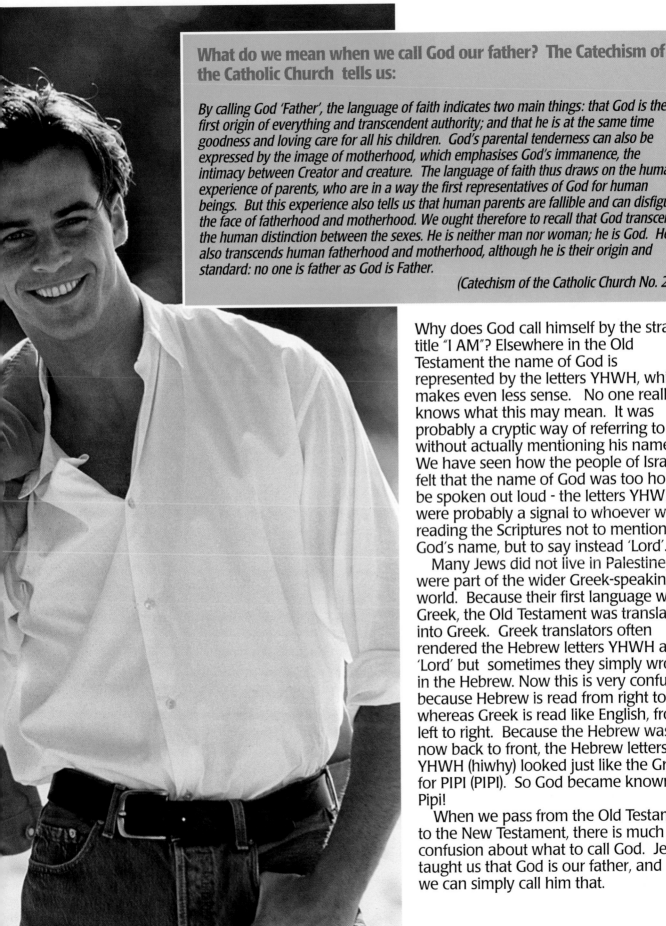

What do we mean when we call God our father? The Catechism of the Catholic Church tells us:

By calling God 'Father', the language of faith indicates two main things: that God is the first origin of everything and transcendent authority; and that he is at the same time goodness and loving care for all his children. God's parental tenderness can also be expressed by the image of motherhood, which emphasises God's immanence, the intimacy between Creator and creature. The language of faith thus draws on the human experience of parents, who are in a way the first representatives of God for human beings. But this experience also tells us that human parents are fallible and can disfigure the face of fatherhood and motherhood. We ought therefore to recall that God transcends the human distinction between the sexes. He is neither man nor woman; he is God. He also transcends human fatherhood and motherhood, although he is their origin and standard: no one is father as God is Father.

(Catechism of the Catholic Church No. 239).

Why does God call himself by the strange title "I AM"? Elsewhere in the Old Testament the name of God is represented by the letters YHWH, which makes even less sense. No one really knows what this may mean. It was probably a cryptic way of referring to God without actually mentioning his name. We have seen how the people of Israel felt that the name of God was too holy to be spoken out loud - the letters YHWH were probably a signal to whoever was reading the Scriptures not to mention God's name, but to say instead 'Lord'.

Many Jews did not live in Palestine, but were part of the wider Greek-speaking world. Because their first language was Greek, the Old Testament was translated into Greek. Greek translators often rendered the Hebrew letters YHWH as 'Lord' but sometimes they simply wrote in the Hebrew. Now this is very confusing because Hebrew is read from right to left, whereas Greek is read like English, from left to right. Because the Hebrew was now back to front, the Hebrew letters YHWH (hiwhy) looked just like the Greek for PIPI (PIPI). So God became known as Pipi!

When we pass from the Old Testament to the New Testament, there is much less confusion about what to call God. Jesus taught us that God is our father, and so we can simply call him that.

The Holy Trinity

The Old Testament was very firm about the fact that there was only one God, but once the Christian Church was formed, it had to work out where Jesus and the Holy Spirit fitted in. If Jesus was God, and the Holy Spirit was God, and God the Father was God, did that mean that there were three gods? Or if there was only one God, how was it that there seemed to be three separate persons? This little conundrum caused all sorts of problems, and a whole batch of heresies. Some did not think that Jesus was really God, while others denied his humanity. Some thought that all three persons of the Trinity were just different roles played by the same person, whilst others thought there were just three gods. The Church rejected all these positions, and put forward its own:

1 The Trinity is one. There are not three gods, but one God in three persons. These divine persons do not divide out the one divinity among themselves, but each of them is God whole and entire.

2 The divine persons are really different from one another. Father, Son and Holy Spirit are not simply names for different roles played by the same person. The three persons of the Trinity have different origins:

It is the Father who generates,
the Son who is begotten,
and the Holy Spirit who proceeds.

3 The divine persons are related to one another. Even though they are separate persons, this does not deny their real unity. They still share one nature or substance.

Some of this is very difficult to understand, and the Church would be the first to acknowledge that the doctrine of the Trinity is a mystery which is not easy to grasp. What is most comforting about the Trinity is the way that God shows himself to be a fundamentally social being — in his essence he is companionship and love. As we become part of the life and love of the Trinity of God we can enjoy a very companionable life now and for ever.

"The Trinity is the family life of God"
St Thomas Aquinas

Heresy

The word 'heresy' comes from the Greek word *heiresthai*, 'to choose'. A heretic was someone who chose to follow a path which rejected the teachings of the Church. In the Greek-speaking world of early Christianity, the word 'heresy' was often used in a very general sense to refer to any philosophical sect or party. So for example in the Acts of the Apostles, the parties of the Sadduccees and Pharisees were referred to as heretics. Here the word was being used in a neutral way to refer to the different religious groups, but in the New Testament and later Christian writings the word was increasingly used in a distinctly derogatory way until it came to represent the heinous sin of turning away from the Church and creating division among Christians.

26

Creator of heaven and earth

God is love, and out of love God created the world. He created the world from nothing. As St Thomas Aquinas says: "Creatures came into existence when the key of love opened his hand." Because creation comes forth from God's goodness, it shares in that goodness. Everything in existence is created by God, and every creature reflects God's infinite wisdom and goodness.

All of us are created in the image of God. Every human being is a reflection of the divine nature of God. Every human person has been made good by God. This means that from the moment of conception every person has a dignity and a worth that cannot be measured. Every person is a reflection of the love and goodness of God. If, along with the whole of creation, we have been created good by a good God, then why does evil exist? If God had made such a fine job of it, then why is the world so full of suffering? If God is completely good and all-powerful, then why is there evil and suffering in the world? Evil

be freely given. Even though God loves his creatures and wants them to be happy, if he also wants them to love, then they can only do so if they are free. God has given us this freedom. We all have choices about how to live. We are free to choose whether or not to love. If God had 'rigged' his creation so that there was no possibility of us really messing it up, then our choices would not have been real choices and our love would have been a sham. As it is, the world is in a mess, but we can love truly and freely!

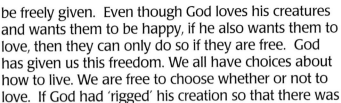

The Bible tells us that, as well as creating the physical world, God created other creatures called angels, who are pure spirit. The word 'angel' comes from the Greek 'angelos' which means 'messenger'. The angels in the New Testament and the Old Testament are the messengers of God. Catholic tradition has it that all of us are entrusted to a 'guardian angel' who cares and watches over us, keeping us from harm.

God is not responsible for the evil we do when we sin, but he does permit it. He permits it because he respects the freedom of his creatures and mysteriously knows how to derive good from it. As Augustine says:

"For almighty God, because he is supremely good, would never allow any evil whatsoever to exist in his works if he were not so all-powerful and good as to cause good to emerge from the evil itself."

In Christian and Jewish tradition, the devil or Satan is an evil figure who fights against God, tricking and deceiving human beings into sin. Satan, also known as Lucifer, 'bringer of light', is a good angel who turned against God. The word 'satan' means 'accuser' in Hebrew — 'devil' comes from the Greek *diabolos* which also means to accuse or slander. In the earlier books of the Old Testament, Satan, 'the accuser', does not embody evil as such, but is a roving, roaming steward whose job it is to check up on human beings and report their misdeeds to God. This is the role played by Satan in the book of Job. It was only later tradition that equated Satan with an evil force and identified him as the serpent who enticed Adam and Eve into disobeying God. Since then, the New Testament and later Christian tradition has continued to see Satan as the embodiment of evil, a powerful opponent who maliciously fights against the goodness of God. However powerful he may be, Satan will nevertheless be defeated — in the end Satan is still a creature and no match for the strength and power of the creator God.

and suffering do exist — so what does that tell us about God? Surely an all-powerful God could just do away with suffering? Looking at human parents can give us a clue about why God allows us to suffer. However much parents love their children, they may still find themselves watching helplessly as their children make mistakes. They do not stop wanting the best for their children, but letting children grow up involves letting them make their own choices. Loving someone involves giving them freedom to choose. No one can be forced to love. Love, by its very nature, has to

Original sin

What is sin? We often think of sins as positively evil actions and we think evil is something tangible and very real. But Saint Augustine is quite clear that evil isn't anything at all. Evil is not a thing, evil is quite the opposite, it is a no-thing. Evil is simply the absence of good. Whenever we do something bad or sinful we are doing something which is not fully good. Augustine believes that all our desires are really for good things — we do not really desire to do evil and wicked things, we always want something good, but sometimes we just don't set our sights high enough, we settle for things that are lesser goods. And this is what sin is — fundamentally, sin is not wanting enough, not desiring enough. We let ourselves be satisfied with things which are not God.

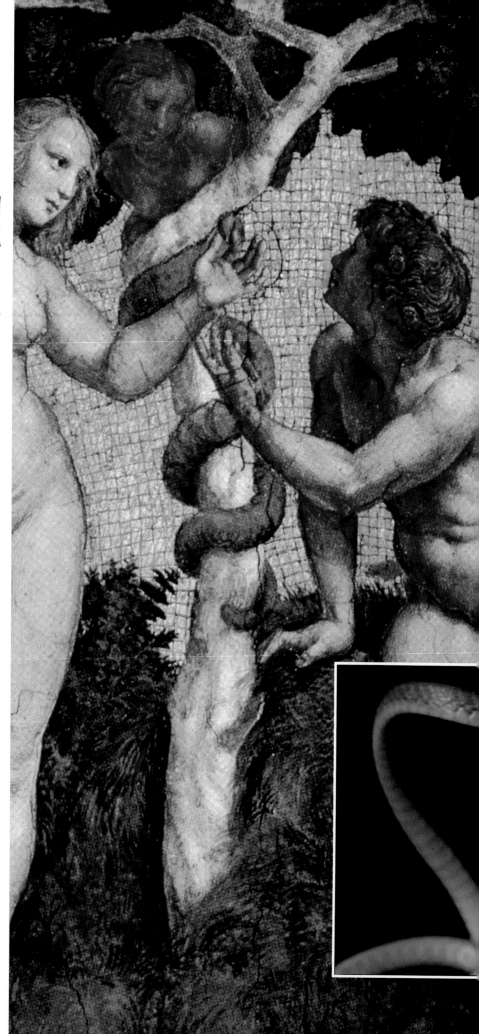

This 'choosing what is not God' is what Adam did in the book of Genesis. The story of Adam and Eve describes how God originally made the first human beings to live in harmony and fellowship with him, and how they turned away from him. God created Adam and Eve in a state of holiness and harmony with the rest of creation — they were not meant to suffer or die. By committing the first sin, Adam and Eve lost their innocence and their immortality. Death came into the world through sin, and from then on a fallen human nature was inherited by the whole human race. All of us are wounded by original sin, the sin of Adam, as we inherit a fallen human nature.

Baptism is the sacrament which wipes out original sin, although we are still weakened by the effects of that sin. The very early Church did not quite know what to make of sins which were committed after baptism. They were unsure about whether or not they could be forgiven. Because of this, many put off being baptised until the last moment, when there was no longer any danger of committing any more sin. They waited until their death beds! The emperor Constantine, for example, was baptised on his death-bed. Saint Augustine put off being baptised and St Ambrose was not even baptised when he was appointed Bishop of Milan. Of course, the Church then developed a theology and mechanisms for dealing with sins committed after baptism — the Sacrament of Reconciliation is one of them.

"And in Jesus Christ, his only Son, Our Lord"

(Catechism of the Catholic Church 422-455)

At the heart of catechesis we find, in essence, a Person, the Person of Jesus of Nazareth, the only Son from the Father...who suffered and died for us and who now, after rising, is living with us forever.
(Catechism of the Catholic Church No.426)

In Hebrew the word 'Jesus' literally means 'God saves'. Jesus is the God who saves us. Jesus is God, but he became a human being in order to save all human beings from sin and death. Jesus became like us so that we might become like him. He became a human being so that human beings could become divine. In the words of Saint Athanasius: 'For the Son of God became man so that we might become God.'

"Jesus Christ is man in his totality. Only God could be. Jesus has his origin uniquely in God; he is God. Yet, born of the Virgin Mary, he is true and total man. This is the glory and offence of Christianity. For, conceived by the Holy Spirit and born of the Virgin Mary, Jesus is not just near to God and resembling man. He is God-man...The sinlessness of Christ answers, then, the question of the true quality of man. The true God is sinless; that we know. But we now learn that the true man is sinless. This is a surprise. The more christified, the more human. The more human, the more divine. For Christ is no maverick; he is simply man, and does not disown descent from Adam but rather glories in his lineage."

(Hugh Lavery, Reflections on the Creed)

Jesus is also known as the *Christ* or the *Messiah*, which means the 'anointed' one. The Jews believed that God was going to send the Christ or Messiah to liberate Israel and establish his kingdom. In Jesus' time, different groups believed different things about what would happen when the Messiah arrived. The Sadducees, for example, believed that the Messiah was an earthly ruler who would throw off foreign rule and restore the kingdom of Israel. The Pharisees believed that the Messiah would defeat evil and raise the dead to life. From then until now, Jews have been waiting for the Messiah. Christianity grew out of this tradition. The very first Christians were Jews who believed that Jesus was the Messiah. They believed that Jesus was the Son of God sent to save humanity. Belief in Jesus lies at the heart of the Christian faith. A belief in Jesus Christ is what makes a Christian a Christian.

If we believe that Jesus really is God, and that he is also a human being, then this must turn upside-down any ideas we have about God as a distant, uncaring creator who stands back and just lets all the horrors of the world be played out before him. We may not be able to understand why God does not just click his fingers and make everything all right, but if we can see that Jesus really was God who became human and shared the horrors of this world, if we can believe this, then we can see a God who has not protected himself from the sufferings we face. Jesus died a very grisly death. God does not distance himself from our pain and suffering. He is there in the midst of all the agonies we suffer. As we suffer, Jesus is crucified.

It is sometimes frustratingly difficult to get a full picture from the Gospels about what Jesus was really like. Almost nothing is said about his life in Nazareth, and even a great part of his public life is not recounted. He spent his first thirty years doing the ordinary mundane things that most people have to do, a life spent in manual labour without greatness or fame. Although we might want to know more about him, we can at least take comfort from the fact that his hidden life at Nazareth gives all of us the blessing of seeing that we can enter into fellowship with Jesus even when our lives seem completely dull and mundane.

"He was conceived by the power of the Holy Spirit and born of the Virgin Mary"

(Catechism of the Catholic Church 456-502)

The Virgin Birth

Jesus was the Son of God, but he was born like any other human being. His mother was a young woman called Mary. Luke's Gospel tells us how the Angel Gabriel was sent to Mary to tell her that she would have a child, and that the child would be the Messiah, the one who would save Israel.

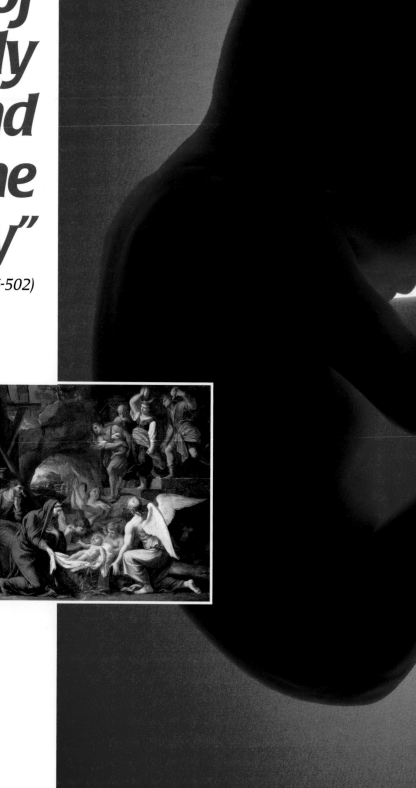

> 'And Mary said to the angel, 'How can this be, since I have no husband?' and the angel said to her, 'The Holy Spirit will come upon you, and the power of the Most High will overshadow you; therefore the child to be born will be called holy, the Son of God.'
>
> (Luke 1:34-35)

Matthew's Gospel tells us the same story but with a slightly different slant. We are told how Mary was betrothed to a man called Joseph, but before they were married she was found to be pregnant. He was about to divorce her when an angel appeared to him and told him that Mary's child was conceived by the Holy Spirit.

Why did God choose to save humanity in this way? Why choose Mary? Why choose to appear in such a way? By conceiving a child in this way, Mary became vulnerable to gossip and rash judgement. For some reason God chose to begin and end his life on earth in tension and pain. He was born in a stable and he died an outcast on the cross.

When faced with the account of how Mary was approached by the angel and agreed to bear the Son of God, many started asking awkward questions like: What if she had said "no?" The Orthodox have a legend that God *did* ask several other women and they all said no. Great debates also went on about whether or not Mary remained a virgin even after she had given birth to Jesus. These discussions went into great detail about the physiological basis of virginity and whether or not a baby leaving the womb would destroy a woman's virginity. Incidentally, the arguments were not helped by the root meaning of the word 'virgin', *parthenos* in the Greek. This word simply meant young girl – though all young girls were, of course, expected to be virgins.

The Immaculate Conception

The doctrine of the Immaculate Conception was promulgated by Pope Pius IX in 1854. It states that Mary was conceived without original sin:

The most Blessed Virgin Mary was, from the first moment of her conception, by a singular grace and privilege of almighty God and by virtue of the merits of Jesus Christ, Saviour of the human race, preserved immune from all stain of original sin.
(Pius IX *Ineffabilis Deus* 1854)

This doctrine, along with the doctrine of the Assumption, has its roots in popular piety. The feast of the Immaculate Conception is celebrated on December 8th in the West, and December 9th in the East. Eleventh century England was the first of the Western European countries to keep the feast, but it was known in the Christian East from the seventh century. The doctrine has a chequered history – some notable theologians such as St Thomas Aquinas and St Albert the Great struggled with it. They thought that once you acknowledged that Mary was conceived without sin, it undermined the whole basis of the doctrine of original sin. If Mary was conceived without sin, then what need was there for Jesus to redeem the whole human race? In the end, it was the theologian Duns Scotus who clarified the doctrine.

The Fathers of the Eastern tradition call the Mother of God 'The All-Holy', *Panagia,* and celebrate her as 'free from any stain of sin, as though fashioned by the Holy Spirit and formed as a new creature'.
By the grace of God Mary remained free of every personal sin her whole life long.

Like us, Mary was saved by Christ, but in a different way. We are saved after birth by union with Christ in Baptism; Mary was saved from the first moment of her existence – she was "conceived immaculate".

The Assumption

The doctrine of the Assumption was defined by Pope Pius XII in 1950. Although Mary died and was buried, her body was not left to decay, but was taken up into heaven. Like the Immaculate Conception, the Assumption is a doctrine which has its roots in popular piety. The feast of the Assumption is celebrated on the 15th of August.

The Assumption means that just as Jesus ascended body and soul into heaven, so did Mary. And just as Mary is now in heaven, body and soul, so also will all God's faithful be.

Many people deny the resurrection; they are not too bothered about the human spirit. Others abuse the human body, either by exalting it in an obsession with style or sexual expression or, at the other extreme, by giving it no importance and treating it as a "necessary evil". The Assumption corrects these false ideas. It reminds us, in St Paul's words, that "our body is the temple of the Holy Spirit, who is in us since we have received him from God... That is why you should use your body for the glory of God."

Mary has always been a rich source of imagery for the whole Church. For example, St Irenaeus says,

'Being obedient she became the cause of salvation for herself and for the whole human race.' Hence not a few of the early Fathers gladly assert:'The knot of Eve's disobedience was untied by Mary's obedience: what the virgin Eve bound through her disbelief, Mary loosened by her faith.' Comparing her with Eve they call Mary 'the Mother of the living' and frequently claim: 'Death through Eve, life through Mary.'

Although both the Immaculate Conception and the Assumption bear witness to extraordinary events, Mary's fate is, hopefully, the same as ours. We too are cleansed from original sin by Jesus, and we too will be taken up, body and soul, into heaven at the final resurrection when all the dead will be raised to life.

Late Medieval Marian paintings depict Mary as a priest. In the same way as the priest offers Jesus' body and blood in the Mass, Mary is shown offering Jesus' flesh to the whole of humanity. Mary is sometimes likened to an oyster, nurturing inside herself the pearl of great price — the kingdom of God.

"Jesus Christ suffered under Pontius Pilate, was crucified, died and was buried"

(Catechism of the Catholic Church 571-630)

The Paschal mystery of Christ's cross and Resurrection stands at the centre of the Good News that the apostles, and the Church following them, are to proclaim to the world. God's saving plan was accomplished 'once for all' by the redemptive death of his Son Jesus Christ.
(Catechism of the Catholic Church 571)

During Jesus' time, Israel was occupied by the Romans. They were particularly brutal rulers and responded very violently to the slightest hint of revolt. Crucifixion was a particularly cruel form of capital punishment which entailed a slow and lingering death. The Romans inflicted this punishment mainly on slaves, mutinous troops and foreign peoples under their rule. Pontius Pilate was the Roman Governor of Judea and Jerusalem at the time when Jesus was killed. He was the one who gave the order for Jesus to be crucified.

Thirty years after Jesus was killed, from 66-70AD, there was a Jewish revolt against Roman rule. The Romans crushed the revolt and destroyed the temple at Jerusalem. The first century historian, Josephus, gives this account of the fate of those fleeing from the city under Roman siege:

When they were going to be taken (by the Romans), they were forced to defend themselves, and after they had fought they thought it too late to make any supplications for mercy: so they were first whipped, and then tormented with all sorts of tortures, before they died and were then crucified before the wall of the city. Titus felt pity for them, but as their number – given as up to five hundred a day – was too great for him to risk either letting them go or putting them under guard, he allowed his soldiers to have their way, especially as he hoped that the gruesome sight of the countless crosses might move the besieged to surrender. So the soldiers, out of the rage and hatred they bore the prisoners, nailed those they caught, in different postures, to the crosses, by way of jest, and their number was so great that there was not enough room for the crosses and not enough crosses for the bodies. (Josephus *Wars of the Jews* 5.449-51)

Among both Jews and Romans, crucifixion was seen as a very shameful way to die. Within Judaism itself, those executed by this method were considered unclean. For example, the Old Testament (Deuteronomy 21:23) orders that the bodies "hanged on a tree" must not be left overnight because they would defile the land. They also had to be buried in a separate tomb. Jesus' followers claimed that they were 'fools for Christ' and instead of being ashamed of the crucifixion of Jesus, they proclaimed it proudly. By being crucified, Jesus had become, in the words of St Paul, 'a curse for us'. Christianity took on the shame of the crucifixion to such an extent that it became its badge or emblem.

By his death and resurrection, Jesus saved humankind. Jesus' total obedience to God wiped out the effects of Adam's disobedience. Adam had disobeyed God and so sin and death entered the world. Jesus' total obedience to God destroyed the effects of sin, breaking its hold and conquering death.

The Church, following the apostles, teaches that Christ died for all without exception: 'There is not, never has been, and never will be, a single human being for whom Christ did not suffer.' Council of Quiercy, 853 AD (*Catechism of the Catholic Church* 605).

How do we make sense of the suffering and death of Jesus? Christian belief is firmly rooted in the fact that by dying and rising again, Jesus saved humanity from sin and death. In the New Testament, and throughout history, the Church has offered different pictures to explain exactly how Jesus' death and resurrection brought about mankind's salvation.

All these explanations are attempts to understand the work of God using human metaphors. Because they use human experiences to explain God's actions, they will always be limited. For example, in the courtroom drama, we may not want to compare God with human judges, or God's justice with our own. Although they can help us to understand what God has done for us, none of them can perfectly explain the mystery of our redemption. So it remains just that: a mystery.

1 One popular explanation is based on the courtroom drama. Humanity is in the dock, charged with crimes that deserve death. For disobeying God and committing sin, the penalty is death. God the judge is forced to admit that mankind is guilty and justice demands that sentence is carried out, but instead of going through with it, God sends his only Son to take the place of humanity. So Jesus takes on our punishment and dies for our sins.

2 Another explanation, which was especially popular in medieval times, is of Jesus the spy. Jesus enters the human race looking and acting just like any other human being, and he fools the devil, who does not realise that he is God. Because death is a punishment for sin, and sinners put themselves under the sway of the devil, Jesus fools the devil by leading a sinless life but still suffering death. Jesus cheats the devil and defeats him, freeing humanity from his clutches.

3 A variation on this theme is Jesus as a fishhook – his divinity is the hook and his humanity is the fleshy bait. The devil sinks his teeth into Jesus' fleshy humanity, but is caught on the hook and defeated.

4 God is also thought of as the redeemer, paying ransom money to release captive humanity. Humanity is taken hostage by sin and Jesus pays the price and sets us free.

"He descended into hell. On the third day he rose again"

(Catechism of the Catholic Church 631-655)

In the Old Testament, everyone who died, good or bad, ended up in *Sheol*. *Sheol* was portrayed as a shadowy place where the dead dwelt in a miserable sort of existence. It was not a place to look forward to, but the end of all that made life worth living. The New Testament carried on this idea of *Sheol* as the place where all the dead go. It uses two words to refer to the realm of the dead: *hades* and *gehenna*.

Hades was the Greek word for the land of the dead. Hades or Pluto was the traditional god of death in Greek mythology.

Gehenna was a Hebrew word which just meant 'the valley of Hinnom'. The valley of Hinnom was a deep and narrow gorge to the south of Jerusalem which became a smouldering rubbish heap. It became an image for the place of punishment for the wicked after death. So when Jesus speaks of 'hell fire' in the Gospels (Matt 5:22; 18:8) the word he uses is *gehenna*.

When the Creed says that Jesus 'descended into hell' it is saying that Jesus really died, and suffered the effects of death that every human being has to suffer. Jesus died, and went to Hades, where all the dead have to go. The Church teaches that Jesus also had a mission to perform when he went to Hades. Because everyone, whether evil or righteous, ended up in Hades, Jesus came to free the just who had gone before him. This is the so-called 'harrowing of hell' which was a very popular theme in medieval times. Jesus went to hell and released those holy souls who were stranded there.

The Gospels tell us that on the third day after his death, Jesus rose. The Resurrection is an historical event. Jesus' human, earthly body was raised from the dead. The empty tomb bears witness to the physical, bodily resurrection of Jesus. After the Resurrection his body bore the marks of crucifixion. When he appeared to his disciples they could still see the marks of the nails in his hands and feet and the hole in his side left by the spear.

The 'Paschal mystery' is the mystery of Jesus' death and resurrection. By his death, Jesus liberates us from sin; by his Resurrection, he opens for us the way to a new life. Jesus' Resurrection opens up the possibility of our own resurrection. For as in Adam all die, so also in Jesus shall all be made alive.

In Jewish law, women were not allowed to be witnesses. They were not allowed to testify or bear witness. The fact that Jesus first appeared to women and specifically used women as the first to witness to his resurrection is a testimony to the fact that in Christ we have discarded the distinctions which separate and divide us as human beings. Other categories of people were also not allowed to testify in Jewish law – children, slaves and shepherds were also excluded. In Luke's Gospel the first witnesses to the birth of Jesus were the shepherds on the hillside. Jesus both came into this world and left it, giving a voice to those usually silenced.

The first people to encounter the risen Jesus were Mary Magdalen and the women who came to anoint his body on Easter Sunday – because Jesus had been killed the day before the Sabbath, his body had been buried in haste. Jesus appeared first to the women, who were thus the first witnesses to his resurrection.

"He ascended into heaven and is seated at the right hand of the Father"

(Catechism of the Catholic Church 659-667)

'...as they were looking on, he was lifted up, and a cloud took him out of their sight. And while they were gazing into heaven as he went, behold, two men stood by them in white robes, and said, 'Men of Galilee, why do you stand looking into heaven? This Jesus, who was taken up from you into heaven, will come in the same way as you saw him go into heaven'

(Acts 1:9-11)

The Bible tells us how Jesus was taken up, body and soul, into heaven. He took his place at God's right hand. He went home. In the Old Testament we are told that no one could see the face of God and live, let alone live with him in heaven. When Jesus ascended into heaven, a human being entered heaven. Jesus opened the doors of heaven to humanity. That means that we now have a place in heaven.

The Ascension has been graphically illustrated in church frescos and wall paintings, from depictions of God's hand reaching down to haul Jesus into heaven, to pictures of the Apostles looking up at a pair of ascending feet, with Jesus heading skyward like a rocket!

Christianity is a material, flesh-and-blood religion. We cannot bypass the physical to reach the spiritual. Jesus ascended into heaven body and soul. We do not reach higher, spiritual truths by rejecting the material world. Heaven will not contain disembodied spiritual beings, but will be full of human bodies – glorified human bodies without the inadequacies we suffer now, but human bodies nevertheless. St Paul has this to say about it:

But some may ask, 'How are the dead raised? With what kind of body will they come?' How foolish! What you sow does not come to life unless it dies. When you sow, you do not plant the body that will be, but just a seed, perhaps of wheat or of something else. But God gives it a body as he has determined, and to each kind of seed he gives its own body. All flesh is not the same: men have one kind of flesh, animals have another, birds another and fish another. There are also heavenly bodies and there are earthly bodies; but the splendour of the heavenly bodies is one kind, and the splendour of the earthly bodies is another.
(1Corinthians 15:35-40)

Jesus' ascension into heaven will be followed by our ascension into heaven. Jesus' glorified body is like what our bodies will become. Jesus' life with God will become our life with God and with each other. Jesus is beyond death and pain and suffering. We see in him our own future, freed from pain and death, when our lives and our loves will not be snuffed out like a spent candle. In Jesus' ascension into heaven we can see our own hopes raised up with him. To the glory of God the Father. Amen.

No seed ever sees the flower

"From thence he will come again to judge the living and the dead"

(Catechism of the Catholic Church 668-682)

We all have some idea of how people are tried and sentenced under the law. The judge solemnly decides on the future of the accused. Judgement is a serious, often pompous affair . When we think of how God will judge us, it is not surprising that we import all the human images of courts and judges and imagine that heavenly judgement will be the same. Perhaps we could do with a healthy burst of contempt of court to unlock ourselves from our own prejudices so that we can be freed to understand what the judgement of God is really like.

In his preaching, Jesus announced the judgement of the Last Day, when all the dead would be raised to life. Those who had lived good lives would enter heaven, whilst the wicked would be condemned to eternal punishment in hell. Not surprisingly, the thought of Judgement has turned many a human heart cold with fear. But Jesus did not come to condemn us, but to save us, to turn us away from destruction. Our fear of his judgement is natural, but remember who it is that will be our judge...

The key to this article of the creed is a pronoun - He. HE will come to judge the living and the dead. And this 'he' is the Jesus who would not cast the first stone, who had tenderness for the failures, who did not despise sinners but dined with them. Possibly we are almost too familiar with these stories of mercy that we fail to register how little they accord with what we would expect. The pious were appalled, the priests and prelates enraged. Simon the Pharisee could not understand how Christ would allow a woman as notorious as Magdalen to approach him, much less anoint him. Yet Jesus did not retract nor murmur an apology. 'Much is forgiven her because she loves much'. Understand this and you see the finger of forgiveness. Forgiveness is the wheat-germ of Christianity, and it is hard to understand, as hard as love.

(Hugh Lavery Reflections on the Creed)

So we can let go of the idea of an angry God punishing us for our sins. all God can do is love us, and if anyone is in hell it is not because God has sent them there, but because he has allowed them to have what it is they really want — hell is a self-made prison. If we choose to reject love, to refuse forgiveness and to lock ourselves away in our own miserable isolation, then we will have put ourselves in a hell of our own making. God the judge only gives us what we have already chosen. And even then he is not acting as an impassive, objective observer. God is not like a cold judge passing sentence upon us, rather, throughout our lives, he is like a distraught lover desperate to save the one he loves. He cajoles, pleads, entices us to open up just enough to let in the saving, loving, renewing spirit of God.

"I believe in the Holy Spirit"

(Catechism of the Catholic Church 683-747)

The third person of the Trinity is called the 'Holy Spirit'. The name 'spirit' is a translation of the Hebrew word *ruach*, which can mean breath, air or wind. When God created the world, he filled it with his breath or spirit. He also breathed life into Adam, the first man:

Then the Lord God formed the man of dust from the ground and breathed into his nostrils the breath of life; and the man became a living being.

(Genesis 2:7)

We are all sustained by the loving, caring spirit of God, the same Spirit that God breathed into Adam at creation and the same Spirit that Jesus breathed on his disciples at Pentecost. The Holy Spirit also breathes life into us. We live the 'spiritual life' when we live a life filled by the breath of God, a breath that fills all the cracks and depths of human experience.

The 'spiritual life' is the life in the Spirit of God, the transforming, fiery, wind-blowing-where-it-will Spirit of God who will blow your life apart at the drop of a hat, and the murmur of a prayer, or when you turn on the news on the radio, or when you pick up your child at school, or when you watch a sick person die or someone you love is broken by unhappiness; or when the bus comes sooner than you expected; or when it doesn't come at all; or when a picture or a film moves you; or a poem makes you think again. In all these things the mighty wind of God is blowing free, through men's minds and hearts and hair.

(Mael Choluim 'The Midnight Hour')

The Holy Spirit is also called the Paraclete – a Greek word meaning 'one called in', an advocate or one who pleads. The Holy Spirit pleads the Christian cause against a hostile world.

The Church has identified and recognised the Holy Spirit through symbols such as the water poured on our heads during baptism, the oil we are anointed with at confirmation, the fire which appeared over the heads of the Apostles at Pentecost, and the dove which settled on Jesus at his baptism. These and other symbols come to represent the presence of the Holy Spirit.

The Holy Spirit is also the giver of gifts. Traditional Catholic catechisms describe the seven gifts of the Holy Spirit: Wisdom, to recognise the things of God; Understanding, to penetrate the mysteries of faith; Counsel, to choose whatever is God's will; Fortitude, to stand firm in the cause of virtue and truth; Knowledge, to discern the difference between good and evil; Piety, to faithfully practise our religion; The Fear of the Lord, which inspires us with a respect for God.

But most of all, the Holy Spirit gives us joy!

When the Spirit of God comes down to a man and overshadows him with the fullness of his presence, then that man's soul overflows with unspeakable joy, for the Holy Spirit fills with joy whatever he touches...'
(Timothy Ware *The Orthodox Church*)

The English Language does not see nouns as masculine or feminine, but other European languages do. In French, for example, a chair is feminine (*la chaise*) whereas a sofa is masculine (*le divan*). In French, as in other languages, there are no set rules that automatically tell you whether something is grammatically masculine or feminine; you can only memorise which is which when you learn the language. To make matters more confusing, different languages can disagree about which things are masculine and which are feminine. Take the Holy Spirit, for example. In Hebrew she is feminine, in Greek it is neuter and in Latin he is masculine. Not surprisingly, this caused a few problems for the early Church, which contained many Hebrew, Greek and Latin speakers. In areas where Hebrew or another Semitic language, such as Syriac, was spoken, the Holy Spirit was thought of as feminine and so images of the Holy Spirit as Mother were common. This meant that the Trinity was made up of a little family group of Father, Mother and Son. These sorts of ideas were openly expressed until about the fifth century when Latin took over as the dominant language.

How we are caught up into the life of the Trinity! The Father, the creator, begets the Son; and the expression of the love between them is the Holy Spirit. Wherever there is love in us, there is the third person of the Trinity of Love – the Holy Spirit.

Dear Friends, let us love one another, for love comes from God. Everyone who loves has been born of God and knows God. Whoever does not love does not know God, because God is love . . . No-one has ever seen God; but if we love one another, God lives in us and his love is made complete in us. We know that we live in him and he in us because he has given us his Spirit.
(*1 John 4:7-8, 12-13*)

The Father begets the Son, and they pour out the Spirit.
The Spirit draws us into Christ, and so to the Father.

46

"I believe in the Holy Catholic Church"

(Catechism of the Catholic Church 748-945)

Our word *church*, the German *Kirche* and the Scots *Kirk* are all derived from the Greek word *Kyriake* which means 'what belongs to the Lord'. The Church is made up of people all 'belonging to the Lord'. The Church has no light other than Christ's. According to a favourite image of the Church Fathers, the Church shines the light and love of Christ onto the whole world. The Church is like the moon, all its light is reflected from the sun.

The Church is Holy
After his death and resurrection, Christ appeared to his disciples and told them that he would be with them until the end of time. Because of this, we can be confident that Christ is with his people, his Church, those who 'belong to the Lord'. Jesus makes the Church a holy place.

The Church is Catholic
The word 'catholic' simply means 'universal'. By saying that the Church is 'catholic' we are saying that in some sense it is universal and so is open to everyone. Everyone is welcome in the Church of God.

Saying the Church is universal does not mean that it is the same everywhere. The Church has always embraced many excitingly diverse and rich cultural traditions and incorporated them into its life and liturgy. Within the unity of the People of God, many different peoples and cultures are gathered together. Among the Church's members, there are different gifts, offices, conditions and ways of life. The great richness of this diversity is not opposed to the Church's unity.

In earlier times the Church saw itself as the only means of salvation. It believed that God chose to save humanity only through the Church.

Some thought that this meant that only baptised Catholics could be saved. The error of this understanding was recognised and the teaching has been expressed differently in more recent times. Vatican II, which ended in 1965, emphasised the more positive side of this teaching – that all are saved through Christ. There are many people of many faiths, those 'anonymous Christians' who, though not directly professing the faith of the Catholic Church, nevertheless are good and honest 'God-fearing' people who are not excluded from the loving, saving work of Christ.

The Church is Apostolic

The early Church put a lot of weight on the Apostles. When there were disputes or arguments about whose teachings to believe, the matter was settled by seeing how true it was to the teaching of the Apostles. It has always been important for the Church to see itself in direct continuity with this teaching, because the Apostles were themselves taught by Jesus. Jesus gave them his spirit, the Spirit of God. God is truth and cannot lie, and in so far as the Church is motivated by the Holy Spirit it acts and speaks in the truth.

Although Spirit-filled, the Church is also a human institution, and full of wounded sinful humanity. It is still a pilgrim people, and though it does in countless ways reflect the glory, truth and splendour of God, it also reflects the broken and sinful state of a lost humanity. So although we rightly expect the heights of sanctity from the Church, it can come as no surprise to discover it is riddled with the effects of original sin. The Church calls for our mercy and forgiveness as much as we call on the Church to be merciful and forgiving towards us.

Some may despair of the Church and see the institution as blockage, as total impediment. This is a danger. For the institution is necessary. True, it may overrate its role and arrogate to itself powers it does not possess. It may fail to see itself as the acolyte of the event, the person and the revelation. Stressing its authority, it may become authoritarian. It may dominate where it should serve. It may silence when it should listen. It may condemn when it should forgive. These are the temptations that come to all in power. History teaches that power, not money, is the author of corruption. Spiritual power is the most potent of all. Yet the Church needs an institution as the body needs a skeleton, for order and for articulation. An invertebrate Church would be a corpse.

Hugh Lavery *Reflections on the Creed*

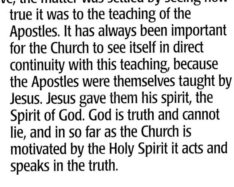

How is the visible communion of the Church ordered?

As Peter was appointed by Christ as first among the apostles so is the Bishop of Rome first among the bishops. Peter was appointed so that the apostles might be one and undivided. In the same way, the Roman Pontiff is the visible source and sign of the Church's unity. "Where Peter is, there is the Church."

(St Ambrose)

Why Peter?

Why Peter? After all he wasn't the brightest of the apostles. It was John's privilege to be "the one Jesus loved". And Matthew, the former tax-collector, was surely a better administrator. Yet Christ singled Peter out. By human standards God's choice of leader was a strange one.

The Church is ordered hierarchically. That is, to enable all members of the Church to reach full communion with Christ, the Church is ordered with a variety of ministries. These ministries are the episcopacy, the priesthood and the diaconate. With their helpers, the priests and deacons, bishops preside as teachers of doctrine, priests of sacred worship and officers of good order.

And so it remains in the Church. Many Christians are surprised at God's choice of leaders for his Church. But none are more surprised than the leaders themselves. Many priests and bishops – including sometimes the Bishop of Rome – remain constantly puzzled that they should be singled out.

One fact, in particular, strikes home: they have not been chosen for their greater holiness. Jesus' invitation to "be perfect, just as your heavenly Father is perfect" is made to *every* Christian. And, without question, very many men and women who are not called to office in the Church respond to that invitation more eagerly and more successfully. Why, then, are certain Christians singled out to succeed Peter and the apostles in the service of Christ's flock?

Jesus formed the apostles after the manner of a college or a fixed group, over which he placed Peter. This apostolic body continues without a break in the order of the bishops. The bishops assembled under one visible head, the Pope, express the unity of Christ's flock.

A communion of love

We have seen that the Church is a "communion of love". This is not a vague and hazy definition. It expresses the essential nature of the Church. Now, we emphasise an equally important truth: *the Church is a hierarchic communion.* That is, the community is ordered a variety of ministries, each subject to the one above it.

This "ordering" is far more than a practical way of preventing chaos. The "ordering" is of divine institution and is Christ's way of making the love of God (which would otherwise be hidden) visible to the world.

We can hardly over-emphasise the practical importance of this truth. Many people today, for example, feel that they can do better without "organised" religion. They feel that they can approach God more effectively without the institutional Church. The truth, however, is that it is God who does the approaching in his Son, Jesus Christ. And Jesus rarely comes to us in a blinding revelation of his glory. He comes quietly to us today, as he did in Palestine, in human form. He comes in a way that we can see him: in his Church.

In short, we enter the invisible "communion of love" by entering into the visible "hierarchic communion". The Church in its fullness is most surely found where there is a bishop in union with the Pope. Such a Church is the surest visible sign of Christ's presence.

So absolute is this truth that the Church recognises that Christ is visibly present even when the bishop, priest or deacon is in serious sin. For although the minister has separated himself from the "communion of love" he nevertheless remains part of the "hierarchic communion" and so a sign of Christ's presence.

"For you, I am Bishop, but with you, I am a Christian. The first is an office accepted, the second a grace received; one a danger, the other safety. If then I am more glad by far to be redeemed with you than I am to be placed over you, I shall, as the Lord commanded, be more completely your servant."

St Augustine of Hippo

What is the visible sign of communion with Christ's Church?

The visible sign of communion with Christ's Church is union with the Roman Pontiff, for Our Lord made Simon Peter alone the rock and key-bearer of the Church

Over the centuries "quite large communities have become separated from full communion with the Catholic Church … Such men who believe in Christ and have been properly baptised are brought into a certain, though imperfect, communion with the Catholic Church". (Dogmatic Constitution on the Church) The division, for example, between the Eastern Orthodox Churches and the Roman Catholic Church grew over centuries of misunderstanding; but their life is especially close, and the Catholic Church can "recommend worship in common given suitable circumstances".

It is, perhaps, more important than we realise to remember that God shows quite a sense of humour in his providential care of men and women. Who cannot smile, for example, at Christ's choice of the simple and somewhat awkward Peter as his first Vicar on earth?

It may seem strange that Christ appointed Peter as his Vicar. But it should not really surprise us that he turned to men of flesh and blood to guide his Church. After all, Christ founded a visible Church so that down the centuries men and women could share in the joys of those who came into contact with the *Word made Flesh.*

"A visible Church," writes Fr. Kenny S.J., "requires a visible head. Since Christ has been abstracted from our gaze, he needs a stand-in, a vicar, a centre of gravity, a focal point, a doctrinal spokesman to gather together, represent, sanction and nourish the thinking of the Christian community." When the world turns to the successor of Peter, it can be sure of turning to a recognisable source of Christ's healing power.

For many people today, the Catholic Church stands or falls on the Papacy. They point to the scandals of the past and suggest the Church is lacking today in constructive leadership. And here, of course, is a serious challenge. But is there not a shining example of the divine humour in the fact that "by divine appointment" the Church is a Church of sinners and not saints?

The title "Vicar of Christ" means that the Pope is the spiritual father of all. We believe, of course, that it is the Spirit and not the institution who is the Giver of Life. But the frail figure of the Pope reminds us that Christ granted the Spirit of Unity to a very weak Peter.

The Church recognises that all people can reach salvation "who through no fault of their own do not know the Gospel of Christ, yet sincerely seek God and, moved by grace, try by their actions to do his will as it is known to them through the dictates of conscience." Such men and women are not visibly united with Christ's Church, but they enjoy in some degree the invisible life of the Church: the grace of the Holy Spirit.

"I believe in the Communion of Saints"

(Catechism of the Catholic Church 946-962)

The Church is not just an earthly institution. Those who have died are still part of the Church, and we are still in communion with them. The living and the dead all belong to Christ and all live in Christ. So when we speak of the Church, we also speak of all those who have died and gone before us, marked with the sign of faith.

Mary Mother of the Church

(Catechism of the Catholic Church 963-975)

Among the saints Mary is pre-eminent. The life of Mary gives us an insight into the communion of saints and so we look at the meaning of her life in more detail. She is not a god, she is one of us.

Why is Mary addressed as 'Mother of the Church'?

Mary was acknowledged as "Mother of the Church" by Pope Paul VI in 1964. She is thus addressed because "through the choice of the Father and the action of the Holy Spirit, she gave human life to the Son of God, from whom the People of God – the Church – receives the grace and dignity of election". Jesus extended Mary's motherhood to all his disciples when, from the cross, he gave her as mother to his beloved disciple, John.

Her title, 'Mother of the Church' is closely linked to her more ancient title, 'Mother of God', which goes back to the Council of Ephesus, 431 AD. The Council, faced with the difficulty of stating that Jesus was both God and man, but not two persons, expressed the truth by stating that Mary, the Mother of Jesus, is Mother of God.

"Devotion to the blessed Virgin reflects the preoccupations of the Church herself, among which, in our day, is her anxiety for the re-establishment of Christian unity … Just as at Cana, Mary's intervention can help to bring to realisation the time when the disciples of Christ will again find full communion in faith." *(Marialis Cultus)*

Very little of Mary's life is recorded in the Gospels. But the mother's role is often not to speak or to act but simply to be there. Surely that is why St John, on two significant moments in Christ's life, reminds us, simply, that "the mother of Jesus was there".

Those two moments are Cana and Calvary. At Cana in Galilee Jesus worked his first sign or miracle. On Calvary he worked his last sign that won life for all humankind. And "the mother of Jesus was there". In the first, Mary brought those in need to Jesus: "Do whatever he tells you." In the last, Jesus brought those in need to Mary: "This is your mother."

For us, as for Jesus, Mary is there as our mother. She accepted him into her heart, and, in a similar way, she accepts us. She presented him to the Father in the Temple and, in a similar way, she presents us. She helped Jesus to walk his first steps and, in a similar way, she helps us. She stood by him in his suffering and, in a similar way, she stands by us. She is always there.

Mary cares for the Church and for every member of the Church as she cared for Jesus. When we fall, by accident or our own foolishness, she comforts and she cares. She guides us until we are restored to full life by the healing grace of her divine Son. Her love and attention enable God's grace to restore us to health.

This truth was clearly taught by Pope Paul VI when, at the close of the Second Vatican Council, he proclaimed Mary "Mother of the Church". In declaring this, Pope Paul wanted to teach us that we should deepen our understanding of the Church by reflecting on the life of Mary. Through prayer, and through study of Mary's life, we learn to realise that she "sums up" all that the Church is about. We can say that the history and purpose of the Church is already fulfilled in her. Everything that the Church means may be discovered in a right understanding of Mary.

And so if we think about the Church and Mary together, we will not fall into the trap of thinking about the Church *solely* as an institution. It is easy to criticise an institution, but it is harder to show bitterness towards one's mother. If we love Mary we will love the Church and vice versa. For the Church is the Body of Christ, to whom Mary gave birth when she consented to be the mother of Jesus at the Annunciation.

It is strange how anyone could cool in their devotion to our Lady, especially in these days when we claim to realise so clearly our need of one another. We need the help of saints; and we need the help of others who, like ourselves, are struggling members of the Church on earth. How much more, then, do we need the help of Mary, who has given us her Son, Jesus Christ, and with whom she now lives in the full glory of the resurrection? To those who ask her help Mary is always there.

a. **Greek Initials** for "Mother of God".
b. **Star** on Our Lady's veil. She is the Star of the Sea... who brought the light of Christ into the darkness of this world... the star that leads us safely home to Heaven.
c. **Greek Initials** for "St Michael the Archangel". He is depicted holding the spear and the sponge of Christ's Passion.
d. **Mary's mouth** is small, symbolising the fewness of her words and the depth of her contemplation.
e. **Red tunic**, the colour worn by virgins at the time of Christ.
f. **Dark blue mantle**, the colour worn by mothers in Palestine. Mary is both Virgin and Mother.
g. **Christ's hands**, placed in those of his Mother, speak to us of the trust we should repose in the prayers of Mary.
h. **Golden crown**, placed on the original picture by order of the Holy See. It is a token of the many favours obtained by Our Lady, invoked as "Mother of Perpetual Succour".
i. **Greek Initials** for "St Gabriel the Archangel". He holds the Cross and the nails.
j. **Mary's eyes are large**: they see all our needs and invite our requests.
k. **Greek initials** for "Jesus Christ".
l. **Mary's left hand**, supporting Christ firmly, speaks to us of the security we find in devotion to the Mother of God.
m. **Falling sandal**, a sign that those who contemplate Christ's passion will enjoy redemption and set foot in his eternal inheritance (see Ruth 4:7-8).

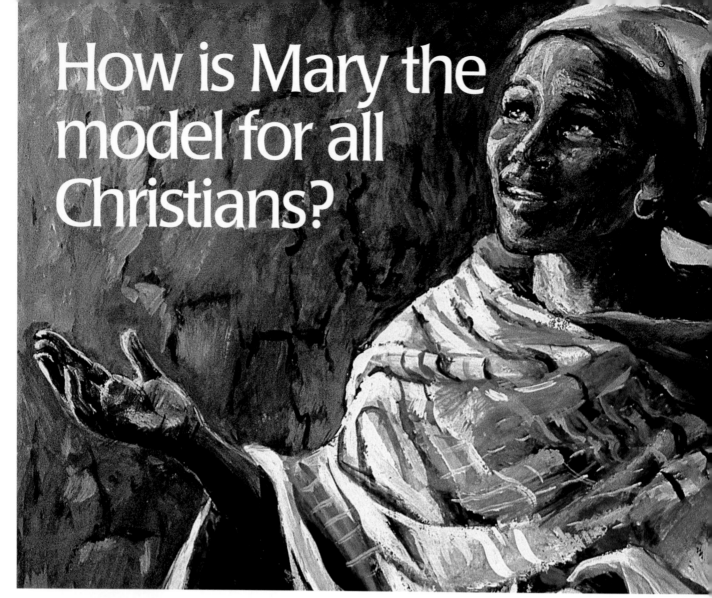

How is Mary the model for all Christians?

The Virgin Mary has always been proposed as an example to the faithful for the way in which, she "fully and responsibly accepted the will of God, because she heard the word of God and acted on it and because charity and a spirit of service were the driving force of her actions". Thus, having conceived the Son of God, she visited her cousin, Elizabeth, to share the Word she had discovered.

"Mary, while completely devoted to the will of God, was far from being a timidly submissive woman; on the contrary, she was a woman who did not hesitate to proclaim that God vindicates the humble and the oppressed … She was a woman of strength who experienced poverty and suffering, flight and exile … and her action helped to strengthen the apostolic community's faith in Christ." (Marialis Cultus)

"The Blessed Virgin Mary offers a calm vision and a reassuring word to people today, torn as we often are between anguish and hope, troubled in mind and divided in heart, uncertain before the riddle of death, oppressed by loneliness while yearning for fellowship, a prey to boredom and disgust. She shows forth the victory of hope over anguish, of peace over anxiety, of eternal visions over earthly ones, of life over death."

We are told that a young painter once brought a picture to Gustave Doré, the French artist and engraver. It was a painting of Christ, and he asked for Doré's verdict upon it. At first Doré was slow to say anything, but when pressed, he at last answered in one sentence: "You don't love Christ, or you would paint him better."

The lives of all Christians should portray Jesus Christ perfectly. We are to be "true images" of the Son. But each of us can say that we don't love him sufficiently, or our lives would paint him better. Love is the great interpreter. Only love can truly portray the life of Christ.

Mary's life most accurately reflects that of her divine Son. She loved Jesus; and so her life, from the moment of her conception to her glorious Assumption, paints the life of Christ and the life of every Christian perfectly.

The Christian imitates Mary. But what does this *mean* ? Clearly, the concrete situations of everyday life that we meet are very different from hers. But the Church reminds us that we are to imitate the *attitude* of Mary in our daily life and especially in our worship.

The Virginity of Mary

Perhaps we can understand this more fully by realising what is meant by Mary's virginity. Quite simply, this means that Jesus had no earthly father. The Gospels are very clear about it and the first teachers of Christianity included the doctrine of Mary's virginity as part of the faith. But all Christians are not called to physical virginity. What, then, does Mary's virginity *mean* to us?

In trying to answer this question we cannot simply presume that virginity is superior to marriage and that therefore it was the "way" chosen for Mary. We have only to recall the dignity given to marriage by Jesus to realise that this is not the answer.

Jesus was born of a virgin so that no one could be confused about where he had come from. The Son of God was born because God in his goodness and love chose to give him. He was *not* born because a man or woman willed it. The absence of a human father for Jesus meant that all humankind might know he is truly of God.

The human nature of Jesus was a pure gift of God. But it was achieved through the Virgin Mary. And so Mary teaches us what it means to completely abandon ourselves to God's will. She accepted the grace of God so completely that, quite literally, the Word of God, Jesus Christ, was born from her.

We learn from Mary's attitude. She was utterly at God's disposal. She was ready to receive God's grace. She responded joyfully to it. She responded joyfully to God's word. She emptied herself, realising her complete dependence on God for all that really matters in life. Mary shows us in her virginity that whatever we give for the sake of the Kingdom of God is repaid a hundredfold in the end.

"I believe in the forgiveness of sins"

(Catechism of the Catholic Church 976-987)

There is no offence, however serious, that the Church cannot forgive. 'There is no one, however wicked and guilty, who may not confidently hope for forgiveness, provided his repentance is honest' (Roman Catechism I, 11, 5). Christ who died for all desires that in his Church the gates of forgiveness should always be open to anyone who turns away from sin. *(Matthew 18:21-22, Catechism of the Catholic Church 982)*

By choosing to sin, we are choosing to settle for something less than God. We are choosing to sell ourselves short and allowing ourselves to become less human, less fully the people that God wants us to be. Sin makes us less human. For this reason, God's response to the sinner is not rage and anger, but gentle pity. When we sin we stand in need of healing. Forgiveness is the way that the healing mercy of God is given to us. Punishment for punishment's sake and vengeance for vengeance's sake have no place in the kingdom of God. Our God is a God of mercy, slow to anger and abounding in love.

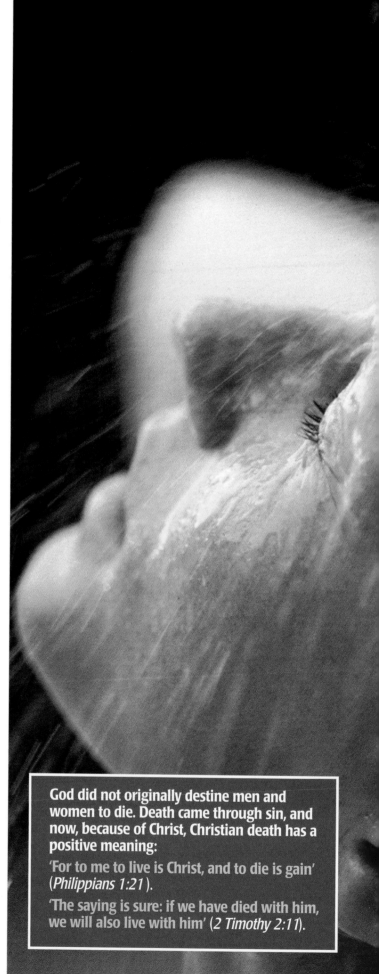

God did not originally destine men and women to die. Death came through sin, and now, because of Christ, Christian death has a positive meaning:

'For to me to live is Christ, and to die is gain' (*Philippians 1:21*).

'The saying is sure: if we have died with him, we will also live with him' (*2 Timothy 2:11*).

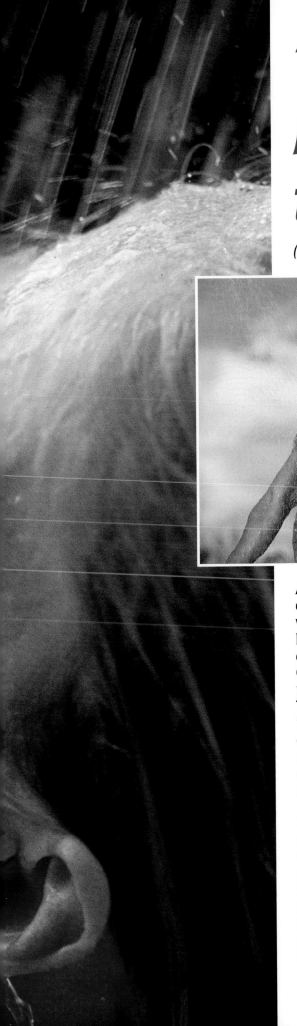

"I believe in the Resurrection of the Body"

(Catechism of the Catholic Church 988-1019)

Christian faith in the resurrection has often met with incomprehension and opposition. On no point does the Christian faith encounter more opposition than on the resurrection of the body. It is very commonly accepted that the life of the human person continues in a spiritual fashion after death. But how can we believe that this body, so clearly mortal, could rise to everlasting life?

Although we believe that Christ will raise us up on the last day, it is also true that, in a certain way, we have already risen with Christ. Christian life is already now on earth a participation in the death and Resurrection of Christ. United with Christ by Baptism, believers already truly participate in the heavenly life of the risen Christ. The believer's body and soul already participate in the dignity of belonging to Christ. This dignity entails the demand that we should treat with respect not only our own body, but also the body of every other person, especially those who suffer.

When we die, our soul separates from our body and our human body decays. The soul goes to meet God, while awaiting its reunion with its glorified body. At the last day, God will raise up our bodies, reuniting them with our souls, through the power of Jesus' Resurrection. God will not only raise up our human bodies, but the whole of creation will be transformed: God will create a new heaven and a new earth.

58

"I believe in life everlasting"

(Catechism of the Catholic Church 1020-1060)

Heaven

We cannot know what heaven will be like; we do not know the fate that awaits us after we die. This mystery of blessed communion with God and all who are in Christ is beyond all understanding and description. Scripture speaks of it in images: life, light, peace, wedding feast, wine of the kingdom, the Father's house, the heavenly Jerusalem, paradise. 'No eye has seen, nor ear heard, nor the heart of man conceived, what God has prepared for those who love him.' *(1 Corinthians 2:9)*

Purgatory

We may feel that we are really not good enough for heaven – what if we die when we are not ready, or before we have repented of all our sins? This is where purgatory comes in. Purgatory is a place of cleansing, where those who have died undergo a final purification to make them ready for heaven. Everyone in purgatory is certain to enter heaven – it's a bit like wiping your feet on the doormat before you go in.

We can never fully repair the damage caused by sin: we need to depend, in the end, on the mercy or "indulgence" of God. An "indulgence" (either partial or plenary) is a remission (in part or in full) of the punishment due for sin after its guilt has been forgiven. This remission is obtained by some "token" gesture of goodwill on our part. Indulgences have often been misunderstood and their abuse was the occasion for Martin Luther's final break with the Church at the Reformation.

The Church recognises that we do not always fully repair the damage caused by our sin in this life. Our final purification begins with death and is completed by what lies beyond death. This purification is known as purgatory. It has been the constant tradition of the Church to pray for the dead, especially in the Sacrifice of the Mass.

There are only two kinds of people in the end: those who say to God, 'Thy will be done', and those to whom God says, in the end, '*Thy* will be done.' All that are in Hell, choose it. Without that self-choice there could be no Hell. No soul that seriously and constantly desires joy will ever miss it. Those who seek, find. To those who knock it is opened.

(C.S. Lewis The Great Divorce)

Indulgences

The story of history is very largely the story of the family. Conflict among members of a family has frequently grown into the larger conflict of war. The peace and prosperity of a country, on the other hand, so often have their roots in a family life which is both industrious and stable.

Perhaps this is why both the Old and the New Testaments begin with the story of a family. The Old Testament, the story of man's continual rejection of God, tells the story of Adam and Eve and their children. It is the turbulent story of a family break-up so violent that brotherly love gives way to hate, jealousy, and eventual murder.

The New Testament, the story of God's love for us, introduces us to a very different family. This is the family of the Father who wants all men and women to share his own life. We believe that we are one Body in Christ, that we are united to each other. So close are we, says Saint Paul, that "If one part is hurt, all parts are hurt with it. If one part is given special honour, all parts enjoy it" *(1Corinthians 12:26)*

It is here, in the vision of the Church as a family, that we find the basis of the doctrine of indulgences. This teaching brings to our attention two separate but related beliefs. Firstly, that our own personal sin harms the rest of the Body of Christ and that, even after we have been forgiven, we need to make restitution and reparation to the community for the damage we have caused. Secondly, the doctrine proclaims the magnificent belief that all God's gifts are for giving away, for sharing. Within the family of the Church, we can benefit not only from our own personal gift of forgiveness and reconciliation but from gifts given by God to others.

The late Bishop Wheeler used to give the following simple explanation of this doctrine to children. A boy goes out into the street and heaves a brick through the sitting-room window. Not surprisingly, his father is very angry; but when the boy says he is sorry, his father forgives him. Friendship and reconciliation are established. But the father goes on to say: "To repair the costly damage you must give me 10p per week out of your pocket money until the new pane of glass is paid for." When this has been agreed and the first payment made, and goodwill is apparent, the father puts his hand into his pocket and says: "I am pleased with the effort you are making. Here is an extra 20p to help pay off the debt more speedily."

An indulgence is concerned with the debt which remains to be paid for the damage done by our sins. Like the boy in the story, we can turn to our family for help. We can share in the treasury which the saints already have in Jesus Christ. When we receive an indulgence, we are enabled to restore the damage done by our sins by relying on the merit of Jesus Christ and his saints.

Hell

God loves us with an infinite love, but he has also given us free will. Since we have free will, it is possible for us to reject God. Since free will exists, hell also exists – because hell is nothing more than the rejection of God.

Hell isthe place where all the wicked who fail to repent end up after they have died. Jesus portrayed it as a terrible place full of fire and pain. Those who end up in this terrifying place are separated from God and denied the joys of heaven. The Church affirms that hell *exists* but does not say whether there is actually anyone there. God has not predestined anyone to go there. God's wish is for everyone to be saved. We may have visions of God damning people to hell, but in the end it is *we* who choose heaven or hell, not God. We decide whether to love and let ourselves be loved.

"Amen"

(Catechism of the Catholic Church 1061-1065)
The Creed ends with the Hebrew word *amen*. In Hebrew, *amen* comes from the same root as the word for 'believe'. Thus the Creed's final 'Amen' repeats and confirms its first words: 'I believe.' To believe is to say 'Amen' to God's words, promises and commandments; to entrust oneself completely to him who is the 'Amen' of infinite love and perfect faithfulness. The Christian's everyday life will then be the 'Amen' to the 'I believe' of our baptismal profession of faith.

Part 2
Celebrating the presence of Christ

Celebrating the Church's Liturgy

(Catechism of the Catholic Church 1066-1206)

The 'Creeds', the statements of what we believe, are only part of the Church's tradition. As well as passing down to us things we believe, the Church has also preserved and handed down to us certain kinds of actions – things we do together. These things that we do are called 'liturgies'. The word 'liturgy' comes from the Greek word *leitourgia* which originally meant any sort of service or duty which was done on behalf of the people. Nowadays we tend to use the word 'liturgy' to refer exclusively to the ceremonies and events that take place in Church.

To someone who has never set foot in a church before, liturgical celebrations may seem very strange and out of touch with everyday living. This is partly due to the way that modern society has lost much of its ordinary 'liturgical' tradition, though we can still see traces of it in the way we sing 'happy birthday' and blow out candles on a birthday cake, or in the way a whole stadium of football fans is silent for a minute as a mark of respect when a player has been killed in an accident. Whether in church or not, liturgy is a very powerful way of drawing people together and expressing what they have in common.

Signs and symbols

Liturgy speaks to us in symbols and signs. It uses the whole range of our senses. Through sight, touch, hearing and smell we take part in the drama that is our faith. Liturgy speaks to us through signs and symbols. Signs use ordinary and everyday objects to point beyond themselves to something more. For example a road sign to Bognor Regis is more than just a piece of metal with black lines written on it. It is a piece of metal that points beyond itself and says something about something else – it says that 'Bognor Regis is that-a-way'. We can understand what the sign means because we understand the code: we can read the words 'Bognor Regis'. Signs only work for us when we understand them. If we don't know the code, then the significance of the signs is lost to us.

When we come to Mass we know roughly what is going to happen. The songs may change, the readings change, the priest's homilies change. But much else remains the same. But far from dulling us by this sameness, the liturgy allows us to be drawn into the presence of God. The liturgy gently leads us into the readings and the songs and the homilies. We don't have to think about what's coming next because we know by heart – and in our hearts – what's coming next. So secure in our knowing of the liturgy, we should be able to lay ourselves for an hour in the arms of a loving God.

What is Liturgy?
(Catechism of the Catholic Church 1066-1075)

We engage in liturgy every time we go to Mass, but we don't often stop and think about it. But that, in fact, is as it should be.

Liturgy is not intended to be mulled over. It is not intended to be difficult. It is not meant to be something new and confusing every time we come to it. Liturgy is about ritual, and ritual is best performed by heart.

It's just like, say, a Christmas family tradition. We're comfortable because we're at home and among people we know well and love. And there's a ritual to how the day is done. We arrive and gather. We talk and swap stories. We open the gifts. We eat. We say thanks. We leave. No one has to say, "What are we going to do next?" We all know. It's tradition, after all. But that doesn't mean there's nothing new. The stories we tell are new. The gifts are new. The meal is freshly prepared.

That's what liturgy is about: placing ourselves comfortably − along with the others around us who make up the body of Christ − in the presence of God and then celebrating the day.

A police officer was driving along behind a car which was obviously being driven by a very careful and cautious driver. So it came as some surprise when it drove straight through a set of red lights, narrowly missing a couple of pedestrians trying to cross the road. The policeman pulled the car over and asked the driver if he had realised that he had jumped the lights and endangered the lives of several pedestrians whilst doing so. The driver looked terribly upset and confessed sheepishly that he hadn't realised what the red lights were for − he was from Orkney , a small island off the North of Scotland where they didn't have traffic lights, and he had never seen one before.

64

A Deep Tradition

The word liturgy means a public service or something done on behalf of the people. Within the Church, liturgy is defined as "the worship of God by the Church".

The early Church (as described in the Acts of the Apostles) provided a great example of how we are to celebrate liturgy, because the believers, we are told, were of "one heart and one mind".

The purpose of the liturgy is two-fold: to give praise to God and to sanctify (make holy) the people of God. The liturgical worship of the Church includes not only the Mass, but also the sacraments, the Divine Office, and the sacramentals. The liturgy is, according to the German theologian A. Verheul, "a personal meeting, under the veil of holy signs, of God with His Church and with the total person of each one of her members". The liturgy is full of signs, but Christ himself is the central sign of the liturgy. He reveals himself in the Liturgy of the Word and also in the Eucharist. In the liturgy, Christ becomes united with the Church and becomes a sign of and for the people of God.

"The Church, therefore, earnestly desires that those who have faith in Christ, when present at this mystery of faith, should not be there as strangers or silent spectators; on the contrary, through an adequate understanding of the rites and prayers they should take part in the sacred action conscious of what they are doing, with devotion and full collaboration. They should be instructed by God's word and be nourished at the table of the Lord's Body; they should give thanks to God; by offering the immaculate victim not only through the hands of the priest but also with him, they should learn to offer themselves." Vatican II

The Church's Liturgy – brings us together as the Body of Christ

There is no point in a sign that points nowhere. The signs and symbols of the Church's worship point us to Jesus Christ and to his words and actions. Everything we say and do when we come together celebrates our union with Jesus.

This union is not, of course, with a Jesus who is dead and buried. The signs in the Church's liturgy don't simply take us back two thousand years to keep alive a half-forgotten memory. The liturgy unites us with a Jesus who is risen and who lives in glory. The signs and symbols of the Church point us to the present; they unite us with the Body of Jesus, a Body filled with the Spirit of God, who draws us into the eternal love of our heavenly Father.

The Church Community is the Body of Christ

The modern liturgical use of the word "community" means a group of people who are bound together by their common faith. As a group, the members of the "community" strive for both their own salvation and for the salvation of all those in the group.

Vatican II says: "God did not create us for life in isolation, but for the formation of social unity." God saves us not as individuals without bonds between us, but as a "single people". From the beginning, God has made covenants with "his people".

Jesus was the epitome of this plan. As the Word-Made-Flesh, by nature he shared unity with all humans. He lived the life of an ordinary man, sharing in the joys and pains of life, just like those around him. In his teaching, he stressed the importance of treating everyone as if they were family. In his prayers, he asked that his disciples might be "made one". He commanded them to bring the good news to all people so that all might become part of the family of God.

In short, Jesus did not come for an elite group. He came that all might be one, just as he is one with the Father.

ty: The
⌐rist
 is one
⌐as
s, and all
⌐f the
⌐gh
 one
⌐so with
 in one
⌐ere all
⌐to one
⌐ther
⌐eeks,
⌐ee persons, and we are all
⌐ink of one Spirit."
(1 Corinthians 12:12-13)

Paul and the Body of Christ

The Church was first referred to as "the body of Christ" by Paul in his first letter to the Church at Corinth. Although this term certainly refers to the intimate relationship between Christ and his early followers, it is more than that. For through faith and baptism we are incorporated into Christ; we are taken into his body, his death and his resurrection. This relationship is nurtured when we listen to Christ's Word and receive his body and blood in communion. So as we partake of his body and blood we bind ourselves all the more closely both with Jesus and with all other believers who share in this communion. Paul speaks eloquently of these relationships throughout his letters to the early Church. For more insight, read:
1 Corinthians 6:15-20; 10:16-17;
all of chapter 12
Colossians 1:18-24
Romans 12:3-8
Ephesians 1:15-23; 4:1-6

What makes us the Body of Christ and the People of God?

According to the teaching of the Catholic Church, these are the characteristics of the People of God:

- We are Christians not by birth, but by being "born anew" in the waters of baptism and by our faith in Jesus Christ.
- We are a Messianic people. Jesus Christ – the Messiah – is the recognised head of the Church.
- Because we belong to God we have dignity and freedom.
- The Holy Spirit dwells within us. We are the temple of the Holy Spirit.
- Our chief law is the new commandment to love each other as Christ loved us.
- Our mission is to be the salt of the earth and the light of the world.
- Our destiny is the kingdom of God, which was begun by God here on earth and must be extended until it has been brought to perfection by him.

> "The Church is a people brought into union from the unity of the Father, the Son and the Holy Spirit."
> (Dogmatic Constitution on the Church, par. 4)

The Church's Liturgy – brings us together for worship

Jesus had two all-consuming passions. He wanted to unite himself fully with human beings. And he wanted to express openly his union with his Father. These ambitions were not achieved during his life on earth.

In his death and resurrection everything changed. In his passion on Calvary, Jesus offered the spirit of forgiveness to every person when he cried out: "Father, forgive them, they do not know what they are doing." And then he gave up his spirit to his Father in his final words: "Father, into your hands I commit my spirit."

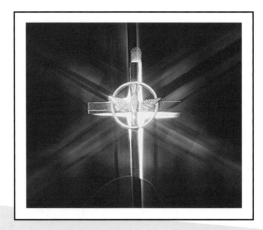

After his resurrection, Jesus said to his disciples: "Peace…Receive the Holy Spirit. For those whose sins you forgive, they are forgiven." The Spirit of God – the spirit of love – is offered to every person in a union so deep that we become the Body of Jesus Christ. The forgiveness which is offered in Jesus' resurrection completes the passion of Jesus to be with every human being, just as it fulfilled his passion to be with his Father.

This union with Jesus is celebrated whenever we come together in his name. And, because we are with Jesus in his own passion to be united with his Father, we do have something to celebrate.

This celebration is "worship". Worship isn't something we have to get through in order to keep God happy. It is recognising that through the gift of the Spirit we are being drawn into the love and intimacy of Jesus and his Father. That is why we make our prayer to the Father, through Jesus, in the power of the Holy Spirit. And, at the conclusion to the Eucharistic Prayer during Mass, the priest says:

Through him, with him, in him,
in the unity of the Holy Spirit,
all glory and honour is yours,
almighty Father,
for ever and ever. Amen.

It was my family's first Sunday in our new parish. But this was not just any "new parish" experience. We had just moved to England from the United States. It was our first time living anywhere else except our hometown.

Everything was a bit strange to us. We didn't know any of the songs, we didn't know a soul in the congregation, and we had a hard time understanding the words of the old Irish priest. My wife and I held each other's hand and secretly wished we were back home.

But our disorientation was short-lived. When it was time for communion I went to the front of the church, held out my hand, and received the precious body of Christ. At that moment the barriers fell away, for I knew I was sharing the same body with everyone back at our old parish, as well as with millions of Catholics around the world who approach the altar every week not because they are worthy but because they are hungry and in need of healing.

We were thousands of miles and an ocean away from family and friends. But we knew we were home. That's the mystery of the Body of Christ.

The Lord's Supper

The words and images of Jesus' "last supper" with his disciples are almost second nature to us. We know the words because we hear them every Sunday at Mass. We all know the famous painting by da Vinci.

And so we think we have an idea of what it must have been like to have been there. And that's just as Jesus intended. For that "Last Supper" was not given as an exclusive meal for his chosen insiders. It was given to them so that it could be repeated over and over—so that it could be "done in remembrance." That holy meal was given to the disciples so that we could do it ourselves.

Down through almost 2,000 years, this simple meal has been at the core of Christian – especially Catholic – worship. It is for this reason that the rest of the liturgy was created. We gather to offer prayer and sing songs and listen to the readings so that we can partake of this bread-turned-flesh and that wine-turned-blood. It is the kind of gift that only an all-loving God could give. God created us and gave us life. He gave us a home where everything we could ever need was provided. When all that wasn't enough for us, he gave himself. That is why we celebrate.

"While they were eating, Jesus took bread, said the blessing, broke it, and giving it to his disciples said, 'Take and eat; this is my body.' Then he took a cup, gave thanks, and gave it to them saying, 'Drink from it, all of you, for this is my blood of the covenant, which will be shed on behalf of many for the forgiveness of sins. I tell you, from now on I shall not drink this fruit of the vine until the day when I drink it with you new in the kingdom of my Father.' Then, after singing a hymn, they went out to the Mount of Olives." (Mattthew 26:26-30).

Do this in memory of me...

When Jesus knew his time on earth was short, he gathered his disciples together for one more meal. The meal itself was either offered on the night before the Jewish Passover or it was actually a Passover meal. They came together in an upper room we now refer to as the Cenacle (from *cena*, the Latin word for supper). His actions were not unusual to them. Offering bread and wine, giving thanks, breaking the bread, sharing food and drink–these were typical Jewish observances. But Jesus gave a new twist to these old rituals when he told them that the bread was his body and the wine was his blood.

By his words and actions, Jesus transformed this Jewish meal into a new ritual tied to his passion and death. In the process, he instilled in his followers a greater understanding of who he was and what was to come.

At the same time, he commanded his disciples to repeat this new ritual and perpetuate it, establishing this memorial to his redemptive death as a sacrament for his new Church. This memorial then, looks back to the Exodus of the people of God, expresses our belonging to Christ and looks forward to eternal life with him.

The Liturgy of the Early Church

"They devoted themselves to the teaching of the apostles and to the communal life, to the breaking of bread and to the prayers....All who believed were together and had all things in common .... Everyday they devoted themselves to meeting together in the temple area and to breaking bread in their homes."
– Acts 2:42-46

In the days following Jesus' death and resurrection, the disciples struggled to build a new Church and a new way of worship. They continued to attend the Jewish synagogue, but they also began to meet in each other's homes for prayer and breaking bread. A new Church was being formed from the ground up.

When the first Christians gathered to celebrate "the Lord's Supper", they met in the late afternoon and the service was followed by a meal. Only toward the middle of the second century did the "Eucharist" as we know it become a rite of its own. At that time, the celebration was moved to Sunday morning and was joined to a service of reading and preaching. A liturgy began to take form.

The early Christians had no churches or temples, and the places they worshipped (mostly their homes) had no religious significance in themselves. Instead, the focus of their worship remained the praying community. They were the Church.

The earliest written description of the Mass comes from Justin the Martyr, who died in 165. In a letter he wrote in 155 to the pagan emperor Antoninus Pius, he explains what Christians did when they gathered:

"On the day we call the day of the sun, all who dwell in the city or country gather in the same place. The memoirs of the apostles and the writings of the prophets are read, as much as time permits.

"When the reader has finished, he who presides over those gathered admonishes and challenges them to imitate these beautiful things. Then we all rise together and offer prayers for ourselves and for all others, wherever they may be, so that we may be found righteous by our life and actions, and faithful to the commandments, so as to obtain eternal salvation.

"When the prayers are concluded we exchange the kiss. Then someone brings bread and a cup of water and wine mixed together to him who presides over the brethren. He takes them and offers praise and glory to the Father of the universe, through the name of the Son and of the Holy Spirit and for a considerable time he gives thanks (in Greek: eucharistian) that we have been judged worthy of these gifts.

"When he has concluded the prayers and thanksgivings, all present give voice to an acclamation by saying: 'Amen.' When he who presides has given thanks and the people have responded, those who we call deacons give to those present the "eucharisted" bread, wine and water and take them to those who are absent."

House Churches

In many places around the world, small groups of people continue to meet in each other's homes to pray. In Latin America these groups are called communidades de base; in Africa, small Christian communities; in Asia, intentional Christian communities. In North America they are known by many names, including house churches and basic Christian communities.

These gatherings resemble the house churches of the early centuries of Christian life. Although each community varies widely depending on the membership and culture, they do share some identifying marks.

- They are small enough for all the members to know one another. Rarely will a community have more than 20 members.
- They meet regularly, often once a week.
- They are not viewed by their members as an alternative to the institutional Church. Rather, they are an authentic form of the institutional Church. They do not view themselves as isolated from the rest of the Church.
- They are based on Gospel values and centred on the Liturgy of the Word and when a priest is available, on the Eucharist.
- While the communities themselves are non-hierarchical, they are generally not anti-hierarchical or against the traditional Church.
- They see themselves as basic ecclesial units.

The Jewish Seder

In recent times, many Christian churches have taken to offering their congregations an opportunity during Lent to experience a Jewish seder meal because of its obvious ties to the Christian Eucharist.

The seder (from the Hebrew word for "order") is eaten on the first two nights of Passover. So if Jesus' last supper was indeed offered on the first night of Passover, he and his disciples were actually gathering for the seder.

The seder is the Jewish celebration of the Exodus from Egypt. During the meal, the Exodus story is retold and re-experienced by the celebrants. This re-enactment of their bondage and deliverance form the heart and spirit of the seder. Specific foods are eaten in set order during the ceremony, including:

- matzoth, the unleavened bread of bondage;
- maror, or bitter herbs (grated horseradish), commemorating the bitterness of slavery;
- baitzah, a hard-boiled egg, symbolic of life's cycle of birth and death;
- zaroah, roasted lamb representing the paschal lamb;
- haroseth, chopped nuts, apples, and wine, symbolic of the clay used by the slaves to make bricks;
- karpas, parsley, lettuce or other greens, as a reminder of the new growth of spring.

Four cups of wine are drunk during the ceremony, and a goblet of wine is placed on the seder table in the symbolic hope that the prophet Elijah, whose appearance will presage the coming of the Messiah, may enter and partake of the wine that awaits him.

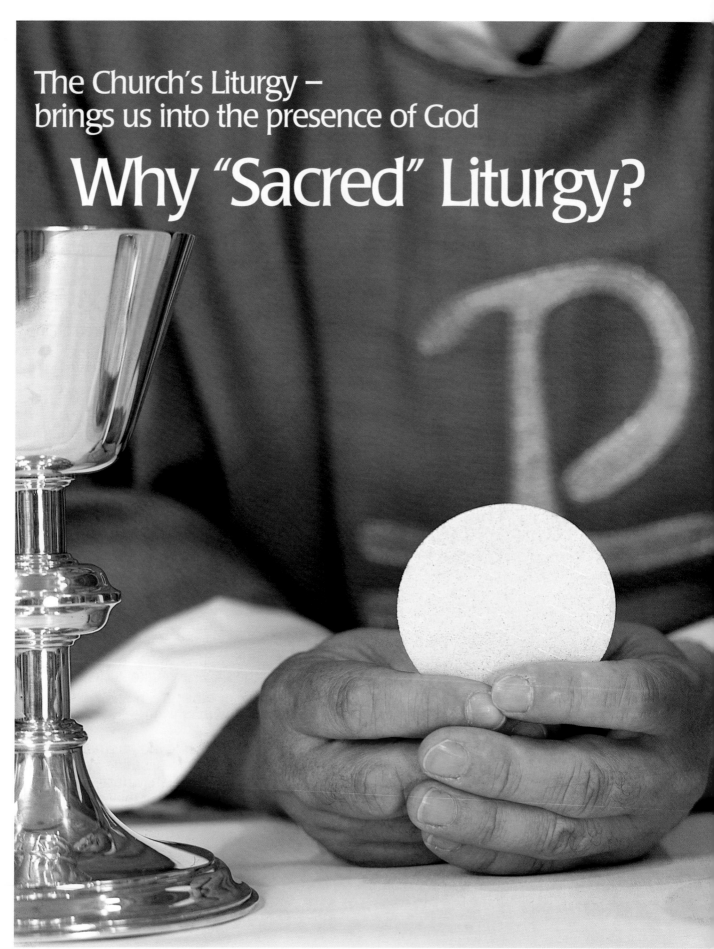

The Church's Liturgy –
brings us into the presence of God
Why "Sacred" Liturgy?

"On the first day you shall hold a sacred assembly..." (Exodus 12:16)

Most people would confess to a few things that they hold sacred. But do we seek the sacred? We should, for when we perceive things to be sacred, what we are perceiving is their connection to God. That's why the liturgy is sacred.

The liturgy is filled with sacred things like sacred vessels and the Sacred Host. The church is filled with sacred furnishings and art. The sacred Scripture is proclaimed. We are surrounded by "sacramentals" like candles, holy water, vestments, the sign of the cross, the rosary, and blessings.

All of these are there to bring us closer to God, to what is sacred. These things are sacred because the presence of God is sacred. A favourite hymn says: "This is holy ground. We're standing on holy ground. For the Lord is present and where He is, is holy." The "sacred" around us creates for us a piece of holy ground upon which we can draw near to God and worship Him.

Within the liturgy, everything that is done is sacred. Every movement of the president's hand, every word uttered and prayed, every song sung, every vessel filled and later cleaned, every step we take towards the altar to receive the body of Christ, all this is sacred because it brings us that much closer to God.

The most sacred symbol within the liturgy is not really a symbol at all. For when we receive the consecrated body of Christ we go beyond sacred signs and enter directly into the presence of God and of Christ. We become sacred.

Our "job," so to speak, is to recognise this sacredness. That's why the liturgy requires our full participation and attention. For when we recognise the sacred in the liturgy, we recognise that all those gathered have entered into the presence of God. And when that happens, the place where we meet becomes holy ground.

Signs, Symbols and Gestures

Sacred signs, symbols and gestures within the liturgy all serve to bring us closer to God. The Mass brings us directly into the presence of God because it is filled with these sacred symbols. They exist within our world, and yet, because of their sacredness, they also reach beyond this world. They help us bridge the gap.

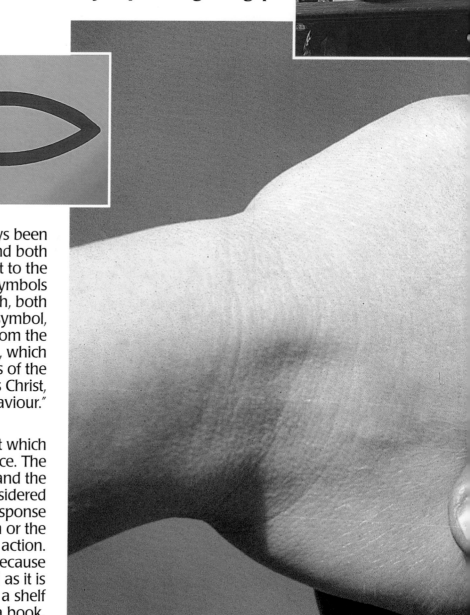

Symbols in liturgy have always been used as a way to call to mind both people and mysteries important to the Christian Church. Early symbols included the cross and the fish, both symbols of Christ. The fish symbol, called an "ichthus", is derived from the Greek letters for the word fish, which also spell out the initial letters of the proclamation of faith: "Jesus Christ, Son of God, Saviour."

A sign is an action or an object which has special religious significance. The crucifix, the Sign of the Cross, and the books upon the altar are all considered signs because they call for a response by the person observing them or the person performing the action. The lectionary is a sign only because we listen to the Word of God as it is read from it. Sitting on a shelf it is just a book.

Gestures are symbols that we perform. We make the sign of the cross and bless ourselves. We genuflect. We stand. We kneel. If we perform these gestures with reverence and attentiveness, they can assist us in moving closer to God. If we perform them purely out of habit, they can be just that – habit. It is our attention and reverence that give gestures meaning. They are not magic.

What does it mean when I....

● Kneel...When we kneel we acknowledge the greater power and high position of God. Like knights before the king, we give our God our allegiance, our reverence and honour.

● Stand...In the liturgy, we stand when we pray. We stand in respect for a loving God who hears our prayers. When we stand before God, it also shows our attentiveness to his Word and his blessings.

● Genuflect...When we touch our right knee to the ground we engage in a simple act of reverence. Genuflection is the appropriate act of veneration before the Blessed Sacrament in the tabernacle.

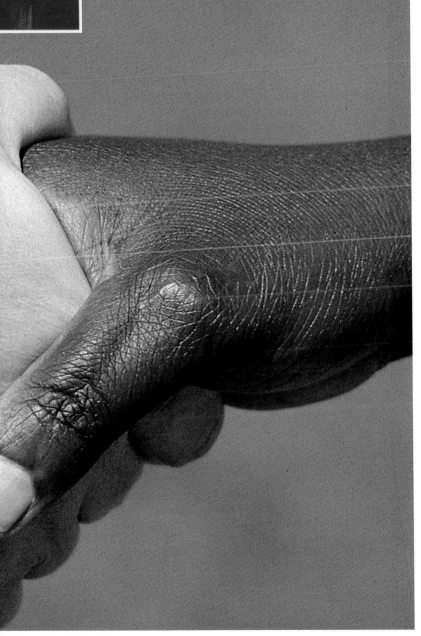

"...Christ Jesus, who, though he was in the form of God, did not regard equality with God something to be grasped. Rather, he emptied himself, taking the form of a slave, coming in human likeness;...he humbled himself, becoming obedient to death, even death on a cross. Because of this, God greatly exalted him and bestowed on him the name that is above every name, that at the name of Jesus every knee should bend, of those in heaven and on earth and under the earth, and every tongue confess that Jesus Christ is Lord, to the glory of God the Father."
(Philippians 2:5-11)

Music and Singing

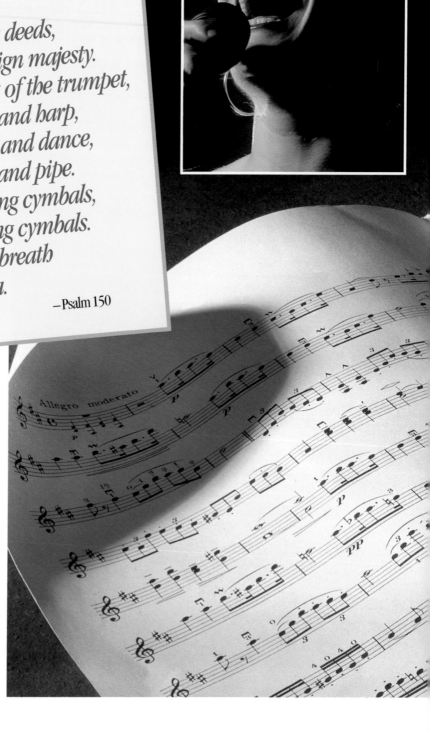

*Praise the Lord in his sanctuary,
praise him in the firmament of his
strength.
Praise him for his mighty deeds,
praise him for his sovereign majesty.
Praise him with the blast of the trumpet,
praise him with the lyre and harp,
praise him with timbrel and dance,
praise him with strings and pipe.
Praise him with sounding cymbals,
praise him with clanging cymbals.
Let everything that has breath
praise the Lord! Alleluia.*

—Psalm 150

According to the Catechism of the Catholic Church, "The musical tradition of the universal Church is a treasure of inestimable value, greater even than that of any other art. The main reason for this pre-eminence is that, as a combination of sacred words and music, it forms a necessary or integral part of the solemn liturgy."

The key to this statement lies in the words "necessary and integral". For while music may be viewed by some as an "add on" to liturgy, it is, in fact, a necessary part of liturgy. The American writer and liturgist Gabe Huck, in his book, "How Can I Keep From Singing?" goes as far as to say: "When people come together for ritual, we expect there to be music."

Back in Old Testament times, David wrote inspired psalms that were often accompanied by instruments. In the days of the early Church, Paul appeals to the Church at Ephesus to "address one another in psalms and hymns and spiritual songs, singing and making melody to the Lord with all your heart." Perhaps St Augustine said it most bluntly: "He who sings prays twice."

So we sing and offer musical praise at Mass not because it's a nice addition to the liturgy, but because it is liturgy. But that doesn't mean that just any old song done in any old way is appropriate for liturgy. Music is especially significant when:

● Is it beautiful and expressive of prayer.
● It has the participation of the congregation.
● It matches the sacred character of the celebration.

Liturgy – for ever and ever

The roots of much of the liturgical year lie in pre-Christian ceremonies, for example Christmas has its roots in the pagan feast of the unconquered sun. The word 'Easter' originates in fertility rites to the German dawn-goddess who was called 'Eastre'. We still celebrate Easter with Easter eggs which have little to do with Christian symbolism and very much to do with pagan symbols of fertility. It is remarkable how successfully the Church has taken over and transformed the old pagan festivals, which celebrated the natural cycles of the year, and given them new Christian meanings.

Worship is natural to humanity

The Church's liturgy follows the natural rhythms of the year and the changing seasons. Colour, smells, sight, sound – all our senses are involved in liturgy. The colours of the priest's vestments at Mass change with the seasons – green for ordinary time, red for martyrs' feast days, white for Easter Day and purple for Advent and Lent. The rhythm of our lives fits into the rhythm of the Church. There are prayers said regularly throughout the day, the 'liturgy of the hours', daily and weekly Masses, the great seasons of Advent, Christmas, Lent and Easter, feast days and Holy days. From the microcosm to the macrocosm, from minutes and hours to the seasons of the year, the liturgy of the Church surrounds and encompasses us so that our everyday existence is drawn into the prayerful rhythm of the whole Church.

Liturgy can be seen as a foretaste of heaven. Through the rituals of the Church, local churches all through the world are joined together. The whole of the believing community is involved, which includes the 'community of saints', and the whole company of heaven. All those who have died join with us and the angels to praise and glorify God through the liturgy of the Church.

From the Outside Looking In

"I was not raised a Catholic, and my limited exposure to "things Catholic" as a child (weddings, funerals, etc.) brought me to this early conclusion: Catholics must be very tired by the time they leave Mass. They sit, they stand, they kneel, they cross themselves, they make funny gestures that I couldn't understand. I didn't understand any of it, except for this: They seemed to be doing all of these things in reverence, and their reverence appealed to me. I longed to kneel before the cross, but we just didn't do that in my church."

The Catholic faith is more than symbolic. It is a faith rooted in Scripture, history, tradition, and the deep-seated beliefs of all who have gone before. Still, to a great extent it is the symbols of this ancient faith that help keep it alive and bring its members into closer communion with Christ and his Church.

Ughh!
Gregory of Tours, who lived in the sixth century, belonged to a monastery which firmly held to the belief that the angels joined them in their prayers. Throughout the day and night the monks would gather to sing the psalms, sitting facing each other in two rows. Hosts of angels were thought to stand between them, singing out with the monks in praise of God. The angels were pressed so closely into the space between the two lines of monks, that the monks were informed that if they desired to spit, they should turn around to avoid spitting on any of the angels which were gathered in front of them.

The Mass itself is the strongest symbol the Church puts forward. The Mass represents the gathered body of Christ, joined together in love and devotion. It represents nearly 2,000 years of Christians gathered in upper rooms, catacombs and cathedrals. It represents a world-wide Church that continues to gather despite persecution, changing cultures and modern influences. But more than any of these things, the Mass symbolises an outpouring of love so great that it can only be understood when we kneel before the cross or accept the precious body of our Lord and say "amen" to the words: "the body of Christ."

The Liturgical Year

The Church calendar, also referred to as the liturgical year or liturgical calendar, is the series of liturgical seasons throughout the year that determines daily Scripture readings as well as the daily assignment of saints' feast days and other commemorations. Although not all Christian denominations make use of the liturgical calendar, the Catholic Church believes the calendar helps create harmony and unity among its vast number of churches and dioceses throughout the world. Vatican II documents stress the importance of creating this unity:

"Holy Mother Church is conscious that she must celebrate the saving work of her divine Spouse by devoutly recalling it on certain days throughout the course of the year....Within the cycle of a year, moreover, she unfolds the whole mystery of Christ, not only from His incarnation and birth until His ascension, but also as reflected in the day of Pentecost, and the expectation of a blessed, hoped-for return of the Lord." (Constitution on the Sacred Liturgy, par. 102)

So although parts of the Mass always remain the same, others change according to what is right and proper for the season or the particular feast being celebrated.

"And on that day you will explain to your son, 'This is because of what Yahweh did for me when I came out of Egypt.' The rite will serve as a sign on your hand would serve, or a memento on your forehead, and in that way the law of Yahweh will be ever on your lips, for Yahweh brought you out of Egypt with a mighty hand. You will observe this ordinance each year at its appointed time."
– Exodus 13: 8-10

December	January		February	March	April	May
Advent	Christmas	Ordinary Time	Lent		Easter	Pentecost

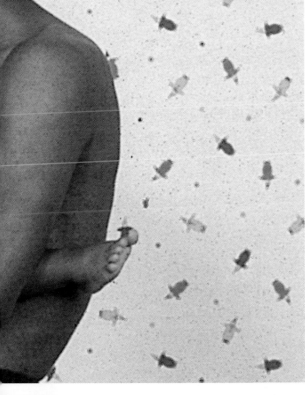

The Year

Advent – The liturgical year begins near the end of our calendar year – in December. Lasting four weeks, advent is a time of waiting and preparation for the birth of the Saviour. Drawing largely on the writings of the prophets who anticipated the birth of Jesus, advent whets our appetite for the glory of Christmas and fills us with hope and longing for "light in the darkness".

Christmas – The Christmas season begins with midnight Mass on Christmas Eve and continues through the day celebrated as Christ's baptism in early January. So rather than believing that Christmas is a one-day affair, the Church holds that it is a season unto itself, a time to meditate on the wonder of Jesus alive in each of us.

Ordinary Time – This first section of Ordinary Time lasts six to nine weeks depending on the date of Easter. It begins with the baptism of Jesus by John in the Jordan and so the beginning of Jesus' public ministry. It's a time to catch our breath after Christmas and get reacquainted with our daily lives. And like the people whom Jesus taught during his ministry, we are treated to readings during this time that show us what an extraordinary teacher Jesus was.

Lent – like Advent, Lent is a period of preparation. For 40 days we are called to spiritually ready ourselves for the focal point of the liturgical year – Jesus' passion, death and resurrection. Lent is about penance and giving up, but it's also about deepening our relationship with Jesus so we can understand these events all the more. It is a time to remember our weaknesses and place ourselves in the loving arms of our Lord. Lent ends with the beginning of the Easter triduum at the Mass of the Lord's Supper in Holy Thursday. The Easter triduum then begins consisting of Holy Thursday, Good Friday through to evening prayer on Easter Sunday. Holy Thursday, Good Friday and the Easter Vigil on Easter Saturday.

Easter – Easter, like Christmas, is a season and not just a day. It begins on Easter morning and continues through to Pentecost. The stories we hear during this seven-week period are vivid reminders that we are not the mourners of a dead prophet, but rather the resurrection people of a living Saviour. Included in this season are the feasts of Jesus' Ascension to the Father and Pentecost – the coming of the Holy Spirit.

Ordinary Time (again) – Back to our regular life with a longer period of ordinary time. This season takes us back where we started – Advent. Feasts during this time include Trinity Sunday, Transfiguration, Assumption, All Saints and All Souls Days.

June	July	August	September	October	November
		Ordinary Time			Christ the King

The Most Important Signs – Sacraments

The word 'sacrament' comes from a Latin word *'sacramentum'*. Within the Roman army, recruits had to take a military oath, called a Sacramentum, which was an oath of loyalty. Then they were often branded or tattooed with the emperor's mark – this was so that if they deserted they could be identified easily. For some reason the early Church Fathers began to use the word sacramentum in a Christian context, perhaps seeing a similarity between the soldier's oath of loyalty and the commitment of the newly baptised Christian's baptismal vows. The permanent change which took place in the life of the newly baptised mirrored the oath of fidelity of the new recruit and the brand on his skin.

The history of sacraments

The seven sacraments of the Church are: Baptism, Confirmation, Eucharist, Penance, Anointing the Sick, Holy Orders and Marriage. The process by which the Church recognised these seven sacraments took place over many centuries. St Ambrose, for example, who lived in the fourth century, saw both baptism and foot-washing as sacraments, while St Augustine thought of the creed, the Our Father, baptism and the Eucharist as sacraments, and St Peter Damien (eleventh century) thought that the anointing of kings, the dedication of churches, funerals and the monastic habit were all sacraments. Sacraments were seen as tangible signs of something holy, and so included what we today would refer to as 'sacramentals' – the blessing of a house or a person, for example. It was only in the middle ages that the term 'sacrament' was narrowed down to the more precise meaning that we think of today. The first Council to officially name the seven sacraments was the Fourth Lateran Council in 1215, but it was not until the Council of Trent in 1547 that it was defined as being a matter of faith that there are seven sacraments.

Revelations of Love

Sacraments are signs which point us to the forgiveness and mercy of God. They reveal God's plan to save mankind from sin and death. Sacraments bring us into fellowship with each other, they offer us healing and forgiveness and they join us to each other in love and service. They are signs of God's love for us, revealing the tremendous goodness of God and his concern for the salvation of the whole world. Sacraments are signs of God's love, but they are also more than just signs.

God is at work in the sacraments, making what they signify a reality. Most signs tell you something, but they don't make it happen. A sacrament is a sign of salvation which brings about the very salvation that it signifies. This is what the Church means when it speaks of the sacraments as 'efficacious' signs. An efficacious sign is a sign which has an effect!

What is a sacrament?

A sacrament is a saving act of Jesus Christ. In the celebration of every sacrament it is Jesus Christ who makes the first move in coming to lift up the person in need of salvation, just as he came to lift up his friend Lazarus in the village of Bethany.

It is an act celebrated in and through the Church which unites us with Christ's worship of his Father. In the celebration of every sacrament of the Church Jesus Christ lifts up the one who believes in order to unite that person with the Father; just as he revealed the glory of God when he raised up Lazarus with the words, "Father, I thank you for hearing my prayer." (John 11:41)

It is an act by which we receive the Spirit of Christ and so are formed in the image of Christ when he emerged from the tomb with new life.

"Since the Lord is no longer visible among us, everything of him that was visible has passed into the sacraments" (St. Leo the Great).

> "St Thomas sums up the various aspects of sacramental signs: 'Therefore a sacrament is a sign that commemorates what precedes it – Christ's Passion; demonstrates what it accomplishes in us through Christ's Passion – grace; and prefigures what that Passion pledges to us – future glory'." (Catechism of the Catholic Church 1130)

In most of the sacraments the Church takes material things – water, wine, bread, oil – and uses them as a vehicle of the Spirit. In this way the sacraments reflect the incarnation, when God took on material flesh and became a human being. The sacraments are a combination of outward, visible signs and inward, invisible, spiritual grace. At Baptism, we have water poured over us and are at the same time cleansed inwardly from sin. At the Eucharist we receive what appears to be bread and wine but which is in reality the body and blood of Christ.

Perhaps it may seem obvious to say that Jesus Christ was the first to live the Christian life. But it does bring home to us that it is meaningless to talk about a Christian life which is not an actual sharing and participation in Christ's life. That is where the sacraments come in. Christ is continually seeking to share his divine life with us, to be born again in each one of us. And the place of our meeting is in the sacraments. As St Ambrose expressed it, "You have shown yourself to me, Christ, face to face. I meet you in the sacraments."

Baptism

(Catechism of the Catholic Church 1213-1419)

Baptism

The word 'baptism' comes from the Greek word *baptizein* which means to plunge or immerse. Baptism has its roots in Judaism where converts had to undergo a purificatory bath as part of the rite of conversion. Jesus began his public life after being baptised by John the Baptist in the river Jordan. After his resurrection, Jesus told his disciples: 'Go therefore and make disciples of all nations, baptising them in the name of the Father and of the Son and of the Holy Spirit, teaching them to observe all that I have commanded you' (Matthew 28:19-20). Throughout history, the Church has followed Jesus' command, instructing catechumens and then baptising them in the name of the Father and of the Son and of the Holy Spirit.

Baptism marks the entry of the believer into the Christian community. Along with Confirmation and the Eucharist, Baptism is one of the sacraments of initiation. It acts rather like a sort of gate which opens into the other sacraments. Through Baptism, we have access to the full sacramental life of the Church. We are freed from sin and joined with Christ, sharing in his divinity and destined for eternal life. Baptism leaves us indelibly marked and permanently changed. Once baptised, we are no longer the person we once were. We have been reborn, dying to our old selves, dying to death and sin, and rising to new life in Christ.

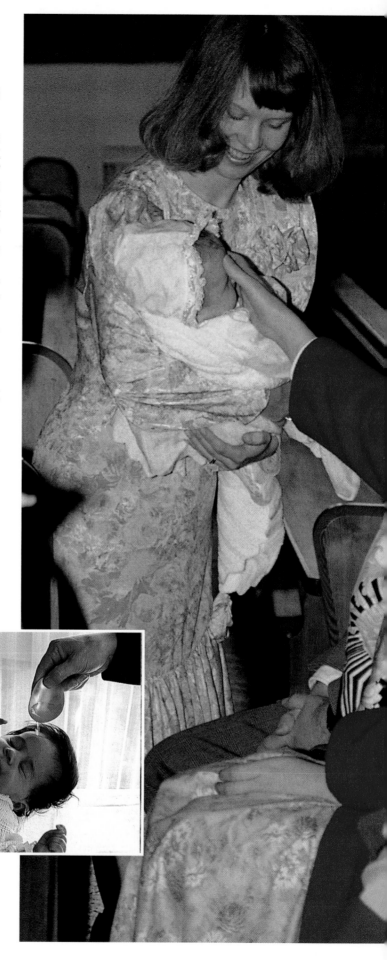

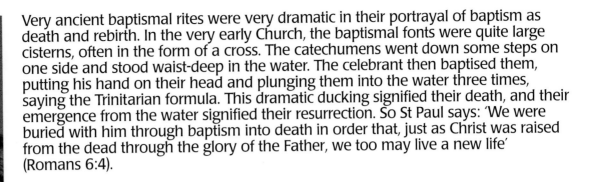

Very ancient baptismal rites were very dramatic in their portrayal of baptism as death and rebirth. In the very early Church, the baptismal fonts were quite large cisterns, often in the form of a cross. The catechumens went down some steps on one side and stood waist-deep in the water. The celebrant then baptised them, putting his hand on their head and plunging them into the water three times, saying the Trinitarian formula. This dramatic ducking signified their death, and their emergence from the water signified their resurrection. So St Paul says: 'We were buried with him through baptism into death in order that, just as Christ was raised from the dead through the glory of the Father, we too may live a new life' (Romans 6:4).

Since the liturgical reforms initiated by Vatican II there are three separate rites for Baptism:

> one for infants
> one for children old enough to understand
> one for adults

The essential part of the baptismal rite consists of pouring water over the head and saying the Trinitarian formula: 'I baptise you, in the name of the Father, and of the Son and of the Holy Spirit.' The usual minister of Baptism is the priest or deacon, but anyone can baptise in an emergency. Although water and the Trinitarian formula make the sacrament valid, the ordinary rite usually includes the anointing of the forehead of the candidate with holy oil. This oil is blessed by the bishop at the Mass of Chrism on Maundy Thursday. In the Old Testament, priests, prophets and kings were anointed with oil, and as the priest or deacon anoints the candidate he says:

God, the Father of our Lord Jesus Christ has freed you from sin, given you a new birth by water and the Holy Spirit, and welcomed you into his holy people. He now anoints you with the chrism of salvation. As Christ was anointed Priest, Prophet, and King, so may you live always as a member of his body, sharing everlasting life.

Once the newly baptised have been anointed they are given a white garment, to signify their new life in Christ, and a candle lit from the paschal candle. Like Christ who is the light of the world, the newly baptised Christian carries the light of Christ out into the world.

Baptism cleanses us from sin. This means that it cleanses us from all the sins which we have committed so far. The early Church had a problem – what if you committed sins after Baptism? Could you be forgiven these too? At first the Church was not sure that it had the power to forgive sins committed after Baptism, and this became such a cause of anxiety that many delayed their baptism for as long as possible because they did not want to fall into serious sin and have no way of remedying the situation. St Augustine was not baptised until he was well into his thirties and St Ambrose waited until he was thirty-four, and then it was part of the ceremony which made him into a bishop!

Obviously this situation was not a very healthy one, and the Church gradually evolved mechanisms for dealing with post-baptismal sin. A system of penances was instituted which became the early form of our modern day sacrament of Penance and Reconciliation.

the Sacraments of Christian Initiation

Confirmation

Sacraments of Initiation

Confirmation originally formed part of the joint rite of Baptism, Confirmation and the Eucharist, which were all given to the new convert at the same time. Even small infants were simultaneously baptised, confirmed and given communion. If children were too small to receive the consecrated bread, a small drop of the consecrated wine was dabbed on their lips. Nowadays adult converts are still baptised and confirmed and receive the Eucharist at the same time, but infants are generally baptised a few days or weeks after birth, receive the Eucharist when they are seven or eight and are confirmed some years later. This time lag between the three sacraments has an historical basis. As the early Church was very much city based, it was easy for the Bishop to be present at every baptism to administer the full rites of initiation which included Baptism, Confirmation and the Eucharist. When the Church grew larger, and moved into rural parishes, it became much more difficult for the Bishop to be present at every ceremony. Because the Church wanted to preserve the tradition of having the Bishop as the minister of Confirmation, the rite became separated from Baptism and the Eucharist, which could be administered by the local priest. Once the separation had taken place, some saw it as a good thing that children should wait until they were old enough to have a fuller understanding of what was happening, and so instead of waiting until the Bishop next came round, they deliberately delayed confirming children until they were much older.

Before Jesus was put to death, he promised his followers that he would send the Spirit to comfort and strengthen them. On the day of Pentecost, the Holy Spirit was poured out onto the Apostles. The sacrament of confirmation is our own Pentecost. When we are Confirmed the Holy Spirit is poured out onto us so that we receive the gifts of the Holy Spirit.

Confirmation is administered by anointing with the oil of Chrism and the laying on of hands. The Bishop places his hands on the heads of the candidates and then anoints their foreheads with holy oil, saying the words: 'Be sealed with the Gift of the Holy Spirit'. In Jesus' time soldiers were marked with their leader's seal and slaves with their master's. By receiving the seal of the Holy Spirit we show that we belong to God. Being anointed is a sign of ownership and belonging, but it also elevates us to a higher position. In the Old Testament, priests, prophets and kings were all anointed with oil.

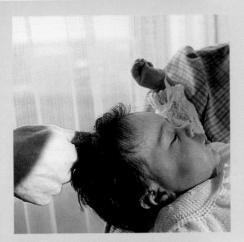

The Eastern churches still keep the more ancient tradition of maintaining the unity of the sacraments of initiation so that their children are baptised and confirmed and receive the Eucharist at the same time. During Confirmation, instead of just anointing the forehead with a sign of the cross, they anoint the forehead, eyes, nose, ears, lips, breast, the back of the hands and the feet.

Although the Church has separated the rites of Baptism, Confirmation and the Eucharist, they still constitute a unity, as, properly speaking, Confirmation completes the baptismal rite. Those who have been baptised but have not yet been confirmed are urged to receive the sacrament of Confirmation to complete their Baptism. This is not to devalue their Baptism in any way, but it does mean that their Christian initiation remains incomplete.

A school chaplain preparing children for Confirmation would tell them how, once they had received the Holy Spirit, their lives would never be the same again. No longer would they be able to lie to their parents, steal sweets from the sweet shop or bully their younger brothers and sisters. Oh no, now they would hear the voice of the Holy Spirit in their heads telling them to "STOP!" what they were doing wrong and start behaving themselves. Perhaps the Holy Spirit does not work in such a crude way, but the school chaplain did have a point. The Spirit of God can comfort and calm us, but can also challenge us and make demands on us that are far from comfortable.

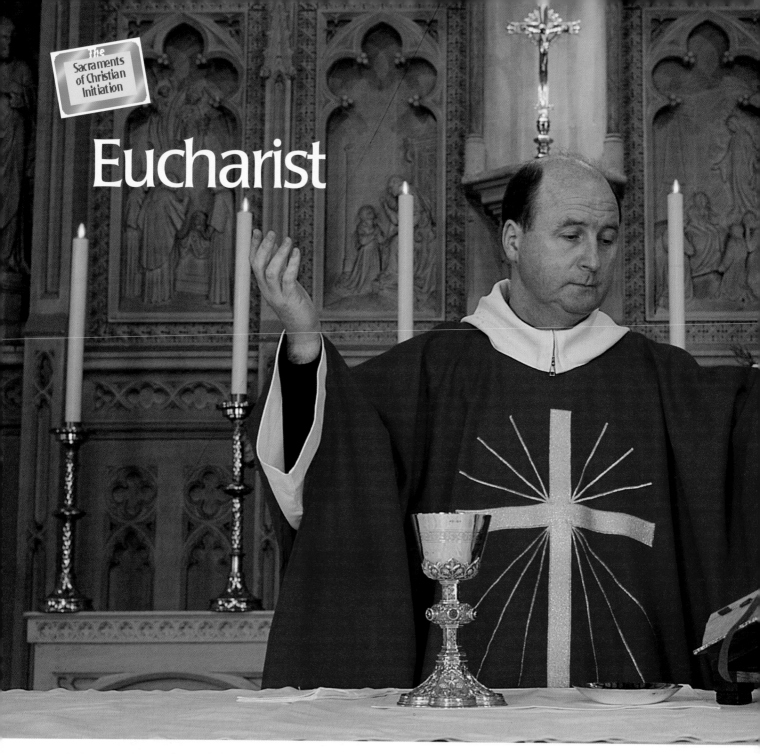

Eucharist

The word 'Eucharist' comes from the Greek word *eucharistein*. It simply means 'to give thanks'. *Eu* means 'well, good' and *charis* means 'gift', so when we say 'eucharist' we are saying 'the gift is good!' In the Eucharist we exchange gifts with God. We offer to him the bread and the wine, and he gives us his own body and blood. The Eucharist is a shared meal. Eating and drinking together is one of the most sociable things we can do, and during the Eucharist we join with the whole of the Church to eat and drink together. But the Eucharist is more than just a cosy meal, it is also a sacrifice. The roots of the Eucharist lie in the Jewish Passover meal which commemorates the delivery of the people of Israel from slavery in Egypt. The story is told in the Old Testament, in the Book of Exodus. In order to persuade a reluctant Pharaoh to let the people of Israel go free, God killed every first-born son. During the first 'Passover' every Jewish household was instructed to sacrifice a lamb and sprinkle its blood on their doorposts so that the angel of death would see the blood and 'pass over' them, sparing the life of their first-born son. When Jesus spoke of himself as 'the lamb of God', and the bread and wine of the last supper as his body

Mass is celebrated every day, but above all on a Sunday – the first day of the week, the day of Jesus' resurrection. The Mass we celebrate today has the same overall structure as it has done throughout the centuries:

It is in two parts,

the liturgy of the word, with readings, a homily and intercessions,

the liturgy of the Eucharist which consists of the presentation of bread and wine, the consecration and communion.

Transubstantiation

The Church teaches that Christ is really present in the bread and wine that have been blessed by the priest at Mass. This means that the bread and wine have become the body and blood of Christ. Although the bread and wine still look and taste like bread and wine, the substance, what is actually there, has changed. The word 'transubstantiation' is used to describe this real change. Transubstantiation just means 'a change in substance'.

When we talk about the Eucharistic celebration we often refer to it simply as 'the Mass'. This is the name it has been given from at least the sixth or seventh centuries. The word 'mass' comes from the Latin word 'missio', the sending. This refers to the words of dismissal at the end of Mass: 'ite missa est' – Go! It is sent forth!' which in today's Mass is translated; 'The Mass is ended, go in peace to love and serve the Lord.' No one quite knows why the Eucharist came to be known as the 'missa' or 'mass', but some think that it is because of the way that monastic prayers were conducted in the early Middle Ages. When the monks gathered for prayers, they were often concluded with a short Eucharistic celebration. These Eucharists sometimes took only ten minutes or so, and as they marked the end of the whole set of prayers, they signalled the end of the service. This, it is suggested, is why the Eucharist came to be known as the 'dismissal', the Mass.

and blood, he was speaking of himself as the Passover sacrifice, the lamb whose blood would be shed so that the people of Israel might go free.

The Mass is the new Passover, with Jesus offering his own body and blood so that we might go free. In other words, as well as being a sacred meal, the Eucharist is also a link with Jesus' death. When we take part in the Eucharist we take part in the Passover meal which he celebrates with us now, shedding his blood so that we might be saved.

Penance and Reconciliation

(Catechism of the Catholic Church 1420-1525)

The Sacrament of Reconciliation is primarily a sacrament of healing. Sin dehumanises us and cuts us off from God and from each other. Many lives are blighted by sin and guilt, by the need for conversion and forgiveness. The Sacrament of Reconciliation gives us the opportunity to express our sorrow for the things we have done wrong, to heal broken relationships, to forgive ourselves and others, to open up the channels of full communication between us and God.

A university chaplain in the USA had a motto which she pinned to the chaplaincy wall: 'We are only as sick as the secrets we keep!' Most of us have things that we would rather others didn't know about us – things we have done or thought that we are ashamed or embarrassed to admit to. Sometimes these hidden secrets can take on much more importance than they deserve, simply because we keep them bottled up and are unable to speak about them. Being able to say something out loud in a place of total confidentiality can be very liberating and healing. Confession is above all a place of healing. It is not a place of judgement or punishment. The point isn't to discover how awful we really are, but to discover how much we are loved by God, how precious we are, to discover our full dignity as children of God, loved by him to distraction. Confession is a place of mercy, where we can lay down burdens of guilt and shame that we carry with us. Nothing we have ever done is too much for the mercy and love of God. No matter what we think of ourselves or of God, we can still be certain that God forgives us, loves us and wants only to heal us.

THE CONFESSIONAL 'SEAL'

The 'seal' of confession is the undertaking by the priest that nothing said by the penitent in confession will ever be repeated. What the penitent has made known to the priest remains 'sealed'. The confidentiality of the confession is absolute. The priest cannot even act upon the knowledge given to him in confession. There have been cases where priests have been prosecuted by civil authorities for refusing to give evidence because that would mean divulging something told to them under the confessional seal.

Once he has heard our confession, the priest says the words of absolution:

> God, the Father of mercies,
> through the death and the resurrection of his Son
> has reconciled the world to himself
> and sent the Holy Spirit among us
> for the forgiveness of sins;
> through the ministry of the Church
> may God give you pardon and peace,
> and I absolve you from your sins
> in the name of the Father, and of the Son, and of the
> Holy Spirit.

The bishop and his priests are usually the only ministers nominated to hear confessions. However, there have been some notable exceptions. In 1349, during a particularly horrific outbreak of plague, people and priests were dying at such a rate that they were unable to have their confession heard before they died. Here is part of a letter that the Bishop of Bath and Wells sent out to his clergy:

> '...you should at once publicly command and persuade all men, in particular those who are now sick or should fall sick in the future, that if they are on the point of death and can not secure the services of a priest, then they should make confession to each other, as is permitted in the teaching of the Apostles, whether to a layman or, if no man is present, then even to a woman...'

He then bound them by the laws of the Church to uphold the confessional seal and maintain the confidentiality of the penitent's confession. This of course was not sacramental confession but an appropriate pastoral solution in a crisis.

Penance

At the beginning of Mass there is a short penitential rite, where we acknowledge that we have sinned and ask forgiveness from God. The word 'penance' comes from the Latin word *poenitentia* which means sorrow or regret, so to be a penitent means to be a 'sorrowing one'. Penance also came to mean the things people did to show that they were sorry. In the early Church, penitents would stand in a special area of the church during the liturgy. They were called 'weepers' because they often just stood and wept throughout the Mass. Here is an account by the fifth century writer Sozomen, of weeping penitents in the liturgy:

> They throw themselves prostrate on the ground with wailing and lamentation. Facing them with tears in his eyes, the bishop hurries towards them and likewise falls to the ground. And the whole congregation of the church with loud crying is filled with tears. After this the bishop rises first and raises those who are prostrate; and after he has prayed in a fitting manner for those who are repentant of their sins, he dismisses them.

Anointing the Sick

Sickness, pain and death were not written into God's original plan for mankind. Part of Jesus' ministry was to heal the sick, and he went about curing those who were ill or disabled. Jesus came to announce that the kingdom of God was now a reality here on earth. One of the signs of this reality was that the sick were healed and the dead raised up, because suffering and death can have no place in the kingdom of God.

The very early Church was already anointing the sick with blessed oil, following the words of St James:

'Is any among you sick? Let him call for the elders of the Church and let them pray over him, anointing him with oil in the name of the Lord; and the prayer of faith will save the sick man, and the Lord will raise him up; and if he has committed sins, he will be forgiven' (James: 5:14-15).

St James' exhortation to anoint the sick was as much a practical response to sickness as it was a spiritual one – oil had long been used medicinally in the world of the New Testament and doctors frequently treated patients by rubbing them with oils. The Church has always had a special mission to the sick, from visiting a sick person at home, giving communion to those who are housebound to building hospitals and clinics. Human beings are made body and soul – the physical side of human life is as much the Church's concern as the spiritual side, and those who are sick and in pain are especially in need of comfort and healing.

A small boy was carrying his little brother up a steep hill. Moved by the sight of the boy obviously struggling under the weight of his burden, a passer-by called out, "Isn't that a heavy load you are carrying?" "No," the boy replied, "It isn't a load; it's my brother."

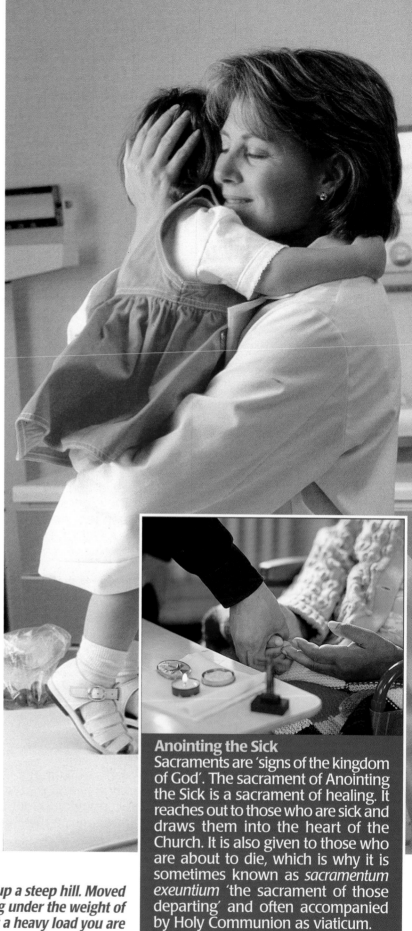

Anointing the Sick
Sacraments are 'signs of the kingdom of God'. The sacrament of Anointing the Sick is a sacrament of healing. It reaches out to those who are sick and draws them into the heart of the Church. It is also given to those who are about to die, which is why it is sometimes known as *sacramentum exeuntium* 'the sacrament of those departing' and often accompanied by Holy Communion as viaticum.

The Sacrament of Anointing of the Sick is administered by a priest or bishop. It begins with a short rite of penance followed by a reading. Then in silence the priest lays his hands on the sick person, and anoints the forehead and palms with oil, saying these words:

Through this holy anointing may the Lord in his love and mercy help you with the grace of the Holy Spirit. Amen. May the Lord who frees you from sin save you and raise you up. Amen.

St Paul once described the burden of his sufferings in a similar way: "The only thing I can boast about is the cross of our Lord Jesus Christ … the marks on my body are those of Jesus," he wrote. Everywhere he travelled Paul took the burden of persecution upon his shoulders for the sake of the Gospel. But his sufferings were not too heavy to bear; for in them he carried Christ his brother.

It is easy to accept God's will when it coincides with our own. The trouble is that it so often doesn't! In carrying Christ we will *always* be asked to carry, too, some of the weight of the cross.

Nothing calls for a more complete change of attitude than that of accepting suffering for Christ's sake. Every fibre of our flesh, every conviction of our mind cries out against pain and rejection. In all the world there is no question asked more often than, "Why suffering?"

We try to think it out. Maybe we start with the Old Testament idea that we are being punished for our sins. From there we go on to think of offering up our sufferings in payment of our sins. We are making some progress, but we have a long way to go yet. We only realise how far when we are faced with suffering in the innocent; maybe in a child who is dear to us. Then we are really left with a big question, *why?* We look to heaven, somewhat reproachfully, for the answer.

We do not have to look too high, no higher than the crucifix on our wall. The moment of suffering can be the moment we look on the crucified Christ for the millionth time, and see him for the first. For there is the Most Innocent One who has suffered the most.

There is an alternative to the burden of the cross. But it is heavier still. It is the burden of hate. A short while before being struck down by the assassin's bullet, Martin Luther King spoke the following words: "I've seen too much hate to want to hate myself, I've seen hate on the faces of too many sheriffs, too many white citizens, councillors, to want to hate myself, and every time I see it, I say to myself, hate is too great a burden to bear …"

"In your minds you must be the same as Christ Jesus: his state was divine, yet he did not cling to his equality with God but emptied himself to assume the condition of a slave, and became as men are; and being as all men are, he was humbler yet, even accepting death, death on a cross." (Philippians 2:5-8)

MAKING SENSE OF SUFFERING

All of us will have our own share of suffering. Mental and physical anguish seem to be an inescapable part of human experience. Sometimes our own suffering and the suffering of others can seem utterly meaningless. Illness, pain and disability seem only to cut us off from those around us, leaving us feeling like isolated prisoners set apart from the rest of the world and tormented by our own bodies.

So much of the suffering in the world does seem senseless. Suffering and death are evils which undermine the wholeness of our humanity. They are not part of God's desire for humanity, and he does not just watch impassive and uncaring whilst humanity suffers. Instead God suffers with us. Through Jesus' suffering and death, God joins his suffering to the suffering of human beings. And by doing this, he transforms human suffering, and gives it a new meaning.

To say that through Jesus' redemptive suffering our sufferings can have meaning isn't to trivialise them in any way, nor does it make the suffering any easier. It still feels just as awful, but what Jesus has done is to take hold of suffering and death and create a situation where it no longer has the ultimate power to separate us from each other or from God. Through joining ourselves with the suffering of Christ, our pain, our sense of isolation and loss can become part of the saving work of Christ, who suffered agonies and died for men and women.

'My God, my God, why have you forsaken me?' His agonised cry of rejection from the cross echoes the cries of countless human beings. Christ has reached to the depths of human suffering and isolation so that even when we feel most abandoned and desolate, Jesus is there with us crying his cry alongside ours. And like him, God will raise us from our bed of pain and sickness and lead us to eternal life.

Holy Orders

(Catechism of the Catholic Church 1536-1666)

Priesthood

Within the Church there are a great many different sorts of ministries to perform. Some may discover their talents in visiting the sick, some in reading at Mass or serving at the altar. Some may be good at welcoming strangers, leading youth groups or organising the music for the liturgy. Some may be called simply to pray.
The Church bears witness to a whole host of ministries, so that each person has a unique contribution to make, however small.
The Church is not a passive organisation, but an active cauldron, bubbling away and bringing life to the whole world.
Among all these ministries of service one stands out as a particular sacrament: the sacrament of Holy Orders, which ordains to the office of bishop, priest or deacon.

Bishop

The word 'bishop' comes from the Greek word *episkopos* which means 'supervisor'. The bishop's primary role is to act as a sign of Christ in the local church, blessing and teaching the people. He is also a sign of unity, healing divisions and protecting the weak and vulnerable.

Priest

The word priest comes from the Greek word *presbyteros* which means 'elder'. The very early Church appointed elders to be community leaders, to preach and administer the sacraments. These elders were chosen for their wisdom and maturity, called to lead their communities with patience and kindness.

Deacon

The word 'deacon' comes from the Greek word *diakonos* which means 'minister' or 'servant'. Deacons can be seen helping bishops and priests at Mass. They share in the pastoral work of the Church, in preaching, proclaiming the gospel and ministering at baptisms and weddings. From the earliest times they have had a special role in caring for the poor and hungry on behalf of the whole Church. Since Vatican II, the office of permanent deacon has been revived, and now married men are often ordained to the diaconate.

prominent role in the Church, especially as priests are required to lead a celibate lifestyle. However, celibacy is not an intrinsic part of priesthood. There is nothing incompatible between priesthood and marriage, and the Church's insistence that priests remain celibate is not based on theological concerns but is a matter of Church discipline. There have always been married priests in the Oriental Catholic rites, and married Anglican clergy who have recently been received into full communion with the Catholic church have been allowed to exercise their priesthood.

The priest's calling or vocation (the word vocation means simply 'calling'— it is from the Latin *vocare,* 'to call') is, along with all believers, first and foremost to preach the Good News of God's love and care for humanity. The priest also says Mass and administers the Sacraments, taking an active role in offering Christ's gift of himself. During the Mass, the priest represents Christ and also acts on behalf of all the people of God. His sacramental priesthood represents the priesthood of the whole Church.

Many religions have sacrifice at the heart of their ritual practices. For whatever reason, whether as a way of feeding the gods or of trying to appease them, many religions are based on a system which involves animal sacrifice. Ancient Judaism was no exception. The temple in Jerusalem acted rather like a huge abattoir, slaughtering thousands of animals each year. Different sorts of sacrifices were made: some were for thanksgiving, some for sin, some were required at different times in the liturgical year. The role of the priest in this sort of environment was very much that of a ritual slaughterer, and his job was to sprinkle the blood on the sides of the altar, offering the blood of the animal to God.

Celibacy

At the present time the Church demands that the majority of priests remain celibate, which means that they cannot marry. Celibacy has a long tradition in the Church. Choosing not to marry can be a valuable witness to Christian values which may differ from the fashions and conventions of contemporary society. A celibate lifestyle can be a radical departure from imprisoning expectations, giving freedom and choice where otherwise there might be little of either. Celibacy does play a

The priesthood of all believers

At our baptism all of us became part of the 'laity'. The word 'laity' comes from a Greek word *laos* which just means 'people'. The laity are the people of God. As people of God, all of us share in the priesthood of Christ. This is why the Church speaks of the 'priesthood of all believers', because when we were baptised, we were incorporated into Christ's priesthood. Every one of us is called to exercise our priesthood within the Church, strengthening and serving each other. The exercise of priesthood means, above all, to serve. The Church speaks of Jesus as our High Priest, the one who offers sacrifices to God on our behalf. But instead of sacrificing an innocent victim, Jesus chose instead to offer himself as the sacrificial animal. Jesus is the priest and victim, offering himself as a sacrifice to God. The priesthood that Jesus exercises is one of self-giving. All those who are called to the priesthood of Christ are called to serve as he did, offering themselves in a spirit of service and love.

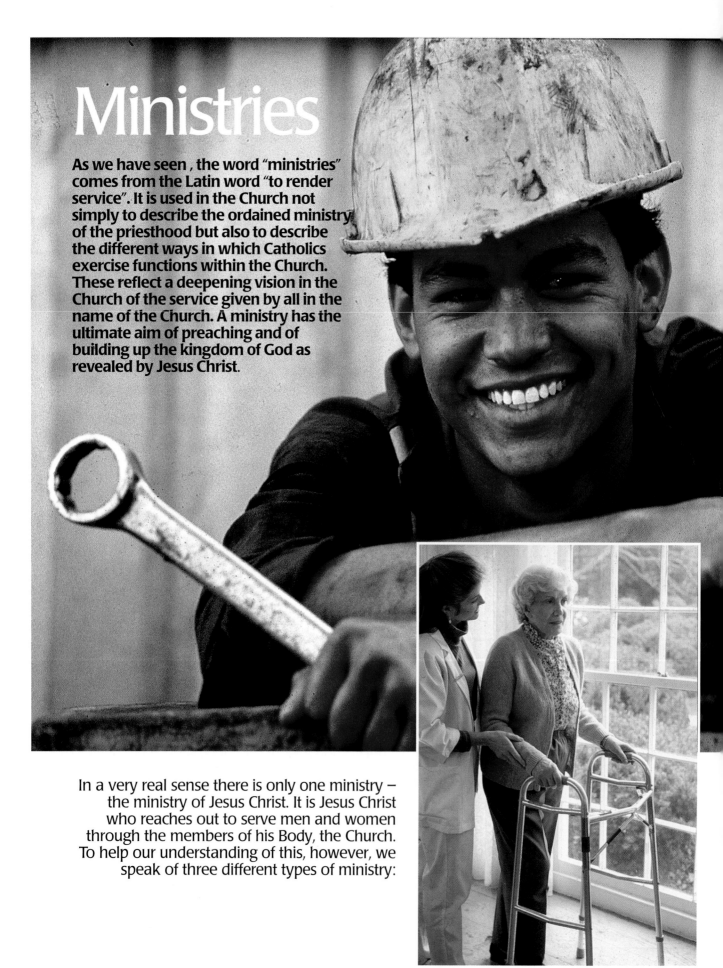

Ministries

As we have seen , the word "ministries" comes from the Latin word "to render service". It is used in the Church not simply to describe the ordained ministry of the priesthood but also to describe the different ways in which Catholics exercise functions within the Church. These reflect a deepening vision in the Church of the service given by all in the name of the Church. A ministry has the ultimate aim of preaching and of building up the kingdom of God as revealed by Jesus Christ.

In a very real sense there is only one ministry – the ministry of Jesus Christ. It is Jesus Christ who reaches out to serve men and women through the members of his Body, the Church. To help our understanding of this, however, we speak of three different types of ministry:

1 Ministries undertaken by those who are baptised.

This refers to any activity which is undertaken without a formal commission from the Church. These ministries would include the work of nurses, teachers, and social workers, for example. It is important, though, to recognise that this type of ministry is not limited to the caring professions. It includes the service of all who work in their local parish and do everyday work in a spirit of Christian dedication.

2 The instituted ministries

These are the ministries officially recognised as forms of service within the Church, such as those of lectors, acolytes, catechists, ministers of the Eucharist.

3 The ordained ministries

These are the diaconate, priesthood and episcopate, and are only exercised by those who have received the sacrament of Holy Orders *(See Supplement part 3).*

Every member of the new people of God is called to serve. The Holy Spirit lives in each one of us, inspiring some to be leaders and teachers, while others have gifts for taking care of those who are sick or poor. There are those who have the patience to do the smallest tasks well and still others with the perseverance to grapple with immense problems.

In short, there are many gifts given to us by the Holy Spirit. The important thing is that we use them in the service of God and our neighbour. This is the command Christ left to every member of his Church. For as members of his Church we have the responsibility of making Christ visibly present to those among whom we live and work. For the visible Church is not just the Pope and the bishops and a world-wide organisation. It is us. And if we don't make Christ present to the people we come into contact with, who else will?

The truth is that the followers of Jesus in every age are united to him in such a way that they form one body with him. With Jesus they are the Church. With them and through them Jesus continues the redeeming work he came to do on earth. Just as Jesus made God visibly present to the men and women of his time so now the Church which he founded, and of which he is the head, makes Jesus present to the men and women of today.

Marriage

Human beings are social creatures. We suffer if we feel lonely and thrive most in the company of those who love and accept us. Our first experience of this love is within our family. The family is where we first encounter the love of other human beings. God loves us, but his love is often most clearly shown to us through the love of other people. The love which we have for each other is part of the love of God. All love comes from God, and all love reflects that love that God has for all of his creation. We call God 'Father' but we only understand what this means because we have an idea of what a human father ought to be like: loving, patient and generous.

Human beings are sexual creatures, and for most people sexual love is the closest form of union they will ever know. The love which a couple have for each other mirrors the love that God has for men and women. The sacrament of Marriage is, first and foremost, a sacrament of this love. The couple echo the words of Christ which are spoken in the Mass: 'This is my body, which is given up for you.' The sacrament of Marriage becomes the sacrament of Christ's love for the whole world. The self-gift of the Eucharist is made truly visible in the love between the married couple.

Not everyone is able to find this sort of love; in parts of the world poverty may prevent some from marrying, or people may have to look after members of their family. Some people simply don't find a partner or their partner may have died. Although the sacrament of Marriage is an important expression of the human need to form committed relationships, it is not the only way. We all need to belong, to be part of a family or group that will accept and care for us no matter what. But we can develop and grow through close, significant relationships without marriage, especially if we belong to a Church which is a true community of love.

With the best will in the world, some marriages do not work. Instead of being a place of love, care and support, they become a place of fear and violence or isolation. In some cases the physical and emotional well being of a family demands that the couple separate. Mercy and gentleness are needed for those who have suffered a broken marriage. The Church does not permit divorce and remarriage, however there are cases where a couple may well have grounds for annulment. An annulment is not just the Church's version of civil divorce, where it is enough to show that the marriage has broken down irretrievably. In order to be granted an annulment, the couple must demonstrate that they were not validly married in the first place. A valid marriage is one where both partners freely consented without fear or outside pressure to the sharing of the whole of their future life together.

Marriage is a sacrament of the self-giving love which two people offer to each other. But the love that a couple has for each other need not end there. Ideally their love should spill out to those around them and become a source of hope and of comfort for others. The support which a married couple can give each other can be a source of great strength, allowing them to serve others in a very powerful way. That is why the priest may give the newly wedded couple the following blessing:

May you always bear witness to the love of God in this world, so that the afflicted and the needy will find in you generous friends and welcome you into the joys of heaven.

The minister of the sacrament of Marriage is not the priest, but the couple themselves. The priest acts as a witness. In the past, a marriage could be valid even without the presence of the priest. In the Middle Ages, for example, it was usually enough for a couple to say 'I marry you' for the marriage to be valid and binding. This meant that even words spoken in the heat of the moment could constitute a valid marriage. This situation did cause problems if the marriage broke down, especially if there were no witnesses and one of the couple denied agreeing to the marriage. In response to these difficulties, the Church demanded that the couple at least have their marriages witnessed by the priest, and in the twelfth century the first marriage rites were developed.

Sacramentals

(Catechism of the Catholic Church 1667-1690)

The seven sacraments of the Church reveal to us the mystery of God's love for each one of us. They are central to the life of the Church and have a very important place within the Church's liturgy, but there is also a whole range of blessings, prayers and devotional practices which are not classed as sacraments, but are related to them.

'Sacramentals' are blessings of people or objects. Every baptised person is called to be a blessing and to bless. By blessing objects and people we dedicate them to God's love and care. A blessing always includes a prayer, and is often accompanied by a specific sign such as the laying on of hands or sprinkling with holy water. So we may bless the food we are about to eat before our meals or say a quick prayer for our children as they head off to school. We can administer some blessings ourselves, but there are others which we might like a priest to do. For example, we might like to bless our food before we eat it, but ask a priest to come and bless our new house.

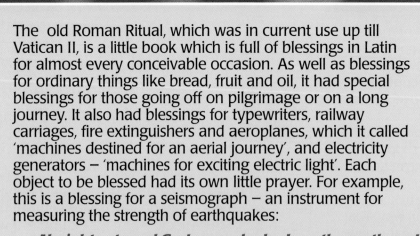

The old Roman Ritual, which was in current use up till Vatican II, is a little book which is full of blessings in Latin for almost every conceivable occasion. As well as blessings for ordinary things like bread, fruit and oil, it had special blessings for those going off on pilgrimage or on a long journey. It also had blessings for typewriters, railway carriages, fire extinguishers and aeroplanes, which it called 'machines destined for an aerial journey', and electricity generators – 'machines for exciting electric light'. Each object to be blessed had its own little prayer. For example, this is a blessing for a seismograph – an instrument for measuring the strength of earthquakes:

Almighty eternal God, you who look on the earth and make it tremble, pour out your blessing on this seismograph. Grant that the signs of the earth's tremblings may be rightly recorded by it and that, for the service of your people and for promoting the greater glory of your name, they may be rightly understood.

Apart from sacraments and sacramentals, there are all sorts of actions and practices which reflect peoples' popular beliefs. Some people may have a particular devotion to a certain saint, for example, or like to visit places of pilgrimage. Others may like to pray the rosary, take part in the Stations of the Cross, dance liturgical dances, attend a prayer group, wear medals depicting a particular saint or even keep a relic of the saint's bones or clothes.

The Church has a very rich tradition of devotional practices to various saints. Saints are simply people who have led good and holy lives and so are sure to be in heaven. Thinking about the life of a saint can inspire us to live in a different way, and we can also ask them to pray for us. This does not mean that we are giving a human being the worship due only to God. Asking a saint for prayers is no different from asking a friend to pray for us.

These are all ways in which the Church's liturgy extends beyond the sacraments. Funerals are also important occasions when we pray for those who have died and surrender them 'into the Father's hands' as they complete the last stage of their earthly journey.

Many local churches have a particular saint as a patron, and have the story of their saint's life painted or carved around the walls. Some may even have the bones or relics of the saint buried in the church. Many saints have their own hallmarks, for example:

Saint Roque is always shown with a dog, lifting his smock to show a huge plague boil on his inner thigh, a reminder of the dog who licked his sores when he was afflicted by the plague.

St Barbara is always depicted with a tower because her father locked her up to stop her suitors from seeing her.

In the past many parishioners were unable to read, and so each saint had to be easily recognisable without the written word. The patron saint of a particular church was thought to have a duty to protect and look after the people who went to church there. In the Middle Ages, it was not uncommon for parishioners to come and prostrate themselves in prayer before the saint's relics if the community was in trouble. There have also been stories of enraged parishioners digging up the saint's relics and shouting at them in rage when the saint failed to deliver the goods!

Treasures of Faith

All sorts of different practices extend the liturgical life of the Church. The seven sacraments are not the beginning and the end of the Church's liturgy. There are other liturgies which are not classed as sacraments, but are nevertheless an important part of the Church's liturgical life.

Benediction and Exposition of the Blessed Sacrament

The primary purpose for reserving the Sacrament outside the celebration of Mass is for the distribution of Communion to the sick. But from the custom of blessing the sick after Communion arose the practice of blessing the people by making the sign of the cross over them with the sacred host in a monstrance or, in a simple form, a ciborium.

(See Supplement part 2)

Stations of the Cross

From the earliest times pilgrims to Jerusalem have retraced our Lord's steps in his Passion. At those points where special events in his journey to Calvary took place they stopped to meditate (Latin, *statio*, a standing still). From this custom sprang the construction of imitations of Jerusalem's "Via Dolorosa" which are to be found in most parish churches around the walls.

(See Supplement part 2)

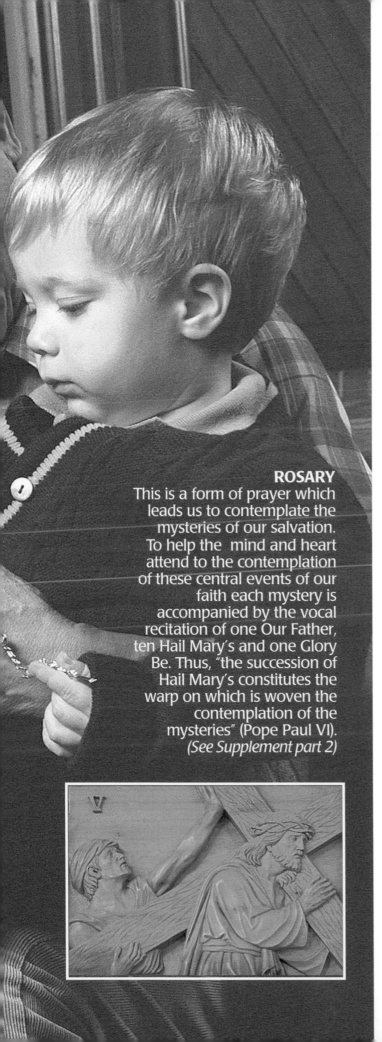

ROSARY

This is a form of prayer which leads us to contemplate the mysteries of our salvation. To help the mind and heart attend to the contemplation of these central events of our faith each mystery is accompanied by the vocal recitation of one Our Father, ten Hail Mary's and one Glory Be. Thus, "the succession of Hail Mary's constitutes the warp on which is woven the contemplation of the mysteries" (Pope Paul VI). *(See Supplement part 2)*

Children's Liturgy

"People brought little children to him, for him to lay his hands on them and say a prayer. The disciples turned them away, but Jesus said: 'Let the little children alone, and do not stop them coming to me; for it is to such as these that the kingdom of heaven belongs.'"– Matthew 19:13-14

Is it any wonder that Jesus gathered the children around him and proclaimed "for such is the kingdom of God?" For although adults seek and yearn for a mature faith, there is much to be said for the faith of a child. Much as a special relationship that exists between the child and his or her parents, children come to God with an unswerving faith that the world has not yet taught them to doubt.

And just as childhood prepares children to be adults in the world, our childhood is also the starting point of our faith. We go to church as children to learn the simple truths of God's love for us and our need to place our trust in God. As we watch our children grow, we try to imagine seeing the world through their eyes. Watching them see the ocean for the first time or standing beside them at the foot of a majestic mountain, we can feel their utter amazement at a world so full of wonder. We lie under the stars on a warm summer night and we can sense their awe at a universe so huge and ever-moving.

Most importantly, we have seen their childlike devotion and faith as they stand before the image of our crucified Lord in church and utter for the first time the word that will bring solace to them for the rest of their lives: Jesus.

Sacred Vessels

"And it came to pass on the day that Moses had fully set up the tabernacle, and had anointed it and sanctified it, and all the instruments thereof, both the altar and all the vessels thereof, and had anointed them and sanctified them..." – Numbers 7:1

The Old Testament is filled with instructions for making and using sacred vessels. Such rules and traditions were and are an important part of the Jewish way of life and worship, and many of those early teachings found their way into Christian rite and ritual. As Christians, we use sacred vessels in the celebration of the Mass because we have the sacred elements of bread and wine that must be handled with respect and adoration.

But in the New Testament, a new sacred vessel found its way into the Christian mind – the Christians themselves. Even before Saul the persecutor became Paul the apostle, the Lord described him in a vision to the disciple Ananias: "...this man is a chosen vessel of mine to carry my name before gentiles and kings and Israelites" (Acts 9:15).

So like the Jewish traditions of sacrifice that have been replaced by the once-and-for-all sacrifice of Jesus on the cross, the sacred

vessels of the Jewish rituals have been replaced by human vessels, however fragile and weak, that can carry Christ and his message to the world. And as these vessels, we need to be mindful that we are made by the hands of the great potter for his own uses. What we are used for – what we are to carry – depends on how the Creator makes us and how we respond to him.

Sacred Art & Furnishings

"Holy Mother Church has always been the friend of the fine arts and has continuously sought their noble ministry, with the special aim that all things set apart for use in divine worship should be truly worthy, becoming, and beautiful, signs and symbols of heavenly realities." – Vatican II

Take a stroll through the National Gallery or any major art museum and you will realise just how important a role faith and religion have played in the development of Western art. Likewise, Western art has played a major role in the development of religion, particularly Christianity. We have ideas of what Jesus and his disciples may have looked like because of the masterpieces hanging on the walls. We know the sorrow in the Holy Mother's face because we have seen it in paintings and sculpture. This close association between the art in our museums and galleries and the faith in our hearts cannot be denied. Art gives images to our faith, and faith gives meaning to the art.

But what about the art in our churches? The Church has always held that its art and furnishings play important roles in fostering worship and spirituality. Because of this, our sacred and liturgical art needs to be excellent and dignified. That need not mean wealth and luxury, and churches should not exist merely as treasure troves of beautiful sacred furnishings. For just as liturgical music must be composed to lead the faithful into prayer, so too must liturgical art and furnishings gently guide the believer into the presence of God. The general instructions of the Mass say:

"The buildings and requisites for worship, as signs and symbols of heavenly things, should be truly worthy and beautiful. At all times the Church needs the service of the arts and allows for popular and regional diversity of aesthetic expression. While preserving the art of former times, the Church also tries to adapt it to new needs and to promote the art of each age. High artistic standards should be followed when commissioning artists and choosing works of art for the church. These works of art should nourish faith and piety and be in harmony with the meaning and purpose for which they are intended."

Vatican II declared that "very rightly the fine arts are considered to rank among the noblest expressions of human genius. This judgement applies especially to religious art and to its highest achievement, which is sacred art." Religious and sacred art, by their nature, are symbols of the creativeness and beauty of God.

Christian Funerals

Catholics, in common with other Christians, believe that death is not the end of life. It is an important move on towards a greater and richer fulfilment of life and all that is good. In the certainty of Christ's resurrection we have confidence in the the complete triumph of Jesus over death. In baptism, every Christian is united with Christ and therefore shares in his triumph over death.

For a Catholic, then, death means that life is indeed changed but not ended. In the midst of our tears of sorrow and loneliness at the loss of a loved one, we have a sure and certain belief in the resurrection and in eternal life.

In celebrating a Christian funeral the Church aims to express our union in Christ with the one who has died, the sharing of that communion by those who have gathered together for the funeral, and the proclamation of our faith in eternal life.

The Christian funeral is an opportunity for the hope at the heart of the community to be shared. It expresses the solidarity of the one family of Christ, its mutual support and fellowship. And it gives the family an opportunity to say farewell in special commendation to God of the one who has died.

The Christian funeral shows the meaning of death in the light of the death and resurrection of Christ, for in him is our only hope.

"The sadness of death gives way to the bright promise of immortality."

Part 3
Life in Christ

Made in the image of God

(Catechism of the Catholic Church 1691-1802)

So far we have looked at what it is that the Catholic Church believes and how and why the sacraments are administered. Believing the right things and regularly receiving the sacraments are a good way of ensuring that we grow and develop into the people that God intended us to be. This next section is concerned with how we treat each other, how we can live lives that reflect the love of God.

Every human person is made in the image of God. When we look at each other, we see God's image reflected back at us. This means that each human life is infinitely precious, each human being has a value way beyond anything we can imagine. Being created in God's image is not something anyone can earn or deserve, we can't *help* being created in the image of God, we were just made that way! And because we can't help it, it also means that we cannot scrub out that image from the faces and the lives of those we meet. God's image is what faces us in the poorest and the most despicable-looking human beings. God's image is there in everyone, regardless of who they are or what they are, or even what they have done.

Learning to recognise God even in the most unlikely candidates can be a life-long task. It is often easier just to pretend that other people, other races, other cultures are not 'like us' and so what happens to them is not really that important. History presents a depressing picture of how easy it is to sink into prejudice and deny others the rights that we enjoy. In the sixteenth century, for example, the European powers set about conquering South America, killing and enslaving the native Indian population. They justified their genocidal treatment of the Indians by arguing that the Indians were not fully human, but an inferior race little more developed than animals. This sort of prejudice is easy to slip into; it is all too easy to see people of other races and cultures as somehow less than human just because they are not like us.

111

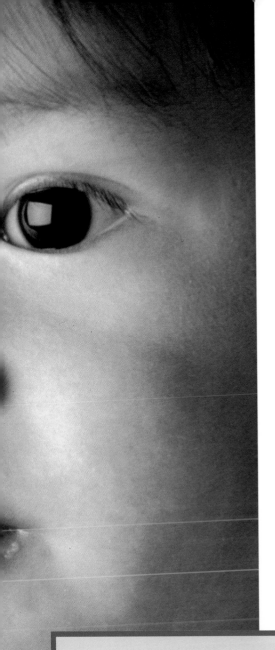

Being made in the image of God means that all of us are meant for Beatitude, enjoying the bliss of eternal life with God. This calling to heavenly bliss is what gives us our desire for happiness, our yearning for fulfilment and love. God has put into our hearts a yearning for love and happiness which cannot be satisfied by anything less than God. True happiness is not found in riches or well-being, in human fame or power. True happiness is found in God alone, the source of every good and of all love. St Augustine prayed to God in his "Confessions":

'How is it, then, that I seek you, Lord? Since in seeking you, my God, I seek a happy life, let me seek you so that my soul may live, for my body draws life from my soul and my soul draws life from you'. (*Confessions* 10, 20)

In New Testament times, many people believed that wealth and success were a sign of favour from God, so that if any disaster struck, they immediately assumed that God was angry with them or they had done something wrong. They thought that when someone was rich and successful it meant that he was favoured by God, whilst those on the wrong end of a disaster had been totally abandoned by him. Their disastrous circumstances meant that God had turned his face away. Jesus turned this sort of thinking on its head. He taught that God had not abandoned those who failed; instead, the failures should rejoice because God was blessing them.

Jesus taught us not to judge happiness by the standards laid down in the world – by wealth, fame and success – happiness comes from finding God, often in the most wretched of situations...

Blessed are the poor in spirit, the kingdom of Heaven is theirs.
Blessed are the gentle: they shall have the earth as their inheritance.
Blessed are those who mourn: they shall be comforted.
Blessed are those who hunger and thirst for uprightness: they shall have their fill.
Blessed are the merciful: they shall have mercy shown them.
Blessed are the pure in heart: they shall see God.
Blessed are the peacemakers: they shall be recognised as the children of God.
Blessed are those who are persecuted in the cause of uprightness: the kingdom of Heaven is theirs.
Blessed are you when people abuse you and persecute you and speak all kinds of calumny against you falsely on my account. Rejoice and be glad, for your reward will be great in heaven; this is how they persecuted the prophets before you.

Matthew 5:3-12

What are the values of the Law of Christ?

We have seen how it is from the heart that good or evil emerge. Good or evil is in our attitudes. Sin is a false attitude of mind and heart. The Law of Christ to love God and neighbour is expressed in the Beatitudes. We will look at each of the eight Beatitudes in turn, for they uniquely contain the Christian attitudes which bring happiness.

The first Beatitude is:
Blessed are the poor in spirit, for theirs is the kingdom of heaven.

This attitude (that of the destitute) is one of total dependence upon God our Father. It is an attitude of constantly turning towards God in prayer and worship. This worship begins in our heart and in our home; its climax is the Sunday Eucharist.

When St Paul instructs us to "pray constantly" *(1 Thess 5:17)* he means us to take this attitude of dependence into every moment of our everyday life. This means recognising that the world and all it contains has been entrusted to us to build up into an acceptable offering to God.

In this way the Christian builds up and possesses the kingdom of God on earth.

The second beatitude is:
Blessed are the meek, for they shall possess the land.

This attitude (that of gentleness and humility) involves patience. Following Christ, who patiently accepted suffering, the Christian is called to "love your enemies and pray for those who persecute you." *(Matt. 5:44)* Suppose there has been anger or hatred. "If you are bringing your offering to the altar and there remember that your brother has something against you, leave your offering there before the altar, go and be reconciled with your brother first, and then come back and present your offering" *(Matthew 5:23-24)*.

Humility is the quality of humus. It is the decomposing and decaying of plant material from which issues rich and luxuriant growth. In the same way, from humility, which is self-dying, comes fruitful and abundant growth.

In this way the meek "shall possess the land".

The third Beatitude is:
Blessed are they that mourn, for they shall be comforted.

This attitude (that of grief) is one of recognising our sin, which leads to repentance; and we learn to recognise the sufferings of others, which leads to compassion. In this way, we follow Christ, who identified himself with a suffering world. Jesus mouned over the spiritual condition of Israel, the root cause of her troubles. "Jerusalem, Jerusalem, you that kill the prophets and stone those who are sent to you! How often have I longed to gather your children as a hen gathers her chicks under her wings, and you refused!" *(Matthew 23:37).*

Such a grief leads to prudent action. Prudence is the grace to know what to do in a given situation. Confronted by sinners, for example, Jesus often showed compassion; yet when the situation demanded it, he was ruthless. And so Jesus, "making a whip out of some cord, drove the money-changers and the people selling cattle and sheep and pigeons out of the Temple saying, 'Take all this out of here and stop turning my Father's house into a market'." *(John 2:15)*

In this way, those who mourn and so act rightly will be comforted.

The fourth Beatitude is:
Blessed are they that hunger and thirst after justice, for they shall have their fill.

This attitude of the Christian (that of "good relations") is one of giving God and human beings what is due to them. We recognise that we can stand with dignity in God's presence – because of God's gift of grace we are being "justified" – and our gratitude for this gift leads us to treat others with the same respect that God does. We are to "hunger and thirst" for justice. "Do not say, 'What are we to eat? What are we to drink? It is the pagans who set their hearts on all these things. Your heavenly Father knows you need them all. Set your hearts on his kingdom first, and on his justice, and all these other things will be given to you as well." *(Matthew 6:31-33)* In this way, those who hunger and thirst for justice shall have their fill.

It we take another's life or property or good name or anything that is his, we are obliged, as far as possible, to make restitution. A person's good name, for example, is more valuable than his property, and if we take it away in unjust judgements we are bound to make every effort to give it back.

The fifth Beatitude is:
Blessed are the merciful, for they shall obtain mercy.

This attitude of the Christian (that of loyal compassion) is one of forgiveness and outgoing love. We give to others what we ourselves have received from God. In this we follow Christ who "came not to condemn the world but that the world might be saved". Jesus' parable of the unforgiving debtor who was excused payment of a fortune by his master but demanded payment of a few pence from a fellow-servant illustrates the injustice of our reluctance to forgive.

God will judge us on the way we share his mercy with others: "If you forgive others their failings, your heavenly Father will forgive you yours; but if you do not forgive others, your Father will not forgive your failings either." *(Matthew 6:14-15)* Our forgiveness must go so far as to win back those who have strayed: as Christ, the good shepherd, seeks out the lost sheep, joyfully takes it on his shoulders, and invites all to rejoice.

In this way, those who show mercy will have mercy shown to them.

The sixth Beatitude is:
Blessed are the clean of heart, for they shall see God.

This attitude of the Christian is one of purity of intention. The gift of God's Spirit frees our actions from motives of pride or self-interest. The disciples once complained to Jesus that the Pharisees had been "shocked" by his statement that, "What goes into the mouth does not make a man unclean; it is what comes out of the man that makes him unclean." But Jesus insisted. "The things that come out of the mouth come from the heart, and it is these that make a man unclean. For from the heart come evil intentions: murder, adultery, fornication, theft, slander." *(Matthew 15:11-20)*

Purity of intention is evidenced in the chaste heart, free from lust. For such an attitude means love for the other person's sake rather than one's own. "You have learnt how it was said: 'You must not commit adultery'. But I say this to you: 'If a man looks at a woman lustfully, he has already committed adultery with her in his heart'." *(Matthew 5:27-28)*

In this way, those whose hearts are set on God will enter into his presence.

115

The seventh Beatitude is:

Blessed are the peacemakers, for they shall be called the children of God.

In this attitude (one of establishing right relations between people) the Christian does God's work of reconciliation. Peacemaking (as opposed to troublemaking) is the most practical fruit of love. Christ's "programme" for peacemaking is first to approach the person who does something wrong and "have it out with him alone, between your two selves … If he does not listen, take one or two others along with you … But if he refuses to listen to the community, treat him like an outcast." *(Matthew 18:15-17)*

Christ's gift of peace is the greatest fruit of his resurrection. He died that we "all may be one". The greatest task of Christians is to find peace among themselves so that God's gift of peace may be offered to the whole world.

The sixth and seventh Beatitudes, concerned with purity and peacemaking, deal with the two instincts most troublesome in society, namely sexuality and aggression. They are only purified by the gift of the Holy Spirit who makes us "children of God".

The final Beatitude is:

Blessed are they that suffer persecution for justice' sake, for theirs is the kingdom of heaven.

This attitude is the most specifically Christian: it is the joyful following of Christ in his suffering and death. When we ourselves are the victims we are to offer the wicked man no resistance. "On the contrary, if anyone hits you on the right cheek, offer him the other as well." *(Matthew 5:39)* And, at his trial, guards standing by gave Jesus a slap in the face.

Following Christ's own practice in the desert, we are to deny ourselves. Our sharing in Christ's death, celebrated in the Eucharist, is to be extended into our everyday life through voluntary penance in the form of fasting and works of charity. The Church especially commends fasting for those who are materially prosperous; and the acceptance of suffering (while still seeking to promote better social justice) for those who are poor.

"Happy are you when people abuse you and persecute you and speak all kinds of calumny against you on my account. Rejoice and be glad, for your reward will be great in heaven." *(Matthew 5:11-12)*

Freedom and good acts

God has created human beings with a great capacity for love and goodness. He has also made us free to choose whether or not we will act in a kind and loving way. The more we choose to do good things, then the more free we become, while the more we abuse our freedom by doing evil, the less free we become. This might sound like a funny sort of freedom, a freedom which only works when we do good things, but we do experience the same sort of thing if, for example, we take up something that is addictive. Take someone who decides to start smoking (this principle is also true for eating chocolate, gambling, taking drugs, driving too fast – anything which gets us hooked). The initial choice about whether to start smoking, or eating chocolate, might be a relatively free one: it might simply be curiosity which invites the first puff or the initial nibble, but after a while the addiction takes hold and gradually the decision about whether or not to have another cigarette or a little more chocolate becomes less of a free choice and more of a compulsion. In the end the smoker chocolate-eater becomes a slave to the addiction, powerless to do anything but give in to the cravings. It is the same with sin. The more we choose to sin, the more enslaved we become and the less able we are to freely choose *not* to sin. Sin is as much an addiction as eating chocolate or smoking cigarettes.

Most of our moral decisions are not grand affairs, but little things, the quality of exchanges between us and our partners, friends, children. They all add up, little by little, to make us who and what we are.

Acting in a loving and kind way is something we can learn to do well. We can get into good habits or bad habits. Many of the ways we behave are made up of patterns which we have learned and developed over a long period of time. We can get into the habit of always saying a kind word and praising someone's good points, of swallowing the urge to criticise and instead trying to find something positive to offer. We can practise trying to understand why people act the way they do, what it is like to *really* be in their shoes, to be quick to try to see their point of view and listen to what they are trying to say. Most of the ways we behave are simply habits built up over a lifetime. Changing habits is often hard, but the more we try to act kindly, the easier it will become because the freer we will become. Most of our moral decisions are not grand affairs, but little things, the quality of exchanges between us and our partners, friends, children. They all add up, little by little, to make us who and what we are.

118

Goodness

Although our human nature has been wounded by sin, we are redeemed and being 'good' is really about being the person God intended us to be, that is most truly and freely ourselves. If we were all to act according to our true selves, we would always do good. Being good need not be something forced or a strain, it is not about trying to pretend we are someone else. In its essence, being good is about being totally, fully, freely and joyfully ourselves. Accepting ourselves as we really are, warts and all, is a necessary step to becoming who we can be. We are all created in God's image as creatures meant for love and eternal happiness. When we act in a way that reflects this , acknowledging both the human and the divine in our nature, then we do no violence to ourselves and ultimately will find peace and joy.

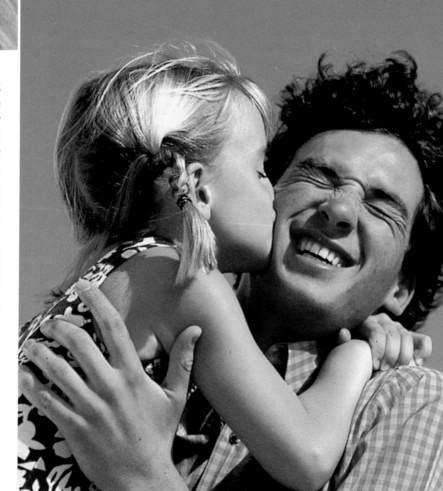

119

If everyone were to act lovingly according to their true, God-given selves, then there would be no need for laws and rules to tell us what to do and how to behave. Because most of us are still learning the art of love, we need the guidance of rules and laws. All rules and laws should have love as their starting point. In the end the only law is God's law which is really not a law at all, but a principle, the principle of love. Laws are good or bad depending on whether or not they encourage people to act according to love.

When deciding whether or not an action is good or bad, the Church has traditionally looked at three different factors:

1. **the deed itself**
2. **the context in which the deed took place**
3. **the intention of the person carrying out the deed.**

Some deeds are just wrong in themselves, for example rape and torture are always wrong whatever the circumstances. It is also never right to do something bad so that good may come out of it. The end can never justify the means. Although some deeds are wrong in themselves, there are others which can be right or wrong depending on the context and the intention of the people concerned. For example, a torturer pulling someone's teeth out is clearly morally wrong to do so. There is no doubt that it is wrong to pull someone's teeth out in order to cause them pain. However, the same action could be morally right if it was done by a dentist who was forced into performing an emergency operation without any anaesthetic. In this case the circumstances in which the action takes place can tell us whether or not it is right. The intention of the person performing the action can also affect whether or not it is morally right. For example, even though our dentist might be morally justified in pulling out the patient's teeth without anaesthetic in an emergency, he would be acting immorally if part of his intention was to cause as much suffering to his patient as possible because his patient happened to be his bank manager who was about to repossess his house! In this case the dentist would be acting immorally, even though he might be doing exactly the same actions and causing exactly the same amount of pain to his erstwhile bank manager. The difference is that in one example he intends to cause his bank manager pain, in the other he does not. So even though an action may be done in a context that would make it morally acceptable, if those concerned do not intend to do good, then they are acting badly.

What is conscience?

Conscience is our ability to make a moral judgement. "Always summoning him to love good and avoid evil, the voice of conscience can, when necessary, speak to his heart more specifically: do this, shun that." *(Gaudium et Spes, art. 16)*
By conscience we reason what we ought to do: it is our consciousness of God's will for us. "Conscience is the most secret core and sanctuary of a man. There he is alone with God, whose voice echoes in his depths." *(Ibid)*

We are obliged therefore:
1. To follow the demands of conscience. "Obedience to one's conscience, even if the conscience is in error, is the best way to the light" *(Cardinal Newman)*. St Paul demanded respect for people whose conscience was in error. He instructed Christians in Corinth not to eat meat offered to idols and then sold in butchers' shops – even though this was permissible – for fear of upsetting those who wrongly considered eating such meat to be sinful.

2. To inform one's conscience correctly. This means drawing on the wisdom of the past and consulting others. Above all, the "voice of conscience" can only be true if it echoes God's voice. By prayer and listening to the word of God our conscience is informed with the attitudes of Christ.

The size of the world depends on your conscience. Conscience can make the world bigger or smaller.

This may seem a very strange thing to say. But it was our Lord himself who told us this. Two people can look at the "lily in the field" and the one sees more than the other. The first sees the stem and petals of the flowers. The second sees all this and something beyond: the Providence of the Father who clothes it more magnificently than "Solomon in all his regalia".

For the second person, the Christian conscience is something more than a "still small voice". His world is bigger and he is too big a person to be crippled by a feeling of guilt when he dares to be unconventional. Such a person can see the whole stage and not just part of the scenery. He recognises the Christian conscience to be a very special spiritual gift we must all pray for. A gift Fr Gerald Vann O.P. used to call "the Vision of the Whole".

The modern Catholic rarely prays for this gift – the Vision of the Whole. Ours is a specialist world. The tremendous growth of our knowledge means no individual can become expert in the whole of any subject. To stay sane, he must specialise in a small area of knowledge.

Contemporary men and women, then, are forced to be "small-minded". And this, because we are people of our time, can constitute a real danger to the quality of our Christian life. When we begin to look at the world through a microscope, we soon become prey to childish fears and anxieties. We become too scared to step out of line, to stand up and be counted, because we imagine ourselves to be alone. Like the Athenians Saint Paul engaged in discussion, we soon forget that God is a real Person who loves us, cares for us, and speaks to us in the depths of our hearts.

Saint Paul reminded the Athenians that God "is not far from any of us, since it is in him that we live, and move, and exist" (Acts 17:28). We Catholics talk too little about God in this way. Ours is too often a distant God who lacks any real vitality. Is it at all surprising then, that for many today God and his Church are merely odd relics from a bygone age?

We must constantly pray for the Vision of the Whole. Speaking one day to his disciples, our Lord described those without such a vision as people who "look without seeing, and listen without hearing or understanding". But then he added: "Happy are your eyes because they see, your ears because they hear." (Matthew 13:16)

Our Lord obviously wants to be involved in the world around us. Conscience is all a question of seeing and hearing. It is the power, a gift of God, to see and hear correctly. To see Christ involved in every human situation. To see Christ involved in our own everyday lives. To listen to him who called himself the Way, the Truth and the Life.

The Virtues

Part of the process of learning how to love is to look at how we fail, to see how and why we sin and to try to change the way we do things. But this is only part of the picture. It is also important to keep sight of the positive, of the things we do well, and have a positive vision of ourselves and of who we want to be. Traditionally, the Church has isolated a number of positive characteristics which, with a little encouragement, can help us to grow and develop into fully loving human beings. All these virtues improve with practice! The more we exercise them, the stronger they become. The four cardinal virtues are:

1 **Prudence –**
   having a shrewd idea of the best way to go about things.

2 **Justice –**
   having a sense of the dignity and the rights of others.

3 **Fortitude –**
   hanging on in there even though it seems exhausting and hopeless.

4 **Temperance –**
   behaving in a balanced and reasonable way.

These all rest on what are known as the 'theological virtues', Faith, Hope and Love.

A Jesuit priest was a lecturer at a university, and gave evening classes on 'The Catholic Faith' to anyone from the local church who wanted to come along. For the first few weeks the whole class was extremely disturbed by the fact that the priest made them question everything about their Faith. One parishioner finally spoke up and asked him why he was trying to destroy their most cherished beliefs. The priest replied, 'I am not trying to destroy your beliefs, but to help you to discover the truth. If something is *really* true, then it will stand up to all my awkward questions!'

Faith

Faith is our ability to believe in the truth. Faith is about believing in the goodness of God and the Good News of the Gospel which tells us that God is a God of love and forgiveness who has broken the bonds of sin and death. To have Faith is not just to passively believe what we have been told, Faith is far more active than that. Faith is an active searching, a voyage of discovery where we are always on the look-out for the truth. To have Faith does not mean that we will never have doubts.

Doubting may lead us to ask healthy questions which can in turn deepen our faith. This may be an uncomfortable process, because sometimes we have to let go of our old certainties in order to discover them again at a greater depth. If we hang on too tightly to the faith we have and never let it be questioned or challenged, then we will smother it and not let it grow and develop. Doubt can ensure that we do not settle for less than the truth.

Hope

Hope, the second of the virtues, follows on naturally from Faith. Believing the message of the Gospel gives us Hope. Hope draws on all our longings for love and for happiness. These longings are given to us by God, and their end always lies in the love of God. Hope keeps us going and stops us from becoming completely discouraged. Hope is a sort of foolish optimism which shines out despite the grim-looking circumstances we may be in. Hope is a refusal to take the world and its miseries at face value; it refuses to give in to despair; it puts light in our eyes even in our darkest moments.

St Thomas Aquinas, a Dominican friar living in the middle ages, gave his cure for hopelessness and despair – a hot bath, lots of sleep, a good sobbing cry, pleasure and the company of a good friend was a recipe designed to lift the most downcast of spirits.

Love

Love is the last of the theological virtues. It is also the greatest. Love is at the heart of all virtue, it is what inspires us to lead good and holy lives. Love is the wellspring out of which pours everything that is good.

Traditional catechisms have spoken of the three theological virtues as 'Faith, Hope and Charity'. 'Charity' comes from the Latin word *caritas*, which simply means 'love'. Nowadays the word 'charity' can have negative connotations – it can have the sense of giving something to somebody out of duty or pity in a way that demeans them, as the expression 'as cold as charity' suggests. It is a pity that the word has come to mean something so cold and dry, because in its essence, charity is a warm, generous and spontaneous outpouring of the love which we have received from God. Love is most alive when we give it practical expression; it is not a dreary giving that stems from fear of punishment or hope of some eternal reward. Love is at its best when it is given just for its own sake. This is the sort of thing that St Basil, who lived from about 339-379 AD, had to say:

If we turn away from evil out of fear of punishment, we are in the position of slaves. If we pursue the enticement of wages... we resemble mercenaries. Finally if we obey for the sake of the good itself and out of love for him who commands... we are in the position of children.

When we love others for no other reason than that we ourselves have been loved, then we do not stand before God as slaves, in servile fear, or as a mercenary looking for wages, but as a child responding to the love of a parent.

Emotions are of themselves neither good nor bad. We cannot help feeling angry or sad or even jealous, but what we *do* with the feelings, how we direct them, is what makes them become good or bad.

"Love is always patient and kind; it is never jealous;
love is never boastful or conceited; it is never rude or selfish;
it does not take offence, and is not resentful.
Love takes no pleasure in other people's sins but delights in the truth;
it is always ready to excuse, to trust, to hope and to endure whatever comes.
Love does not come to an end...
In short, there are three things that last: faith, hope and love and the greatest of these is love."
St Paul *(1 Corinthians 13:4-13)*

Sin

In the Old Testament, the Hebrew word for sin literally means 'to miss the mark'. In the New Testament the Greek word for sin has the same meaning as the Hebrew. Sin is essentially about 'missing the mark'. The picture that both the Hebrew and the Greek words give us is of someone aiming an arrow and just failing to hit the target. The Church has traditionally picked up on this understanding of sin. When we sin we miss the target. St Augustine, writing in the fourth century, and St Thomas Aquinas in the thirteenth, both talked about sin in this way. Augustine believed that at the heart of every human being is a deep yearning for love and for God. All of us have a longing which can only be fulfilled by God. We sin when we set our sights too low, when we settle for things that are not God. This means that when we do sin, the answer isn't to put ourselves into a moral straight-jacket, unable to trust ourselves to move freely and take risks in case we commit more; the answer instead is to open our hearts, to let our hearts love freely and deeply so that we can get in touch with our deepest desires. Once we have done this, then perhaps we will come to the conclusion that nothing less than God will do.

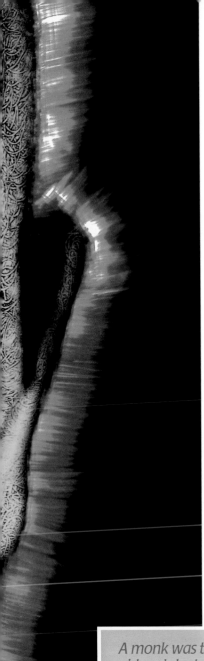

The Church has traditionally divided sin into two main categories: mortal sin and venial sin. The word 'venial' comes from a Latin word *venia* which means 'grace' or 'pardon'. Venial sins do not radically cut us off from God. When we commit venial sins we are not totally rejecting God, but we are failing to live up to our full potential. Venial sins are the result of our failing to love as fully and deeply as we can. Wounded by sin, we are not the fit and healthy people that God made us to be, instead we are weak and wobbly, and keep falling over as we try to run towards God our Father to throw ourselves into his arms.

Mortal sin is very different from venial sin. Mortal sin is the complete rejection of God. No one knows if anyone has ever committed a mortal sin. We only know that mortal sin is a theoretical possibility because God has given men and women freedom, and if our freedom is real it must allow for the possibility that we can turn away completely from God. Throughout history there have been people who have done the most terrible things, who have acted so brutally that we might reasonably wonder whether or not there could possibly be any hope of salvation for them. But we are told by Jesus that where there is love, there is God, and is there really any human being who has never loved at all? We do not know the secrets of another's heart. With the exception of the person who has consciously rejected God, God only knows whether anyone has ever been in a state of mortal sin. We must never make such a judgement.

A monk was travelling on an errand for his monastery and on the way he met a beautiful girl and slept with her. Filled with remorse and shame, he rushed back to his monastery and threw himself at the feet of his confessor. 'I have committed the most terrible sin,' he said and wept bitterly. His confessor was a wise old man and after he had given him absolution, he said to the young lad: 'For your penance, say two 'Our Fathers'. Now go in peace my son'. The young monk was very unhappy with the penance he had been given: he felt it was much too light for the enormity of what he had done. He went straight to the Abbot. 'Father Abbot', he said, 'please hear my confession, I have done the most terrible thing, but my confessor only gave me two 'Our Fathers' as a penance.' The old Abbot heard the young monk's confession and told him that the two 'our Fathers' was quite adequate a penance for his sin. The young monk went away distraught. Then he saw St Columba coming up the road. 'Father Columba!' he cried 'You are a very holy man, and a healer of souls, please hear my confession, because I have done the most terrible thing!' So St Columba heard the young monk's confession and how he had gone to his confessor and his Abbot and the light penance they had given him. 'For your penance for committing the sin of fornication with the woman on the road, I give you two 'Our Fathers', but for the sin of pride in thinking that your sin was more important than it really was, I give you six months on bread and water!'

The New Law

The New Law is the Law of Christ. This does not contradict the Old Law as summarised in the Ten Commandments, but it sheds a totally new light upon it. It sheds this light in three principal ways:

1 Jesus established order among the various laws that had grown up in the Jewish tradition. He established love of God and of neighbour as the centre of his moral code: "You must love the Lord your God with all your heart, with all your soul, with all your strength and with all your mind, and your neighbour as yourself." (*Luke 10:27*)

God's Law

God has revealed his law in nature. Even though totally ignorant of God, all men and women "can point to the substance of the Law engraved on their hearts" which is recognised by conscience. (*Romans 2:15*)

This natural law was expressed in the Old Law or Law of Moses. The giving of the Ten Commandments was the formative event of the Old Testament by which the Jews were separated from other nations to become God's own. The Commandments "sum up the fundamental demands of the human conscience with an accuracy and sureness rarely attained by the pagan philosophers". For the Jews the fulfilment of the Law meant salvation.
Jesus did not come to abolish the Old Law but to complete it. The Old Law was written on tablets of stone, but the New Law is written in men and women's hearts. The Old Law led to confusion and self-righteousness, but the New Law is ordered and leads to intimacy with God.
The Old and the New Law cannot be mixed. As Jesus explained, "Nobody puts new wine in old wineskins; if he does, the wine will burst the skins and the wine is lost and the skins too." (*Mark 2:22*)

2 Jesus called for perfection in his followers. Under the Old Law imperfections had been tolerated because of "hardness of heart" (*Matthew 19:8*). But Jesus set the example in "being perfect, as your heavenly Father is perfect" (*Matthew 5:48*). This is the perfection of the Good Samaritan who "loves his enemies".

3 Most importantly, Jesus offers us the means by which we can become perfect. He offers us the gift of the Holy Spirit. He gave us the Holy Spirit to enable us to overcome sin. After his resurrection, he breathed on the Apostles, saying, "Receive the Holy Spirit. For those whose sins you forgive, they are forgiven..." (*John 20:23*)

128

The Ten Commandments

(Catechism of the Catholic Church – 2052-2082)

Introduction

Since the fourth century, the Ten Commandments have been used as part of the Church's catechetical teaching. These Commandments were a central part of the old Jewish Law, and were traditionally thought to have been physically written by God on tablets of stone. The Old Testament tells the story of how the prophet Moses went up Mount Sinai and how God gave him the stone tablets containing the ten commandments which would form the heart of the Jewish Law. Jesus did not deny the importance of the Ten Commandments, but instead of taking them at face value, he pointed to the principle which lay behind them. In the end, all law and every commandment is based on love – love of God and love of neighbour.

When Jesus was asked which was the greatest of the Commandments, he replied:

'Love the Lord your God with all your heart, and with all your soul, and with all your mind. This is the first and greatest commandment. And the second is like it: love your neighbour as yourself. All the Law and the Prophets hang on these two commandments'
(Matthew 22: 37-40; Mark 12:30-31; Luke 10: 25-28)

The Ten Commandments are:

1 You shall worship the Lord your God and him only shall you serve.
2 You shall not take the name of the Lord your God in vain.
3 Remember to keep holy the Lord's day.
4 Honour your father and your mother.
5 You shall not kill
6 You shall not commit adultery.
7 You shall not steal.
8 You shall not bear false witness against your neighbour.
9 You shall not covet your neighbour's wife.
10 You shall not covet your neighbour's goods.

GEORGE · WHIELDON · 1860

Many of the paintings, the stained glass windows and the carvings in our churches are illustrations of different parts of this way of passing on Church teaching. For example, baptismal fonts were carved with pictures representing the seven sacraments or stained glass windows showed little scenes depicting the seven works of mercy. A wander round some of our older churches can be quite an instructive lesson on the basics of Church teaching.

Although the Ten Commandments remained an important part of the Christian faith, they were joined by a number of other teachings which together formed the basis of Christian belief. In the Middle Ages there was an enthusiastic movement to give both priests and parishioners a better grasp of their faith. This was an age before printing, when all books had to be laboriously hand-written and most ordinary people could not read or write. This meant that anything they learnt had to be passed down by word of mouth and learnt by heart. Much of church teaching was condensed and itemised and put into lists which could be easily remembered. These lists formed a sort of skeleton which could then be fleshed out. Although this was a very useful way of helping people to remember the Church's teaching, it did make it all look a bit like a set of holy shopping lists! However, it was such a successful way of teaching ordinary people that it was used throughout the Middle Ages and beyond. It still influences the structure of modern catechisms and even very recently the majority of Catholic children were still learning the same lists by heart.

Apart from the Ten Commandments there were the two commandments of Jesus to love God and neighbour, the twelve articles of the Creed and the seven petitions of the Our Father. These together formed the central part of the Church's teaching. In addition were the seven corporal works of mercy, the seven spiritual works of mercy, the seven virtues, the seven vices, the seven sacraments, the seven gifts of the Holy Spirit, the six sins against the Holy Spirit, the twelve fruits of the Holy Spirit, the eight beatitudes and the four sins crying to heaven for vengeance!

During this time, yearly confession of serious sin was made compulsory for all the faithful. The seven vices (also known rather more dramatically as the Seven Deadly Sins) were used as a convenient way to examine the conscience. The seven vices were matched by their corresponding virtues:

The Seven Vices	The Seven Virtues
1. Pride	1. Humility
2. Covetousness	2. Liberality
3. Lust	3. Chastity
4. Anger	4. Meekness
5. Gluttony	5. Temperance
6. Envy	6. Brotherly Love
7. Sloth	7. Diligence

Each virtue was a medicine to cure its corresponding vice. The Italian poet Dante said that the souls in purgatory would all be practising the virtues - those who needed to be cured of bad language would learn to sing and speak beautifully, whilst those who needed to be cured of lust would learn to kiss properly.

The First Commandment:
You shall worship the Lord your God and him only shall you serve

A quick flick through the Old Testament leaves a very strong impression that the people of Israel spent much of their time worshipping other gods. Ancient Israelites didn't go in for atheism, which denied the existence of God. Their tendency was very much in the opposite direction. The Old Testament prophets are frequently heard bewailing the fact that the Israelites have yet again gone off after the gods of their Canaanite neighbours.

The high god El, the bull god, was the father of all the gods: kindly, old and wise. He was a powerful symbol of virility, which was why he was often portrayed as a bull. He was the figure the Israelites were worshipping when they made the golden calf in the desert.

El's consort was called Asherah. She was the queen of heaven.

Baal was the storm god, the god of thunder and rain. He rode on a chariot made of clouds and threw down thunderbolts from heaven.

Anat was the goddess of hunting and war, a tomboyish figure who delighted in nothing more than a good fight.

Mot was the god of death who lived underneath the earth in a slimy pit.

In contrast to this rather flamboyant tapestry was the God of Israel. Israel's God refused to let his people think of him in the same way. No images were to be made of him, and no myths told about him. The only story the people of Israel could tell about him was what he had done for them. He refused-point blank to give any indication of what he looked like: all they knew was what he had told them, that he had made human beings in his own image.

The mistake of the Canaanites was that they had made gods in *their* image; they had created their own gods. In our modern age we are still drawn by the glitz and glitter of false gods. Many people are still sacrificed to the false gods of power and wealth. Part the world lives in abject poverty while the other part lives in wealth and splendour. False gods can be simple, ordinary things like money, power, beauty, success, a bigger house or a better job. Whatever it is, once something has become so important that it pushes away the desire for God, then it has become an idol and a false god.

Usually God works through us. When we touch others with healing and compassion, our hands become the hands of God. We too feel his hands on us through the touch of other people. God has chosen to minister to his suffering world through the hearts and the hands of his people. When we serve each other with love and kindness we not only serve God, who dwells within the person we serve, but we also act as a channel for his love and care. The seven corporal works of mercy are the traditional representations of the way in which Christians have always been called to love their neighbour. They include feeding the hungry, giving drink to the thirsty, clothing the naked, sheltering the homeless, visiting the sick and burying the dead. They are based on the passage in Matthew's Gospel when Jesus explains how any act of kindness to the least human being is done to him:

'Lord, when did we see you hungry and feed you, thirsty, and give you to drink? And when did we see you a stranger, and took you in, or naked, and clothe you? Or when did we see you sick, or in prison, and come to you?' And he answered them, 'Truly I say to you, so long as you did it to one of the least of my brothers and sisters, you did it to me.' (Matthew 25: 37-40)

The seven corporal works of mercy are echoed by their spiritual counterparts, which are aimed at ministering to the spiritual well-being of others. The spiritual works of mercy include instructing, advising, consoling, comforting, forgiving and bearing wrongs patiently.

Statues and representations of Jesus or the saints can never replace the real thing, any more than a photograph of can be the real person, however good a likeness it is. A statue of Jesus is not Jesus himself, and when we go to church in order to pray in front of the statue, we are not praying to the statue itself, but using the statue to focus our minds on Jesus. Being human, it is often hard to pray into thin air, but it is easier to have something to focus on – just so long as that thing does not become and end in itself, but points beyond itself to draw our attention to God.

Second Commandment: *You shall not take the name of the Lord your God in vain*

This verse has traditionally been translated from the Hebrew as 'You shall not take the name of the Lord in vain', but in its original context the Hebrew probably meant something like: 'Don't use the Lord's name for mischief.' The Israelites believed that words had their own power. A curse or a blessing had a life of its own, and did its harm or its good regardless of the subsequent wishes of the person who had spoken it. This meant that words were very powerful but also very dangerous. Once a curse had left someone's mouth there was no way to recall it. A curse or a blessing was significantly strengthened if God's name was used in it because the Israelites thought that the name of the Lord was the most powerful of all.

This meant that people could not afford to take it lightly. Hasty or rash words could have devastating consequences. A rash oath or a curse spat out in anger could not be taken back and did its damage and destruction like a bullet fired from a gun. Nowadays we don't literally think that words fly about like darts ready to attack their victims, but it is true to say that angry, hurtful words said in the heat of the moment can leave a very long and lingering trail of hurt and destruction.

There are many other ways of 'using the Lord's name for mischief'. It is all too easy to wheel God in to justify cruel or uncharitable actions or attitudes to others. History is full of religious wars and persecutions, all done in the name of God. The second commandment calls us to resist the temptation to use God as an excuse for judging others in a harsh and intolerant way, but instead to act kindly in the name of God – as we can see in the popular 'prayer of St Francis':

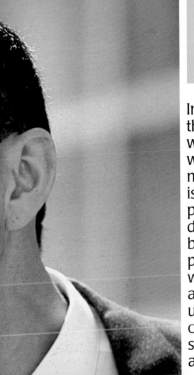

> *Lord make me an instrument of thy peace..*
> *Where there is hatred, let me sow love;*
> *Where there is injury, pardon;*
> *Where there is doubt, faith;*
> *Where there is despair, hope;*
> *Where there is darkness, light;*
> *Where there is sadness, joy;*
> *O divine Master, grant that I may not so much seek*
> *to be consoled as to console, to be understood as*
> *to understand, to be loved as to love.*
> *For it is in giving that we receive, it is in pardoning*
> *that we are pardoned, it is in dying that we are*
> *born to eternal life.*

In court, witnesses are asked to take an oath and swear that they will tell the truth, the whole truth and nothing but the truth. God *is* truth, and when we swear an oath we are calling on God to witness to the truth of what we say. A vow is a free and deliberate promise made to God. When we marry we promise to stay faithful to our partners until death. This promise is made with God as a witness. Priests and religious also make vows and promises. Religious take vows of poverty, chastity and obedience. The difference between a vow and promise is that one is made to a human being and the other is made to God. The Church does, however, have the power to release someone from a religious vow if circumstances arise which make inadvisable to keep the vow. Vows and promises are not about binding people in misery and subjection. They are there to enable us to come closer to God and to love more fully. When they have the opposite effect and begin to destroy and cripple our humanity and strangle our capacity to give and receive love, then they are taking us away from God.

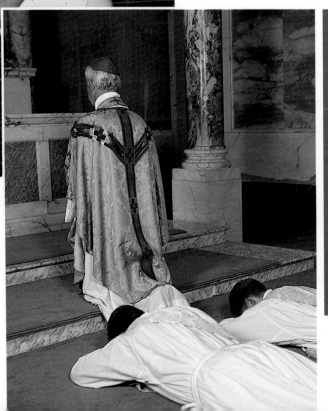

Not all vows are binding – for example if I promise to cut off my hand if God saves my son from a life-threatening disease, then I am not bound by that promise because it is damaging and unreasonable. The point of vows is not to make bargains with God – God does not need to be bribed, threatened or enticed in order to give us good things – he loves us and wants us to be happy. The last thing he wants is for us to imprison ourselves by rules and vows of our own making in the mistaken belief that it is the only way we can get him to do anything good for us! People are also not bound by a vow if they are coerced, or if they didn't understand the real meaning of the vow they were making. In certain circumstances, the Church has procedures to release people from vows which they have made.

Third Commandment: Remember to keep holy the Lord's Day

In Genesis we are told that God made the heavens and the earth and then on the seventh day he had a rest. The Sabbath day has traditionally been a day of resting. Christians moved their Sabbath to a Sunday because Jesus rose from the dead on a Sunday. Judaism still hold its Sabbath rest on a Saturday. It starts with the appearance of the first star on Friday night and ends with the first star on Saturday evening.

Holidays are called holidays because they were originally holy days, when people downed tools and took the day off to commemorate a particular event or to celebrate a saint's feast day. In mediaeval times the number of holy days would have added up to several weeks a year, and it meant that people often had a day off in the week as well as Sundays. When the Protestant Reformers took over in England they banned these holy days on the grounds that devotions to saints were superstitious nonsense and that holy days only encouraged idleness and vice. This move by the Reformers was greeted with dismay by the working population and with glee by the employers who wanted to gain the maximum profit from their workers, which meant giving them fewer holidays.

Life has its own rhythm of work and rest, and in order to keep the balance between working and leisure, all of us need ample time to just relax and enjoy being by ourselves or with our friends or families. We also need time for prayer either alone with God or with each other. Sometimes it is very hard in this pressurised world of ours to squeeze out enough time to rest and recharge our batteries. It is difficult to justify spending time doing nothing, time spent just 'being' on our own or with others. There is a lot to be said for just wasting time. Our Sundays are days for rest and relaxation, when we can waste time to our heart's content. We don't always have to be busy or useful, to have something to show for every minute that we have lived on this earth. God rested on the seventh day, so let's join him on Sundays and all have a holy waste of time!

Modern Orthodox Jews are strict about their Sabbath observance. They are very careful to keep the Sabbath holy. In Hebrew, the word 'holy' literally means 'set apart', so that holy things are things which are set apart by God. In order, then, to keep the Sabbath holy, it must be a day set apart from all the others. The Orthodox Jews go to great lengths to ensure that the Sabbath remains special and to keep it holy and set apart. The Sabbath is above all a day of rest, and so they are very strict about what work can and cannot be done on the Sabbath. Those things which are essential must be done in a different way from normal. For example, if a doctor has to write an emergency prescription on the Sabbath, then it should be written with the left hand if the doctor is normally right-handed, and with the right hand if the doctor is normally left-handed. This means that whatever work has to be done, the Sabbath is still set apart as a day which is special from all the others.

Sunday is the day when parishes get together to celebrate the Lord's resurrection, to go to church, listen to the Gospels, share the Eucharist and meet together. The Church has always encouraged all Catholics to go to Mass on a Sunday. This is known as the Sunday observance. The obligation to go to Mass on a Sunday is also fulfilled by going to a vigil mass on Saturday evening. There are other days throughout the year on which the Church urges people to go to Mass. They are known as Holy Days of Obligation, and include feasts such as Christmas Day, (the day on which Jesus was born) and the Ascension (when Jesus was taken up to heaven). These Holy Days of Obligation are set by the local bishops and may vary between different countries. Those who are travelling, looking after someone who is ill or are ill themselves are not required to go to Mass on Sundays or Holy Days.
(See Supplement part 3)

Fourth Commandment:
Honour your father and your mother

The Hebrew word for 'honour' is one which also has the meaning 'to be heavy, weighty'. (It is the same word as 'liver' in Hebrew because the liver is the heaviest organ.) In Hebrew thought, by honouring someone you made them weighty, you let them count in your decisions, you made them into people of substance. As St Augustine says in his 'Confessions': 'My love is my weight.' Love makes us and others more solidly human. By giving honour to our parents we let them count, we give them weight.

THIS POEM WAS PINNED UP ON THE WALL OF A CHILDREN'S HOME:

If children live with criticism they learn to condemn.
If children live with hostility they learn to fight.
If children live with ridicule they learn to be shy.
If children live with shame they learn to feel guilty.
If children live with tolerance they learn to be patient.
If children live with encouragement they learn confidence.
If children live with appreciation they learn to appreciate.
If children live with fairness they learn justice.
If children live with security they learn to have faith.
If children live with approval they learn to like themselves.
If children live with acceptance and friendship they learn
   to find love in the world.

At first sight, it looks as if this commandment to honour father and mother is telling children to be obedient to their parents and to respect those in authority. Undoubtedly, the ancient Israelites were keen that children should respect and obey their parents, but in its original context this commandment would have probably had a slightly different slant. It was more likely to have been aimed at adult children whose parents would have been elderly and dependent on them for food and shelter. At that time, Israel had no social security system and so elderly parents would have been totally dependent on their offspring. Commanding them to honour their father and mother was simply urging them to behave kindly to their elderly parents, to treat them gently and with dignity and to see to it that they are well cared for. In its original context, this commandment was not teaching blind obedience to authority, but commanding that authority itself be exercised justly and kindly, in a way that paid attention to those who were vulnerable and weak, and to those unable to fend for themselves.

'Jesus called them together and said, 'You know that those who are regarded as rulers of the Gentiles lord it over them, and their high officials exercise authority over them. Not so with you. Instead, whoever wants to become great among you must be your servant, and whoever wants to be first must be slave of all.' (Mark 10: 42-45; Matthew 20: 25-27; Luke 22: 25-26). If we are to take the words of Jesus seriously, we come to see that authority is primarily a service, not the exercise of power. When we are in positions of authority over others, we are at their service, putting ourselves at their disposal and working for their good.

Most of us will at some point be placed in positions of authority, but we will also find ourselves under the authority of others, who may or may not exercise their authority in justice and love. What do we do in the face of authority that is unfair and acts against those it is supposed to serve? What do we do when authority is used to coerce or dominate others, when it is misused and abused? This is a difficult question, but the Church has always taught that Christians are not bound to obey authorities which have abused their position. In order to be legitimate, all authority must be exercised in a just way for the good of all. All authority derives its ultimate legitimacy from God, and so is bound by the commandments and laws of God. Once it departs from these, then it ceases to have legitimacy in the eyes of God and his Church.

Many of the early Church Fathers shunned the responsibilities of high office because they thought that they were completely unworthy and inadequate to the task. In the fourth century Augustine was made a priest unexpectedly and against his will and wept profusely throughout the whole ceremony. St Ambrose fled from Milan rather than let himself be appointed bishop, and a monk from Egypt called Ammonius cut off an ear in his efforts to avoid the bishopric – and when he saw that this would not prevent him being appointed he threatened to cut out his tongue as well!

Fifth Commandment:
You shall not kill

In Hebrew there are a whole range of different words which all mean 'to kill', but talk about different sorts of killing. For example, one word means 'to slay', others 'to slaughter', 'to kill sacrificially', or 'to smite, pierce'. The word used here in the fifth commandment means 'to murder' or 'to kill unlawfully'. The Old Testament law did permit killing in several circumstances – as a punishment for certain crimes, for example, or killing in self-defence or in battle. The fifth commandment was not originally intended to forbid all killing.

If we move on to the New Testament we can see that Jesus did not accept the Old Testament commandment at face value. He dug deeper to unearth the principle which lay beneath the law, the principle that every human life is of infinite value and cannot just be thrown away. Jesus told his disciples: "You have heard that it was said to the people long ago, 'Do not murder, and anyone who murders will be subject to judgement', but I tell you that everyone who is angry with his brother will be subject to judgement." (*Matthew 5:21-22*). Here Jesus is saying that it is not enough to just follow the letter of the law and neglect the principle that lies behind it. If we hate someone, then we have already violated the principle of the law which says that their life is sacred.

It is possible to obey the letter of the law in ways which violate the spirit of the law. The law says that you must not drive faster than 30 m.p.h. in a built-up area. This is also an expression of the principle of respect for life. But if someone drives at thirty miles an hour through a crowd of children playing in the street, he may be obeying the letter, but he is certainly breaking the spirit of the law. On the other hand, it is possible to break the letter of the law while keeping to its spirit. An ambulance driver, taking one of the children to hospital after he has been hit by our car-driver may drive faster than that speed limit, precisely in order to save the precious human life. Sometimes, it seems, we need to break the letter of the law in order to uphold its spirit.

Respect for human life begins as soon as human life begins. At the moment of conception a new human being comes into existence. A very small and hard to recognise one, certainly, but one which will become more recognisably human as it grows older. Every one of us was once an embryo. The Church is clear that abortion, the killing of an unborn child, violates the principle of respect for human life. Euthanasia, deliberately shortening the life of sick or old or handicapped people, is also against this commandment.

All laws are really principles which have been put into practice. If the principle is wrong in the beginning, then the laws which follow will also be wrong. So a law which pays no regard to human life is based on a false principle, and must be rejected by those who obey God's law. Such a law might be one which leads to the taking of life, such as the race laws of Nazi Germany, or one which fails to defend human life.

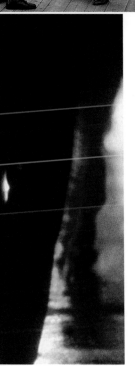

Although deliberately shortening someone's life violates the fifth commandment, there are cases when it is morally acceptable to take actions which will shorten someone's life or threaten the life of another. For example, if someone is dying of cancer the doctor may prescribe strong pain-relieving drugs which may well speed the death of the patient. In this case the intention is not to shorten the life of the cancer-sufferer, but to relieve their pain. There are times when a good action may have unintended but foreseeable consequences which may lead to the death of another. If what we intend is good, then sometimes the unintended consequences are morally acceptable if they cannot be avoided. This is why it is sometimes acceptable to use violence in self-defence or in defence of the weak and innocent. If someone attacks you or attacks someone else and killing them is the only way you can prevent them from killing you or the other person, then you have not violated the fifth commandment because your real intention was to protect life. This rather complicated conundrum is known as the principle of 'double effect'.

Double effect also underlies the Church's "Just War" teaching. This was formulated not to sanction war, but to try to limit both the circumstances in which parties go to war and the damage done once war breaks out. Just War teaching says that you may never use military violence unless there is a major injustice to be corrected, unless you have the authority to correct it and unless you are actually able to do so. You must be sure that the harm you do trying to correct it will not be worse than the harm caused by the original injustice. If any of these are lacking, you may not go to war. Even when it is lawful to go to war, there are many things which are forbidden: attacking civilians, torturing prisoners, deliberately destroying whole areas of countryside, and so on. If this was applied to modern weapons, many of them would be condemned: the use of all weapons which kill indiscriminately is immoral. This would include the use of nuclear and biological weapons, anti-personnel mines and the bombing of civilian areas.

Sixth Commandment:
You shall not commit adultery

The Old Testament law forbidding adultery has, to our modern ears, a slightly unfortunate twist. A married woman committed adultery if she slept with another man, but her husband only committed adultery if he slept with a married woman, and then the offence was against the woman's husband, not against his own wife. The Old Testament law on adultery was clearly not an ideal expression of the principle that a husband and wife live faithfully to each other and treat one another with love and respect. Other parts of the Old Testament express this principle a little more clearly. For example, the Song of Songs speaks of the love between a man and a woman, and the prophets see the fidelity of a husband and wife as a sign of God's love for Israel.

Jesus said, 'You have heard that it was said, 'You shall not commit adultery', but I say to you that everyone who looks at a woman lustfully has already committed adultery with her in his heart.' (*Matthew 5:27-28*). Jesus did not take the Old Testament Commandment at face value, but looked beneath it to the principle that lay behind it. Within marriage, or any sexual relationship, there has to be a reverence for the other person which goes deeper than just obeying the letter of the law. Even now, there are many actions which can take place within a marriage that are legal but unkind. Sexual love demands a reverence for the other person, a delight in them and a willingness to give ourselves to them.

People are not objects
The sixth Commandment is opposed to seeing others as objects. This is why pornography contradicts the sixth commandment. Pornography is wrong not because it gives some people pleasure, but because it treats the bodies of other people, people who are made in the image of God, as mere objects. There is no reverence, no tenderness, no self-giving in such an encounter.

The gift of children

One of the gifts of sexual love is that of children. Sexual activity is not just geared towards the love of the couple, but is also intended to renew the whole human race by bringing new life into the world. This is why the Church teaches that married couples should be open to the gift of children. This doesn't mean that couples have to have as many children as they can as fast as they can. Responsible parenting is at the heart of Christian family life. People are rational beings, able to plan their lives and to act accordingly, and spacing children and timing their arrival often makes good sense. What is important is that the planning must take account of the morality of the methods used.

Some people find themselves attracted to others of the same sex. The Church says that the attraction itself is not sinful. It teaches, however, that the genital expression of the love between a couple of the same sex can never be approved because homosexual acts are not open to the gift of life. In spite of this, the Church is insistent that no one should be discriminated against on the basis of their sexuality. All love is a sharing in the life of God. And the love between two homosexuals is no exception. The Catechism of the Catholic Church states that homosexual persons "must be accepted with respect, compassion, and sensitivity. Every sign of unjust discrimination in their regard should be avoided." (2358)

Adultery in the gospel

In John's Gospel we are told how Jesus was presented with a woman taken in adultery. She was guilty under the Law and the penalty was to be stoned to death. But Jesus refused to condemn her. There is often a tendency to treat 'sexual sins' as the worst sorts of sins. This is understandable, as our sexuality concerns the deepest parts of ourselves, where we are often most vulnerable. This means that we can hurt one another on a personal level more deeply in sexual matters than in many other ways. This is why it is so important to act justly and to take good care of those we love and those who love us. However, it is important to separate out a healthy respect for sexual justice from a more narrow-minded sort of prudishness. It is not fair to treat sexual sins as if they are in a category all of their own. Jesus refused to participate in stoning the woman caught in adultery – even though her accusers were perfectly within their legal rights to treat her in that way. Those who fail in their efforts to love need mercy, forgiveness and encouragement. The way of the Gospel is one of patience, love and forgiveness, not a sort of self-righteous condemnation.

Seventh Commandment: *You shall not steal*

At the heart of the Church's teaching about property is the picture painted in the book of Genesis. God entrusted the earth to the whole of humankind, to till the soil and enjoy its fruits. At that time there was no private property because there was no need for it. At the heart of the Church's teaching on property is this vision that at the very deepest level the earth and its goods belong to the whole human race. Private property is partly necessary to protect the weak and defend their claim to a share in the goods of the earth. People need security and the resources to provide for their own needs and the needs of their dependants.

The principle underlying the Seventh Commandment is that everyone has a right to share in the fruits of the earth. The traditional church teaching on this matter is a radical departure from the sorts of things that we hear from many politicians! Here is a summary of the Church's view:

There was once a Rabbi who was not very well off, in fact he owned nothing but a single cow. He got to know a family that was very poor and so he gave them his cow. His own children asked him the next day why there was no milk. The Rabbi told them that they no longer had the cow. They asked him what had happened to the cow and he answered, 'It has gone to heaven.'
What you give to the poor goes to God...

143

Landowners

Owning land and property brings with it obligations. Those who possess wealth have a responsibility to use its fruits for the good of all. They also have a responsibility to care for the earth and not to squander its resources or pollute and destroy its ecosystems for private profit and short-term gain. Whoever holds land or property holds it in trust for future generations.

Employers

Employers have a duty to ensure that they are giving their workers a fair share of the wealth that they have helped to create. Every labourer has a right to enjoy safe and decent working conditions and a fair wage. All work is aimed both at the well-being and satisfaction of the worker and at releasing the goods of the earth so that they can be distributed fairly among all peoples.

Justice between nations

So called 'economic migrants' are quite entitled to travel wherever they wish in search of better living conditions, especially if they come from a country which is very poor. The world belongs to everyone regardless of national boundaries. Richer countries have a duty to share their wealth with the poorer ones, not out of kindness, but out of justice, because by holding on to wealth the richer countries are stealing what is not theirs. St Gregory the Great wrote:

"When we attend to the needs of those in want, we give them what is theirs, not ours. More than performing works of mercy, we are paying a debt of justice." (Regula Pastoralis 3, 21)

Debt and Usury

Usury – charging interest on a loan – was condemned throughout the Church's history. In the nineteenth century, however, the Church ruled that people could lend money at moderate rates of interest. In the Old Testament usury was particularly frowned upon because at that time those who needed loans were desperately poor that any interest placed on the initial loan only served to cripple them further in a cycle of poverty and debt. Even today many people are struggling under the burden of debt repayments because the interest they are being charged does not allow them to pay off their loan. Many poorer countries pay back more in interest than they received in the initial loan. Demanding money from those too poor to pay amounts to stealing.

144

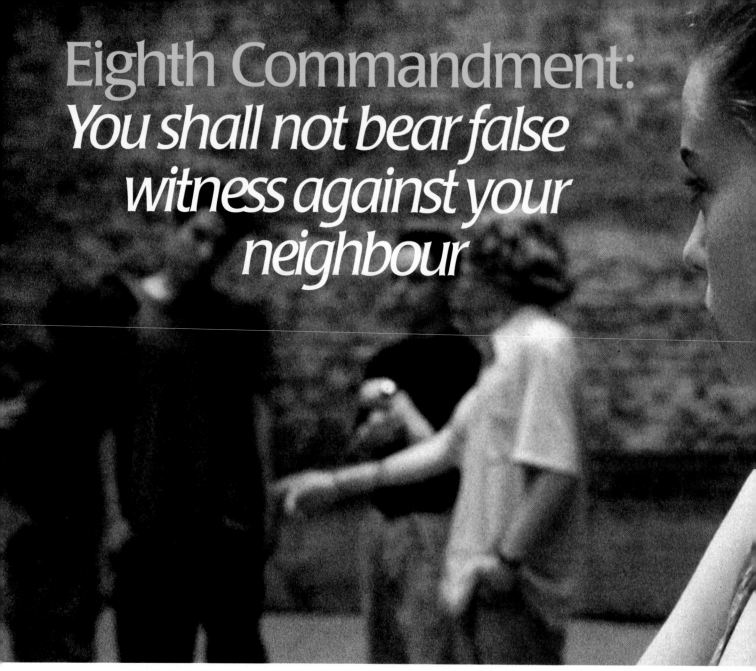

Eighth Commandment:
You shall not bear false witness against your neighbour

Like our own legal system, that of the ancient Israelites depended on witnesses. To give a false testimony is a very serious offence because it can lead to the wrongful conviction of someone. In many cases, the justice of the courts is dependent on the honesty of the witnesses. It was the same for the ancient Israelites. The principle behind this commandment is that of truth. We are all called to witness to the truth. Witnessing to truth is not always easy. It is often difficult to discern where the truth may lie, and even when we do, it is sometimes even harder to speak up about it, especially when we have a lot to lose by doing so.

Natural Law

God is truth. God is the origin of all that is good. We can find God's truth through the natural world and through ourselves. God built into creation his ways and his laws. Gods law, the law of love and justice, is built into the very fabric of all creation. Because God's laws are written into the very being of the world, they are accessible to everyone, and because all people are created by God, they have the law of God written into their hearts and minds. This means that everyone has within them the capacity to know what is good and true and to recognise whether or not something conforms to the law of God. The way in which God's laws are translated into the fabric of creation is known as 'natural law'. That part of us which God has created know what is right is known as our "conscience".

Truth in Christian teaching

Although creation speaks clearly of God's ways through the natural law, and our conscience gives us a built-in capacity to know what is good, sin and ignorance can often blind us and prevent us from recognising God's law. Because of sin, we cannot wholly trust ourselves to discern the natural law. This means that we need guidance from outside ourselves, and this is why we need Revelation – that is the way in which God reveals to humankind his laws and his ways. Over the centuries, God has guided his Church, not allowing it to fall into serious error. This means that in important matters of faith (what we believe) and morals (how we act) the Church is prevented from making wrong judgements. This is called "infallibility". It means that we can trust the Church – though that doesn't mean that we have to agree with everything that any individual says – not even the Pope. It is the bishops as a body who spell it out, and no individual can take over this role. However, the authority of the Pope is part of the Church's infallibility. He is the one who is the "Vicar of Christ and successor of Peter" – the one Jesus entrusted as leader of the apostles. His task is to preach the faith, and to strengthen the bishops in unity with each other. In moments of crisis when the Church is threatened with division, he has a special role of declaring the truth of the faith. We are not, however, expected to look constantly at the Pope for an answer to all our questions.

Witness for truth
The word 'martyr' comes from the Greek word *martyrion* which means 'witness'. The early martyrs were witnesses to the Gospel. We don't need to die glorious deaths in order to witness to truth. If we live according to the Gospel, then everything we do will act as witness to the truth and the good news of God's love and forgiveness.

In El Salvador recently, a brutal military regime committed many atrocities and subjected most of the population to a reign of terror. Many people were taken away by the army and the death squads in the dead of night and never seen alive again. Sometimes their bodies would appear in the streets the next day. Relatives were often too afraid to claim the bodies of their loved ones for fear that the army and death squads would come after them too. In this climate of terror the Catholic Church set up a human rights office whose main work was simply to document the disappearances, tortures and murders that took place within their country. Many of those who worked on this project received death threats and many were themselves tortured and killed. Sometimes simply witnessing to the truth can claim a terrible price from us and may even cost us our lives.

Ninth and Tenth Commandments: *You shall not covet your neighbour's wife. You shall not covet your neighbour's goods*

The final two Commandments, the Ninth and the Tenth, are concerned with not hankering after another's goods. We live in a society that encourages us to spend, spend, spend! We are continually bombarded by adverts and promotional offers, all trying to get us to want more and to spend more to get it. Many of the goods we buy have a 'built-in obsolescence' – they are actually designed to fall apart within a very short time so that we have to go out and buy more. All this rush to consume doesn't even ensure that we will enjoy these things once we have them. It is often just the opposite. Once we have a new car, or a new computer or a new football strip, then another one comes onto the market that is bigger or better, and suddenly the pressure is on us from all sides, to want the newest and the brightest and to discard the old, now obsolete, item that we only bought last week.

The prison of possession

Trying to hang on to the things we have will not help us to enjoy them any better. In fact, the more we grasp and cling the less likely we are to actually allow ourselves to sit back and enjoy things. It is all too easy to be possessed by our own possessions, when we become slaves to our wants and our desires, when we are too occupied with the ownership of things to enjoy them for themselves. The urge to possess things presents us from enjoying them properly. It also stops us enjoying each other properly, because ownership of property is something that alienates the haves from the have-nots, and makes us competitors, fighting each other for a bigger slice of the cake. That is why St Thomas Aquinas says: "No possession is joyous without a companion." Having something is much more fun if it is shared and enjoyed, if it becomes a way of bringing us closer to each other. We are made for friendship, company and love, and the goods of the earth are given to us to enable us to live together like that, not to drive us to squabble over them. As St Paul says, "The love of money is the root of all evil."

Letting others go, letting them be free to live the way they choose is often a very hard thing to do. It can mean letting those we love die, letting them leave us with only grief, sorrow and an overwhelming sense of loss. Ultimately, we are going to lose everything: our goods, our loved ones, and even our lives. But if we practise letting go now, every day surrendering all we love to God, then in him we will eventually receive everything again. It is as Jesus cried on the Cross: "Into your hands I commend my spirit."

I have had worse partings, but none that so gnaws at my mind still — perhaps it is roughly saying what God alone could perfectly show, how self-hood begins with a walking away and love is proved in the letting go.
C.S. Lewis

Freedom

These commandments are about freedom, then. Freedom from the need to own and possess things. But also about freedom in relationships. When people truly love each other, they are not possessive. Love is meant to set people free, not to trap them. A loving mother and father take joy not in dominating and controlling their children, but in helping them to grow up, to learn about freedom, to learn how to make their own decisions wisely. In marriage, love does not lead to jealousy and one partner trying to control the other, but in letting them be themselves.

P.S.

Although it is important not to get caught up in wanting more and more things, in looking always at what other people have got and wanting more for ourselves, there is something to be said for wanting to create a fairer society. If, for example, you work a forty hour week and receive just enough to feed your family, and then someone arrives who does exactly the same work as you and gets paid twice as much, then you might quite rightly feel that there is an injustice being done. This commandment not to hanker after the goods of another is not an excuse for injustice.

148

Part 4 Prayer

Introduction to Prayer

(Catechism of the Catholic Church 2558-2758)

Praying is the most natural thing in the world. God didn't just make us and then walk off and leave us to it. God continually holds us in being, sustaining us every minute of the day. The life we live, every breath, every movement is possible only because God continues to hold us, filling us with his Spirit and breathing life into us. God is closer to us than we can ever imagine – he has built into us an intimacy with him that is quite astonishing. We are already filled with God, we are already part of God. The natural expression of this bond between us and God is prayer. Prayer is our depths speaking to the depths of God. Through prayer we can share our joys and our sadness, finding refreshment and peace.

Images of God

Many problems that we may experience in prayer come about because of the way we think about God. If we imagine God to be a harsh, authoritarian figure who is very critical and takes offence at our slightest mistake, then of course we will find prayer anything but spontaneous or easy. It's very hard to be open and trusting with someone if we feel that we are being judged. God loves and accepts us, he isn't the big judge in the sky waiting for us to put a foot wrong, so there is no need for us to worry about what we say or the way we say it. Relationships thrive best when people can be honest with one another. Honesty is at the heart of good communication. The more honest we can be with God, the better. Praying is not like going off to visit royalty when we must be on our best behaviour and self-consciously trot out formulaic expressions! Talking to God is more like visiting our closest and most trusted friend, where we can just flop down and put our feet up and where we can really be ourselves – cry, shout, laugh, get angry, be sad – knowing full well that our friend cares and accepts us and will not be shocked at anything we say or do.

The essence of prayer is a sort of child-like trust and simplicity. But we can also express ourselves in more formal prayers, through the liturgy of the Church. Formal set prayers can often be very comforting. There are times when our own words fail us, and it is sometimes a relief not to have to find our own words. Sometimes the poetry and rhythm of more formal prayers can say what we want to say better than we could − rather like two people reciting poetry to each other when they are in love. When Jesus was dying on the Cross he used the familiar words of one of the psalms, "My God, my God, why have you forsaken me?" This psalm must have expressed for him, the desolation that he was feeling. The words are the first line of psalm 22:

'My God, my God, why have you forsaken me?
I have cried desperately for help,
but still it does not come.
During the day I call to you, my God, but you do not answer,
I call at night, but get no rest...

My strength is gone, gone like water spilt on the ground,
All my bones are out of joint;
my heart is like melted wax.
My throat is as dry as dust,
and my tongue sticks to the roof of my mouth.
You have left me for dead in the dust...'

The psalms were the set prayers of the Jewish faith, passed down through the centuries. They were written to be sung, and Jesus would have been very familiar with them. The early Christians brought the psalms with them when they broke away from Judaism, and today they are still an integral part of the Church's prayer. During Mass we read or sing one of the psalms, and they are also part of the morning and evening prayer of the Church.

Prayer is simple. We don't have to be experts in anything in order to pray. We don't need to be great theologians to understand all the teachings of the Church, do intellectual somersaults or know every inch of the scripture by heart. Anyone can pray well − praying well is simply being honest and open with a God who loves us.

Ways of Prayer

When we talk to other people our 'body language' is important. What we say is affected by how we say it. Whether or not we make eye contact, if we touch the other person or turn away from them, if we fold our arms defensively, yawn, stare blankly into the middle distance – all these things can dramatically change the meaning of the words we use. When we are speaking, our bodies are important. Likewise we can pray using certain gestures: sitting, standing, kneeling, with our arms outstretched or held together. In the early Church people were urged to pray with their hands outstretched in memory of Jesus on the cross. This is still the case when the priest holds out his hands in prayer during Mass. Early Christians were also urged to pray standing up, as standing was meant to recall the resurrection. This was thought to be particularly appropriate on Sundays and during the Easter season when the resurrection was especially remembered. In the very early Church people were not generally encouraged to kneel, though kneeling was thought to be proper when fasting or confessing sins.

"It is a mistake to ignore the body in prayer. It is an even greater mistake to think that the body is a hindrance to prayer on the grounds that it is material, not spiritual. My body is me. It is the external sign of my soul. What my body performs are my actions. What I receive with my soul I receive through my bodily senses: sight, touch, taste, hearing, smell. It is therefore important to let the body become involved in prayer. If the body is not allowed to co-operate in prayer it will prove a hindrance to prayer by staging a revolt of boredom, or noisy distractions. The Catholic instinct recognises this and has always enlisted the co-operation of the body in prayer by genuflections, bows, signs of the cross, appeals to the ears, eyes and even the sense of smell in incense."
John Dalrymple, Simple Prayer

Early Christians were obliged to observe the set hours for prayer which we now only associate with priests and religious. Up until the fourth century *all* Christians were supposed to pray six times a day. The first prayer was at 9 a.m., the second at midday, the third at 3 p.m. and the fourth just before going to bed. The fifth prayer was at midnight, which meant getting out of bed, and the sixth at cockcrow that morning. They would say the Lord's prayer (the 'Our Father'), some psalms, some spontaneous prayer and a hymn. Today the Church still keeps to this general format in its observance of the 'canonical hours', the daily set of prayers and readings that punctuate the day.

Traditional Prayer

The Church has a tradition of formal methods of prayer which some people find very helpful. For example, contemplative prayer involves emptying ourselves of thought and distractions in order just to be silent in the presence of God. Meditation involves a more active use of the imagination and the emotions, taking a passage of scripture, for example, and imagining ourselves there as we play back the scene in our mind.

The Rosary

The rosary is also a form of meditation. It was developed in mediaeval times as a popular substitute for the set prayers and psalms which made up the liturgy of the hours. The rosary was a simple way for ordinary people to meditate on the main events in the story of Christ. The rosary is divided up into three main sections, each one containing five 'mysteries', or aspects of the salvation brought by Jesus: five joyful, five sorrowful and five glorious mysteries. So, for example, the joyful mysteries lead us to meditate on how the angel Gabriel appeared to Mary, Mary's visit to her cousin Elizabeth, the birth of Jesus, Jesus' presentation in the Temple as a baby and his being found in the Temple when he was a boy. The joyful mysteries meditate on the early events of Jesus' life and the joy of the coming of the Messiah; the sorrowful mysteries look at Jesus' suffering and death; the glorious mysteries celebrate his resurrection and the hope of all believers. Whilst we quietly recite the Our Father, the Hail Mary and the Glory Be, the Rosary allows our minds to dwell on each of these mysteries, letting the richness of their meaning to unfold in our hearts and minds. *(See Supplement part 2)*

The Hail Mary

The Hail Mary begins with the greeting of the angel Gabriel, 'Hail Mary, full of grace, the Lord is with thee' and continues with the greeting of Mary's cousin Elizabeth, 'Blessed art thou among women and blessed is the fruit of thy womb.' When we say the Hail Mary we join the angel Gabriel and Elizabeth in greeting the mother of the coming Messiah. The second part of the Hail Mary goes on to describe Mary's position, 'Holy Mary, Mother of God'. We all participate in Mary's motherhood and share in the fact that she too is our mother. When Christ is born in our hearts, then we too join in the motherhood of Mary. When Christ dwells in our hearts she becomes our mother. The Hail Mary then continues with the request for her to pray for us at the only two certain points in our lives: 'pray for us sinners now, and at the hour of our death'. The only two moments that we can be absolutely sure of are the present moment and the moment that we will die. Because God chose to bring his Son into the world through Mary, there will always be an intimate connection between her and her son Jesus. This is a relationship in which we share when we let Jesus' love reign in our hearts.

Pray without ceasing...

Many members of the early Church took very seriously the words of St Paul, who urged Christians to 'pray without ceasing' (1 Thessalonians 5:17). Some were content to just offer their whole lives to God so that everything they did and thought became a prayer. Some observed the set hours during the day, which effectively served to sanctify the whole cycle of the day. Others, such as St Augustine, thought that just wanting to be with God was enough, and their loving was a continual prayer. Those such as the Desert Fathers took these words of scripture so literally that they went to the desert so that they could pray continually without any distractions. Their big worry was what to do at night – how could they keep on praying when they were asleep? One solution was to pray a short prayer so often during the day that they would still be reciting it in their sleep! Prayers like this one were very popular: 'Have mercy on me, O God, according to your great mercy, and according to the multitude of your mercies blot out my iniquity.' Almsgiving was also seen as a way of 'praying continually.' If you gave alms to the poor, the money itself would pray for you as it did the will of God, feeding the hungry and clothing the naked, and the prayers of the poor who had been helped would be joined to those of the almsgiver.

An introduction to the "Our Father"

(Catechism of the Catholic Church 2759-2865)

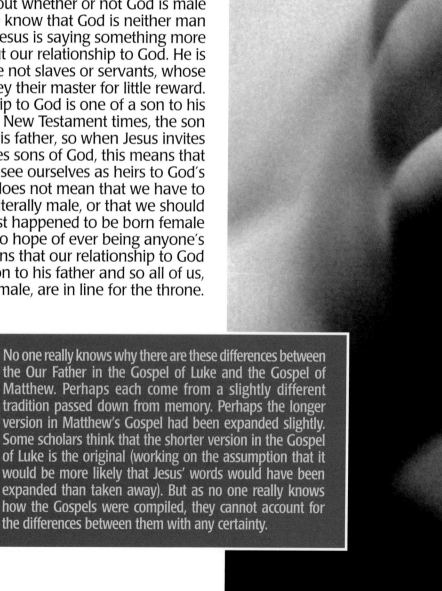

In New Testament times, it was common practice for Rabbis to teach their disciples how to pray. Jesus' disciples fully expected him to teach them how to pray, but the Our Father is the only example in the New Testament of a prayer taught by Jesus. This prayer has been at the heart of all Christian understanding of how to pray and has been the vocal prayer of all Christian communities.

When Jesus prays 'Our Father' he is not making a statement about whether or not God is male or female – we know that God is neither man nor woman – Jesus is saying something more profound about our relationship to God. He is saying that we are not slaves or servants, whose role is only to obey their master for little reward. Our relationship to God is one of a son to his Father. Also, in New Testament times, the son inherited from his father, so when Jesus invites us to call ourselves sons of God, this means that we can all see ourselves as heirs to God's kingdom. This does not mean that we have to see God as literally male, or that we should worry if we just happened to be born female and so have no hope of ever being anyone's 'son'! It just means that our relationship to God is *like* that of a son to his father and so all of us, male and female, are in line for the throne.

No one really knows why there are these differences between the Our Father in the Gospel of Luke and the Gospel of Matthew. Perhaps each come from a slightly different tradition passed down from memory. Perhaps the longer version in Matthew's Gospel had been expanded slightly. Some scholars think that the shorter version in the Gospel of Luke is the original (working on the assumption that it would be more likely that Jesus' words would have been expanded than taken away). But as no one really knows how the Gospels were compiled, they cannot account for the differences between them with any certainty.

Jesus taught his disciples a very simple prayer:

Our Father, who art in heaven,
hallowed be thy name.
Thy kingdom come.
Thy will be done on earth, as it is in heaven.
Give us this day our daily bread,
and forgive us our trespasses, as we forgive those who trespass against us,
and lead us not into temptation,
but deliver us from evil.
(Matthew 6: 9-13)

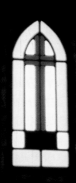

We find two versions of the 'Our Father' in the New Testament, a shorter one in Luke's Gospel and a longer one, the one we normally use, in Matthew's Gospel. The version in Luke's Gospel goes like this:

'Father,
hallowed be thy name,
thy kingdom come.
give us each day our daily bread.
Forgive us our sins,
for we also forgive everyone who sins against us.
And lead us not into temptation'
(Luke 11:2-4)

Fascinating connections

The 'Our Father' is similar to various Jewish prayers of New Testament times. It fits in with a kind of prayer known as a tephillah qezarah, a 'short prayer' which was supposed to be recited in moments of trouble or danger. Here is an example: 'Perform your will in heaven and bestow satisfaction on earth upon those who revere you, and do that which is good in your sight. Blessed are you who hears prayer.' The 'Our Father' is also very like a Jewish prayer called the Kaddish, a prayer prayed in the synagogue after the sermon. The Didache is a very early Christian set of teachings (*'Didache'* simply means 'teaching'). It was written in the first century AD and has a version of the Our Father which it commands Christians to say three times a day. This fits in with Jewish liturgical practice – Jews were also urged to say a prayer, the eighteen benedictions, three times a day. A condensed or abbreviated version was also available which was of comparable length to the Our Father. The version of the Our Father in the Didache also had a doxology tagged onto the end: 'For thine is the power and glory for ever'. After each of the eighteen benedictions, the Jews would say a doxology (*doxa* is the Greek word for 'glory', a doxology is a prayer glorifying God). This tradition of adding the doxology onto the 'Our Father' was carried on into Christian liturgy, and these prayerful additions became so closely associated with the Lord's Prayer that they are often taken to be part of the prayer itself. This is why some denominations add 'for thine is the kingdom, the power and the glory, for ever and ever' onto the end of the Our Father, even though it is not part of the original prayer that we are given by Jesus in the Gospels.

The Seven Petitions of the Our Father

The 'Our Father' has traditionally been divided up into the introduction – "Our Father, who art in heaven", and then seven petitions. Since at least the time of Augustine in the fourth century, the Our Father has been used as a way of teaching people about prayer.

Our Father...

The shorter version of the *Our Father* in St Luke's Gospel does not have "Our Father, who art in heaven", but simply begins with the word "Father". Some scholars wonder whether the original prayer of Jesus was simply "father", especially as the words "our father in heaven" could be found in other Jewish prayers, and so it was likely that Jesus' prayer would be changed to something more familiar. But no one really knows – perhaps Jesus prayed the *Our Father* twice and used different words each time.

Our Father, who art in heaven,
hallowed be thy name;
thy kingdom come;
thy will be done on earth as it is in heaven.
Give us this day our daily bread;
and forgive us our trespasses
as we forgive those who trespass against us;
and lead us not into temptation,
but deliver us from evil.

The *Our Father* was originally spoken in Aramaic, a language related to Hebrew. Aramaic was probably Jesus' mother tongue. The word Jesus used for 'father' was originally an Aramaic word, *abba*. The word *abba* means 'papa' or 'dad'. When we say the *Our Father* we are speaking to God in a very intimate way, not as a distant figure but as a close and comfortable member of the family. It is this rather shocking intimacy that Jesus is wanting to get across to his disciples when he teaches them this prayer.

When we pray the words *Our Father* we are saying that God is not just 'my' father, but everyone's. We cannot exclude anyone from God's loving care, we cannot label some 'in' and others 'out'. God is the father of all.

Who art in heaven...

Where is heaven? We often think of heaven as being 'up there' somewhere vaguely in the sky. But heaven is not really a place 'out there'. Heaven is where God is, where his love and peace hold sway. We have heaven in our hearts, in our communities. Wherever there is love and goodness there is a little slice of heaven. When we say *"Our Father who art in heaven"* we are not banishing God to the outer corners of the sky; far from it! We are acknowledging his presence, his immanence in our world, our lives, our loves, our hearts. Wherever goodness and kindness and love are flourishing, we can see heaven and touch the dwelling place of God. Nor does this mean that God is only to be found in the midst of our happiness and joy: he is constantly at work in even our darkest moments, supporting and transforming, giving life and peace. As St Paul says:

"For I am certain of this: neither death nor life, no angel, no prince, nothing that exists, nothing still to come, not any power, or height or depth, or any created thing, can ever come between us and the love of God made visible in Christ Jesus our Lord."
(Romans 8:38-39)

First Petition: *Hallowed be thy name*

In the Old Testament God's name stood for God himself. Sometimes referring to God as 'his name' was a roundabout way of mentioning him without having to say his name out loud. The name of God was thought to be too holy to mention and he was often known in Hebrew as simply *ha-shem* 'the name'. So when we pray that God's name will be made holy we are praying that God himself will be given the reverence and honour due to him. Giving reverence to God also means acknowledging his place as ruler of the world.

To hallow is older English for 'to make holy', so in modern English instead of saying 'hallowed be your name', we would say 'May your name be made holy'. The *Our Father* is such a well-loved and often-used prayer, that to change its wording to bring it up-to-date with the norms of modern English would involve changing the words that many hold very dear. This is why the *Our Father* is still full of older English: 'thee', 'thou' and 'art'.

Second Petition: *Thy kingdom come*

Throughout the Old and the New Testaments there is a great longing for the time when God will rule the world in full glory and power. The kingdom of God will be ruled by justice and love. There will be no more sadness, no poverty or loneliness.

The petitions of the 'Our Father' all assume that, when we pray, we *do* somehow effect what is happening and that our prayers will actually bring about the things we pray for. The problem is that sometimes God's answer to our prayers may not be exactly what we expect...

Third Petition: *Thy will be done on earth as it is in heaven*

It is often very hard to honestly pray for God's will to be done. Jesus' agony in the garden of Gethsemane is an illustration of how difficult it can be to do the will of God. God's will may not always be our will. Often when we pray, we pray for what we want, or for what we think we want. What we want for ourselves may not always be the best thing in the long run – for ourselves or for others. God's will may well be different from ours. It is very difficult to let go and pray for God's will to be done. His will may well involve loss and grief for us in the short term. It is very hard to trust God with the people and the things that we hold most dear.

A man on a boat suddenly realised that his boat was sinking. He prayed that God would save him – he was sure that God would save him, so he just sat down and waited. After a while he saw a huge ocean liner on the horizon. The ship hailed him on the radio and asked if he was OK. "Oh yes" he said, "I'm fine." Then a helicopter flew overhead and hailed him on the radio, asking if he needed assistance as they could see that his ship was in difficulties, "Oh no, thank you" he replied, "I'm fine." Then a fishing boat came by, and seeing that his ship was beginning to sink, offered to come alongside and take him on board. "No, no," said the man, "I'll be perfectly all right". Then his ship went down and the man drowned. When he got to heaven he was very upset and said to God, "You told me that if I believed in you and prayed for something, then I would get it. I prayed and believed that you would save me, but you left me to drown!" God replied to the man, "I tried very hard to save you, but you wouldn't let me. I sent an ocean liner, a helicopter and a fishing boat to try to save you, but you sent them all packing. What did you expect!"

The original Greek text of this verse of the Our Father is slightly ambiguous. It can either read "thy will be done on earth as it is in heaven" or "thy will be done both in heaven and on earth". The traditional reading assumes that God is in complete control in heaven, and the earth just needs to knuckle under and follow suit. The alternative reading seems to say that God isn't in complete control of heaven – or else why pray for God's will to be done on earth *and* in heaven?

Praying for God's kingdom to come may make unexpected demands on us. God may well choose to use *us* as instruments of his kingdom-building. He may choose to use our hands and hearts to bring the kingdom of heaven about on earth. God can use anyone to answer prayer. He can even use the person who is doing the praying. So when I pray, "Thy kingdom come", I am inviting God to use me as an instrument, to use me to help bring about that kingdom, where everyone will live in the joy of God's love.

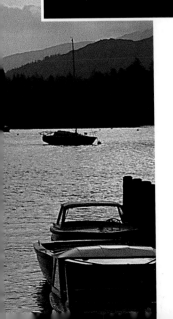

Fourth Petition: Give us this day our daily bread

This simple petition is a prayer asking for the daily necessities of life, for the food for the day ahead. When Jesus taught this prayer, he probably meant something very simple – that we should ask for the basic necessities of life from God. Even if we work for our daily bread, as most people do, it still comes to us as a gift from God. It is good to foster a healthy dependence on God. Asking for our *daily* bread reminds us not to store up and amass wealth, what we need for tomorrow, or next year, but to live simply, trusting that he really will supply us with all our needs. Of course this doesn't mean that we pray our prayer and then sit back and relax, waiting for God to deliver everything to our door! But it does mean that we can trust him to see that our basic needs are met.

Give *us* today our daily bread is praying not just for ourselves. It is not just saying "give *me* today *my* daily bread", but praying also that others will receive their daily share as well. Praying this prayer may well involve us in action – we may be the ones God chooses to answer this prayer. All Christians are called to feed the hungry, clothe the naked, give to the poor. We are all called to play our part in distributing the earth's goods in such a way that everyone can have their 'daily bread'.

The test of the quality of our prayer is not so much how we feel when we are praying, but the quality of our lives. It is tempting to judge our prayer by how we feel when we pray. We do this automatically. When prayer is smooth and easy and there have been few distractions, then we feel close to God. On another day, however, when it has gone badly and has been interrupted with distractions, then we have not felt the presence of God at all. It is a mistake to judge our prayer by how we felt while we prayed. The best test of the quality of our prayer is to look at our conduct outside prayer.

Fifth Petition:
Forgive us our trespasses as we forgive those who trespass against us

The word 'trespasses' has come down to us from the very earliest English translations of the New Testament. As early as 1380 it was used in Wycliffe's translation of the Lord's prayer. It is more difficult for us to grasp the full meaning of what it means to 'trespass' against someone, because the word has changed its meaning since 1380. Nowadays we tend to use the word 'trespass' to mean walking over someone else's land without their permission. Originally, though, the word had a sense of infringing not only land, but the rights and dignity of another. To trespass against someone was to injure them or do them an injustice.

When we ask God to forgive us as we forgive others, what are we saying? Are we really saying that God should only forgive our sins so long as we forgive the sins done to us by other people? What about all those we just find it impossible to forgive? If we cannot forgive someone, does that mean that God will not forgive us? This seems to be what this petition of the "Our Father" does say, and as if to underline the point, Jesus says directly after the "Our Father", "If you forgive others when they sin against you, your heavenly Father will also forgive you. But if you do not forgive others their sins, your Father will not forgive your sins."(Matthew 6:14-15)

There was a report some time ago from the United States about a group of people called "Murder Victims families for Reconciliation". Many of the members of the group had had their loved ones brutally murdered and had gone through the court cases convicting the murderers. They had been advised that if they could punish the murderer to the fullest extent of the law then they would feel better. Many of these families pursued the harshest sentence, but then felt let down and cheated when they didn't feel any better. Whilst not trying to play down the extent of their grief and loss, they discovered that revenge didn't help them – in fact their hatred and desire for revenge only deepened the violence and damage which had already been done. Healing and peace only came with reconciliation and forgiveness. When Jesus taught this prayer he saw clearly that those who cannot learn to let go of their hates and resentments will be eaten away by them and will have no peace. It is not until we can let go of hatred and a desire for revenge that we will be open to the healing, forgiving touch of God.

Although it can be very difficult to forgive others, sometimes it is even harder to forgive ourselves. How many of us are struggling with terrible burdens of guilt and shame, tormenting ourselves with how bad we really are? It is sometimes all too easy to hurt those we love, to make mistakes, to say too much, to say too little, to not have noticed, to not have said goodbye. "I drove too fast, I didn't see the other car, I shouldn't have let him go out that late, I wish I had noticed how bad he looked and had taken him to the hospital right away..." And on and on and on, the world is full of people painfully trying to come to terms with their part in what has happened. But however much we may want to, we cannot turn back the clock. Instead we are just left with our own painful memories, replaying the past again and again in our minds, wishing that somehow we could go back and change the way it was. But in the end, what we really need is to forgive ourselves, to let ourselves be healed.

Sixth Petition:
Lead us not into temptation

The original Greek sentence which is usually rendered in English as 'lead us not into temptation' is difficult to translate. The Greek 'lead us' cannot be translated by a single English word because the sentence means both 'do not allow us to enter into temptation', and 'do not let us yield to temptation'. If we bear both these meanings in mind when we pray this petition, then we can get the general gist of what it means.

When we are tempted, we are always tempted by something which appears to us to be a good thing. We are not tempted by badness, but we may be tempted to do something bad in order to get something good out of it. For example, if Joey wants to have a new stereo, there is nothing wrong with that; wanting a stereo is a perfectly reasonable desire. But if he goes about mugging old people in the street to get his stereo, then clearly there is something wrong. His desire for the stereo is a good thing, but he has succumbed to the temptation to mug old people rather than to try to save up the money himself. At the heart of our temptations are good things, but the problem is that often we may become obsessed with having that one good thing and ignore all the bad consequences that would follow if we tried to get it.

Seventh Petition: *Deliver us from evil*

The word 'deliver' in Greek is a very urgent and dramatic one: it suggests being snatched away from a place of danger. When we ask God to deliver us from evil, the image is of a very desperate plea for an SAS-type rescue mission to save us.

The world is full of suffering and pain. It is also full of people succumbing to temptation and making choices which inflict pain and suffering on others. When we ask to be spared temptation, we are asking that we might not contribute to the misery in the world. When we ask to be delivered from evil, we are asking not to be on the receiving end of it.

When we pray the "Our Father" in the Mass, the priest picks up the theme of the last line and talks about what it means. He says, "Deliver us, Lord, from every evil and grant us peace in our day, in your mercy keep us free from sin and protect us from all anxiety, as we wait in joyful hope for the coming of our saviour, Jesus Christ." Being delivered from evil is about being delivered from any sort of harm and distress. We are asking to be saved from whatever it is that troubles us, or causes us distress and pain. We believe in a God of resurrection and life. Our hope lies in the fact that, however bad a mess we make of everything, at least we know that God can put it right again. We believe in a God of resurrection, a God of healing and peace who can transform our world and make it whole again.

Supplement

SECTION 1
The Church in History

NO. 1 THE APOSTOLIC PERIOD

This is the period when the Church of the Apostles, reflecting on the words of the Lord Jesus, expressed their faith in written and spoken form. Their writings make up the New Testament. We include a short glossary of well-known terms associated with the New Testament, which are here listed in alphabetic order:

Apocrypha: (meaning "hidden things"): Name given to those writings similar to the inspired books of the Bible but not recognised by the Church as part of the canon of Scripture. In the apocryphal *Infancy Gospel of Thomas,* for example, Jesus is shown turning twelve clay birds into real sparrows on the sabbath. In non-Catholic usage the word "Apocrypha", is used to describe the Books of Esdras, Tobit, Judith, Maccabees, etc. which are accepted as Scripture by Roman Catholics.

Apostle: One of the twelve chief disciples appointed by Jesus to be the foundation of his Church. The "Apostolic Succession" means that the college of bishops, with the Bishop of Rome at their Head, enjoy direct succession from the Apostles.

Canon: (meaning "rule"): The term given to the collected books of the Bible recognised by the Church as the inspired Word of God and hence to be taken as the "rule" of faith.

Dead Sea Scrolls: The popular name given to numerous manuscripts discovered on the shores of the Dead Sea by a shepherd boy in 1947. They include most of the Old Testament books and evidence of the life and hopes of a Jewish "monastic" community at Qumran at about the time of Christ. It is thought that John the Baptist and some of his disciples may have been members of this community.

Didache (meaning "teaching"): A manuscript of great value because it dates from apostolic times and is evidence of how the liturgy was celebrated in the early church. It shoes that the Mass had the same essential features that it has today.

Evangelist: Originally means "Preacher of the Good News", but now generally reserved for the authors of the written Gospels: Matthew, Mark, Luke and John.

Gospel (meaning "god-spel", i.e. "good news"): The Gospel in its written form is often divided between the "Synoptic Gospels" of Matthew, Mark and Luke which give a "synopsis" or one view of the life and teaching of Jesus and are clearly dependent upon each other, and the "Gospel of John" which reflects a different tradition in the apostolic Church.

Inspiration: The term refers to the special impulse and guidance of the Holy Spirit given to human beings so that what is written is truly the Word of God. "Since everything asserted by the inspired authors or sacred writers must be held to be asserted by the Holy Spirit, it follows that the books of Scripture must be acknowledged as teaching firmly, faithfully and without error that truth which God wanted put into the sacred writings for the sake of our salvation." *(Vatican II)*

Interpretation: The Church, under the inspiration of the same Holy Spirit by whose power the sacred books were written, understands and explains the true meaning of the Scriptures. This means investigating what meaning the sacred writer really intended and what God wanted to reveal by means of his words.

Versions of the Bible: The languages in which the Bible was originally written (Hebrew, Aramaic and Greek) are not generally understood and so need to be translated. Many English-language "versions" are approved by the Church. In the United Kingdom today the *Revised Standard Version* and the *Jerusalem Bible* are most commonly used in the liturgy.

NO. 2 THE PATRISTIC PERIOD

This is the period (up to about A.D. 800) when the Church reflected on the Apostolic Traditions to produce outstanding Christian "Fathers" in the faith. These great teachers were often associated with the Councils of the Church to produce a period of profound deepening in the understanding of the Faith.

We include a short glossary of well-known terms associated with this period, which are here listed in alphabetical order:

Apologist: The name given to one who explains and defends the faith. The first great "apologist" was St Justin, a layman, who was martyred in A.D. 165.

Apostasy: The renouncing of one's Christian faith. Persecution in the early Church resulted in many "apostates" and controversy arose as to how those who wished to return to the Faith should be treated. Some tried to insist on re-baptism; others refused pardon altogether. The solution of insisting on suitable penance was taught by Pope St Stephen in A.D. 255.

Council of the Church: A meeting of all bishops solemnly convened or approved by the Pope to regulate matters of doctrine and discipline. After the Council of Jerusalem in A.D. 51 (recorded in Acts 15) there have been 21 such General (or Ecumenical) councils in the history of the church, the last being Vatican II in 1962-65. The Orthodox Church only recognises the first seven councils, which were particularly important in the growth of the Christian Faith.
1. Nicaea (A.D. 325) Settled the Arian heresy by affirming that Jesus Christ is "one in substance" with the Father. The "Nicene Creed" proclaimed at Mass has developed from this Council.
2. Constantinople (381) Ratified Nicaea I
3. Ephesus (431) Affirmed that Jesus Christ is truly God

and truly man: and that Mary is the "Mother of God".

4. *Chalcedon* (451) Affirmed that in the person of Jesus the two natures are united unconfusedly, unchangeably, indivisibly and inseparably.

5. *Constantinople II* (553) Condemned various heresies.

6. *Constantinople III* (680) Affirmed that in Jesus there are "two natural wills and energies, undivided, unseparated and unmixed…"

7. *Nicaea II* (787) Condemned Iconoclasm (a heresy which forbade the use of images of Jesus and the saints).

The decrees of a General Council, having received papal confirmation, are the most solemnly binding. "What God has spoken through the Council of Nicaea remains for ever," said Saint Athanasius. These early Councils of the Church were important in explaining, in human terms, the great central mysteries of the Most Blessed Trinity, the divinity of Christ and the humanity of Christ.

Doctor of the Church: A title of honour given by the Church to outstanding teachers in the Faith. There are about 30 such Doctors. The only women are St Teresa of Avila, St Catherine of Siena and St Therese of Lisieux. The only Doctor from the British Isles is St Bede the Venerable.

Father of the Church: A title given to the great Christian writers of the first twelve centuries. Many of them are Doctors of the Church. These include:

St Athanasius (293-373) The "Father of Orthodoxy" and the man most responsible for destroying the Arian heresy (the most dangerous heresy in the Church's history) and for clarifying Catholic belief in the Trinity. *St Augustine* (354-430) The most influential of the Fathers and "doctors of grace". In his *Confessions* he wrote: "Thou has made us, O Lord, for thyself, and our heart shall find no rest till it rest in thee."

St Jerome (342-420) Was the greatest Doctor divinely given to the Church for the understanding of the Scriptures. Translated the Bible from the original Hebrew into the living Latin of his day. This *Vulgate* (i.e. popular) version became the official version of the Church.

St John Chrysostom (347-407) The most prominent doctor of the Greek Church and "the greatest preacher ever heard in a Christian pulpit". Known as the "golden tongue".

Father of the Desert: A monk or hermit of the fourth century who lived a life of prayer. The most famous, St Anthony, laid the foundations of the monastic system.

Tradition: (i) The process of handing on the whole of the doctrine, the life and worship of the Church. (ii) The living heritage itself.

NO. 3 THE EASTERN SCHISM

This is the period of developing friction between Christians who recognised the primacy of Rome and Christians who recognised the primary of Constantinople. The final break came, it is regarded, in 1054; and endures to this day. We include a short glossary of well-known terms associated with this period, which are here listed in alphabetical order.

Crusades: The series of expeditions, with the aim of recovering the Holy Land from Islam, beginning in 1095 and lasting over two centuries. The crusades helped to strengthen the papacy and also provided a base for a common religious purpose in Western Europe. It gave rise to two principal Military Orders founded to help pilgrims: the Knights Templar and the Knights Hospitaller (Knights of St John).

Friar: A member of the "Mendicant" (meaning "begging") Orders (as opposed to a member of the more ancient "Monastic" Orders). The four "great" Orders of Friars are:

1. *Dominicans* Founded by St Dominic in 1216 to fight the Albigensian heresy, which held that Christ was an angel with a phantom body. The Dominicans realised that the fine education and organisations of the heretics could only be opposed by employing similar techniques.

2. *Franciscans* Founded by St Francis in 1223 with the ideals of poverty and humility.

3. *Carmelites* Founded from a group of hermits by St Simon Stock in 1247.

4. *Austin Friars* Founded from several congregations of hermits, brought together in 1256.

Each of these four Orders has a Second Order (of nuns) and a Third Order (of the Laity).

Heresy: The denial of defined doctrine of the Catholic Faith (different, therefore, from *schism* – see below). The need to combat heresy has often led to the formulation of revealed doctrine by the Church.

Monk: A member of a Monastic Order who takes solemn vows to God and lives under a fixed rule. The Monastery is governed by the abbot. In the Eastern Orthodox Church all monks follow the rule of St Basil drawn up in 356. In the Western Church the principal architect of monasticism was St Benedict, who drew up his Rule about A.D. 540. The monk's day is taken up with the Divine Office, spiritual reading and work.

Oecumenical [Ecumenical] Patriarch (meaning "universal Father"): This is the Patriarch of Constantinople. Since the break with the Bishop of Rome (who has the title "Patriarch of the West"), he has enjoyed honorary primacy in the (Eastern) Orthodox Church. In ordinary use today, the word "Ecumenism" has come to mean the attempt to recover the universal unity of Christians.

Orthodox Church: The largest body of Christians after the Catholic Church. Today, it consists of a federation of thirteen members who acknowledge the primacy of the Oecumenical Patriarch. They do not acknowledge the primacy of the Bishop of Rome but "they possess true sacraments, above all – by apostolic succession – the priesthood and the Eucharist, whereby they are still joined to Rome in a very close relationship". *(Vatican II)* Particular efforts have been made in recent years to heal the schism. Much of the discipline of the Orthodox Church is different from the Roman Church (e.g. priests are generally married, baptism is by total immersion) but such customs would not have to change.

Rite: A form of ritual or worship. Most Catholics in the Western Church follow the Roman or Latin Rite. There are also several Rites in the Eastern Churches: some of these Churches are in communion with Rome; others are not (see *Orthodox Church*). Some of these Eastern rites are more ancient than the Latin Rite. All Rites enjoy an equal dignity.

Schism: The separation from the unity of the Church. It is not a heresy *(see above)* but involves the denial of papal supremacy. The Orthodox Church is a schismatic Church. The Western Schism (Great Schism) of 1378-1415 split the Roman Church when rival claimants to the Papacy (antipopes) began the process of fragmentation which led into the "Reformation".

Summa Theologiae (or Summa): Was the work of St Thomas Aquinas. Divided into three sections, it was written in 1266-73 as a handbook for the systematic study of theology, and has served as a basis for such study down to our present day.

NO. 4 THE REFORMATION

This is the period of religious upheaval between the 14th and 17th centuries which gave rise to Christian Churches separated from communion with the Bishop of Rome and divorced from the traditional teaching of the Church. We include a short glossary of well-known terms associated with this period, which are here listed in alphabetical order:

Anglicanism: The faith and practice of religious bodies in communion with the Archbishop of Canterbury, who enjoys a primacy of honour. These bodies are generally found in the British Commonwealth. In today's form, Anglicanism dates from the Acts of Supremacy and Uniformity (1589) and the Act establishing the Thirty-nine Articles. The Anglican Church "has remained faithful to the aim of 'comprehensiveness' which inspired the Elizabethan Settlement and is in consequence undogmatic in its attitude to religion". *(Bishop C. Butler)*

Anglican Orders: The denial by the Catholic Church of the validity of Anglican Orders was expressed in Pope Leo XIII's Bull *Apostolicae Curae* (1895). The basis of this denial is lack of due intention and defect of form. The question of validity of Anglican Orders is often a sensitive one, especially as the Catholic Church recognises that "among Communions separated from the Roman See in which some Catholic traditions and institutions continue to exist, the Anglican Communion occupies a special place." *(Vatican II)*

Calvinism: A religious body founded by John Calvin as part of the "Reformation" movement about 1540. It upholds a strong union between Church and State and is noted for its doctrine of predestination.

Counter-Reformation: The term used to summarise the revival of the Catholic Church in response to the "Reformation" movement: although certain "counter" measures against abuses within the Church were already under way back in 1517 when Luther began his attacks.

The movement for reform expressed itself principally in the foundation of new religious orders and in the Council of Trent.

Lutheranism: A religious body founded by Martin Luther. Traditionally, Luther's act of fixing his ninety-five theses to the door of the University Church of Wittenburg began the "Reformation" movement; but the causes and growth of the Reformation are, of course, less capable of simple definition. Lutheranism accepts one order of clergy only and the chief feature of its worship is the sermon.

Missions: The task of spreading the Gospel was the first act of the apostles after Pentecost. In the "Reformation" period it received fresh impetus with the discovery of "new worlds". In addition to the spreading of the faith to the Americas the Gospel was carried, principally by the Jesuits, to India, the Far East, Japan and China,

Society of Jesus (Jesuits): Founded by St Ignatius Loyola in 1534 "for the greater glory of God", the Jesuits have probably since been the most influential religious order in the Church. More flexible, but more disciplined, than others it undertook the work of education and missions, the success of the latter personified in the work of St Francis Xavier, one of St Ignatius' first companions. Many were martyred, among the most prominent being St Edmund Campion who was put to death in the reign of Elizabeth I. The Jesuits' success was a source of jealousy within the Church, and enemies of the Church came to use the term "Jesuit" as a form of abuse. The *Spiritual Exercises* of St. Ignatius remain the foundation of Jesuit Spirituality.

Seminary: A college for training priests. The spiritual and intellectual weakness of the parish clergy, which had been a contributory cause of the Reformation, was overcome by the decree of the Council of Trent which ordered the establishing of diocesan seminaries. The seminary remains the principal means of training future priests.

Tridentine: Of the Council of Trent. This Council (1545-63) defined Catholic teaching in those areas brought into question by Protestant reformers, especially with regard to justification, the Mass and the Sacraments. Discipline within the Church was strengthened to overcome the effects of previous laxity. The so-called "Tridentine Mass" dates from 1570. This provided the form of the celebration of the Mass in the Latin Rite until 1969 and reflected the need of the Reformation period for care and uniformity in the celebration of the Eucharist.

NO. 5 SOCIAL UPHEAVAL

This is the period, from the mid 17th century to world War I, when profound social and economic upheavals transformed the way of life in Britain, Western Europe, and the U.S.A., from being predominantly agricultural to predominantly industrial. New concepts of freedom, liberty, and the organisation of society brought fresh challenges for the Church in the world of thought, industry,

and politics. We include a short glossary of well known terms associated with this period, which are here listed in alphabetical order:

Atheism: (meaning "without God"): term applied to the belief that the existence of a personal God must be denied. In the mid 19th century Karl Marx proposed atheism as "the cornerstone of a brave new edifice of humanity transformed by total revolution."

Encyclical: A formal pastoral letter written by the Pope on doctrinal, moral, or disciplinary matters. Such a letter is known by the Latin phrase with which it opens. Among the many encyclicals of this period, the most important was *Rerum Novarum,* the pastoral letter of Pope Leo XIII, in 1891, which came to be known as "The Charter of the Working Man".

Free Churches: Protestant Churches which are completely independent of the established Church of a particular country. In England the Baptists, Methodists, Congregationalists and Presbyterians formed a union in 1896 known as the National Council of the Evangelical Free Churches. These churches, with their emphasis on the importance of preaching and the obligation of each member of the congregation to witness to the Gospel, played a key role in the social upheavals of the Industrial Revolution.

Modernism: The accelerated developments of this period in the fields of science, philosophy, and historical criticism, together with changed social conditions, led to renewed study within the Church of the challenge of preaching the Gospel in a manner suitable for the times. The Modernist movement, as it came to be called, was initially encouraged by Leo XII but was condemned for certain errors by Pius X in the decree *Lamentabili* (1907). The term "modernism" came to be used by some in the Catholic Church in a derogatory way. However, the movement grew out of a genuine desire to preach the Gospel in a relevant manner.

Oxford Movement: Usually dated from John Keble's Oxford Assize Sermon in July 1833, on "National Apostasy". The general aim of the movement was to restore the ideals of the pre-Reformation Church to the Church of England. Many of its members eventually became Catholics and two of them, Newman and Manning, became Cardinals. A legacy of the movement remains in the Church of England as the Anglo-Catholic wing.

Papal States: Those territories controlled by the Church from 756 to 1870 when they were annexed by Italian troops. In 1929 the Lateran Treaty recognised the Vatican City as a sovereign state, guaranteeing the political independence of the See of Peter.

Vatican Council I: (1869-1870) This Council, held under Pius IX, concerned itself chiefly with the condemnation of materialism, pantheism, the relation of faith to reason, and the way God reveals himself through the words of Scripture. The Council is best known for its definition of the universal jurisdictional primacy of the Pope and his infallibility when pronouncing solemn dogmatic definitions. The work of the Council was left unfinished when Piedmontese troops, intent on forming a unified Italy, occupied Rome.

NO. 6 THE MODERN WORLD

This is the period embracing the tragedy of two World Wars and unparalleled scientific advances which led up to the Second Vatican Council (1962-1965) – the most authoritative general teaching of the 20th century Church. We include a short glossary of well-known terms associated with this period, which are here listed in alphabetical order.

Apologetics: A term used frequently in the first half of this century to describe those studies concerned with the defence of the Church's teaching and credentials against her critics. Contemporary apologetics (more frequently referred to as "fundamental theology") is concerned more with the believer and his search for the reasons that make his faith intellectually honest, morally responsible, and authentic. At the same time, it invites us to seek the meaning of our life in that same faith.

Catholic Action: A term first used by Pius X and later defined by Pius XI as "the participation of the laity in the Church's hierarchy". Under his inspiration Catholic Action was given a charter to establish and restore Catholic life to family and society while the movement assumed many different forms around the world.

Code of the Canon Law: In 1904 Pius X announced his intention of codifying almost 2,000 years of Church Law in a single volume. This mammoth task was completed in 1917. The decision to revise the Code was made by Pope John XXIII in 1959 and this revision was completed in 1983.

Communism: A theory of politics based on the assertion of Karl Marx and Friedrich Engels that all human life is determined by economic facts. Under Lenin, the successful leader of the October revolution in Russia, the theory gave rise to the powerful Communist party system and State which became a formidable opponent of the Church.

Subsidiarity: A term which first appeared in the Encyclical *Quadragessimo Anno* of Pius XI. He asserted as a fundamental Christian principle that, "all social activity should be to the help of individual members of the social body but never to destroy or absorb them".

Vatican Council II: The 21st Ecumenical Council of the Church was convoked by John XXIII in November 1962 and closed by Pope Paul VI in December 1965. The Council enacted four constitutions, nine decrees, and three declarations, setting the seal on three of the chief movements of this century in the Church – the biblical movement, the liturgical renewal, the lay apostolate. *Constitutions:* These were:

The Dogmatic Constitution on the Church, setting forth the Church's understanding of her own nature, taking its Latin title *Lumen Gentium* from the opening words, "Christ is the light of all nations". Its first chapter, "The Mystery of the Church" presents the vision of a Church which is at once divine and human, embracing all people of good will who make up the subject of the second chapter, "The People of God". Dogmatically, the most important chapter is the third in which the bishops of the Church are seen to constitute a "college" collectively responsible for the work of the Church. Other chapters deal with the laity, the call of all to holiness and the role of the Blessed Virgin Mary.

The Dogmatic Constitution on Divine Revelation, setting forth the Church's teaching on how God reveals himself to us. The transmission of this revelation is recorded in written form in Scripture; its transmission by word of mouth is part of the tradition of the Church. Both Scripture and tradition spring from the one source.

The Constitution on the Sacred Liturgy, setting forth the Church's teaching on worship as the heart of her life. It instructed that "texts and rites should be drawn up so that they express more clearly the holy things which they signify. Christian people, as far as possible, should be able to understand them with ease and to take part in them fully, actively, and as befits a community."

The Pastoral Constitution on the Church in the Modern World, setting forth the Church's attempt to "speak to all people in order to shed light on the mystery of humanity and to cooperate in finding the solution of our time". It is addressed to "the whole of humanity".

Decrees: The nine decrees covered the following subjects: The Pastoral Office of Bishops, Ecumenism, the Oriental Catholic Churches, the Ministry and Life of Priests, Education for the Priesthood, the Renewal of the Religious Life, the Missionary Activity of the Church, the Apostolate of the Laity, the Media of Social Communication.

Declarations: The Council issued three formal declarations on religious freedom, the Church's attitude to non-Christians, and Christian education.

SECTION 2
The Church at Prayer

NO. 1 THE MASS

In the sacred liturgy the power of the Holy Spirit acts through sacramental signs. Actions, symbols, words, clothes, music, buildings, are the living faith and flesh of the worship performed by Jesus Christ the priest and his Body the Church. We include a short glossary of well-known terms associated with the Mass which are here listed in alphabetical order.

Altar: The table on which the sacrifice of the Mass is offered is treated with the utmost respect by the Church (the priest anoints, incenses, kisses it) as a sign of Christ. The altar sometimes contains some relics of the saints and into the stone are cut five crosses recalling our Lord's five wounds.

Altar Linen: Since the 8th century the altar has been covered by one or several white linen cloths as a precaution against spillage from the chalice. The following linens are also used at the altar.
Corporal: A square of fine linen spread on the altar on which are placed the chalice and paten. So called since it holds the Body *(Latin, Corpus)* of Christ. When not in use it is held in the *Burse.*
Purificator: A strip of white linen used to clean the chalice.
Pall: A small square of stiff linen used to cover the chalice.

Candles: A symbol of Christ, the "Light of the World". There are four kinds of candle used in the Church:
a] *The Paschal Candle,* placed on the sanctuary from the Easter Vigil to Ascension Day.
b] *Altar Candles,* used during the Mass.
c] *Blessed Candles,* used in solemn processions, e.g. the Easter Vigil.
d] *Votive Candles,* burnt before images of the saints in petition or thanksgiving.

Chalice: The most ancient of all the sacred vessels is the cup in which the wine at Mass is consecrated. It is mentioned in all three scriptural accounts of the institution of the Eucharist and differs little from the drinking vessels normally in use at the time.

Ciborium: A vessel shaped like the chalice but with a cover, in which the consecrated hosts are reserved in the tabernacle and from which the priest distributes Holy Communion.

Concelebration: The celebration of the Eucharist by two or more ministers.

Liturgical colours: The Church has long appreciated that the proper use of colour can help the community to appreciate the mood and spirit of a particular season or feast day. Accordingly Innocent III (1198-1216) introduced a colour sequence which is still followed today. *White* is worn on feasts of Our lord, Our Lady, confessors and virgins, and Sundays during the Easter Season. *Red* is used at Pentecost and the feasts of the Apostles and martyrs. *Violet* is used during Advent, Lent, vigils of certain feasts and funerals. *Rose* is often used on the third Sunday in Advent and on the fourth Sunday in Lent. The use of *black* for funerals now varies from place to place.

Paten: A shallow plate usually of gold or silver on which the large host rests before and after consecration.

Vestments: The Mass vestments originate from the ordinary secular dress of the Roman Empire in the first centuries of Christianity. The principal vestments are:
Amice A square or oblong piece of linen to which two long tapes are attached at the upper corners. Worn like a scarf, it is symbolic of "the helmet of salvation".
Alb (Latin, albus – meaning white) A long white linen garment, a symbol of purity, it is a survival of the ancient tunic or undergarment. It is held neatly in place by the:
Cincture: A long cord worn around the waist.
Stole: A long thin band of silk worn around the neck and shoulders, suggestive of the "yoke of the Lord". It is worn by the priest in the solemn celebration of all the sacraments (the deacon wears it over one shoulder only).
Chasuble: The outermost garment worn by the priest. It is a circular piece of cloth cut in the centre for the head. Over the centuries the shape has been altered to allow greater freedom of movement. The colour of the stole and chasuble varies with the liturgical season (*cf. Liturgical colours*).
In addition to these vestments, the bishop wears the:

Mitre: Originally a soft, low cap, it has developed into a high, stiff hat consisting of two stiffened pieces of cloth joined by soft material.

Pectoral cross: (*Latin,* pectus – meaning breast). A cross worn suspended from the back by a chain or cord.

Ring: Worn on the right hand as a symbol that he is wedded to his diocese.

NO. 2 THE SACRAMENTS

The purpose of the sacraments is to sanctify, to build up the Body of Christ, to give worship to God. Because they are signs they also instruct us and by words and objects nourish, strengthen, and express our faith. We include a short glossary of well-known terms associated with the administration of the sacraments which are here listed in alphabetical order.

Baptistery: The room or place laid aside for the celebration of baptism. The early Christians referred to it as the *fons* (pool) and today the central feature – a large stone vessel containing the baptismal water – is known as the *font.*

Baptismal Name: In the first few centuries of the Church the custom of changing one's name at baptism to express some Christian idea in a name such as Irene (peace) became common. The fourteenth century saw the custom become law and the Ritual of the Council of Trent (1624) instructed parish priests to persuade parents to give their children saints' names and not "strange, laughable, obscene, or idolatrous ones".

Confessional: Place set aside in a church for the celebration of the Sacrament of Penance. The traditional confessional, introduced by St Charles Borromeo in sixteenth-century Milan, was a simple box-like construction with a metal grille between the priest and penitent. Present-day confessionals are variations on the original design but the introduction of "face to face" confession has led to the construction of reconciliation rooms of varying designs around the world.

Gregorian Chant: The form of singing (chant) described by Pope St Pius in 1903 as "the special chant of the Latin Church, who received it alone from the Fathers, has carefully preserved it in her records, and commends it to the faithful as her own". Tradition attributes this form of chant to St Gregory mainly because he gathered the chants of his day into the *Antiphonal.*

Homily: The term used to describe the form of preaching that takes place during a liturgical celebration. The homily, based on the scripture readings and liturgical theme, is regarded as an integral part of the Mass and must always be given at Sunday and feastday Masses. It is also regarded as an essential part of some of the other sacraments.

Oil: Oil is the symbol of strength and has been used from the most ancient times for the consecration of kings. There are three kinds of oil used in the celebration of the sacraments:

Oil of Chrism: Used in the sacraments of baptism, confirmation and orders. These sacraments give the candidate a share in the priestly "character" of Christ (the title "Christ" meaning "the anointed one"). It is also used in the consecration of churches.

Oil of Catechumens: Used in the celebration of baptism and so called because it was originally used for anointing those who were about to be baptised.

Oil of the Sick: Used in the sacrament of Anointing of the Sick. Each year, the three Holy Oils are blessed by the bishop on the morning of Maundy Thursday (Chrism Mass), usually attended by all the priests of the diocese.

Rubric: The directive in a liturgical book describing how prayers are to be recited and ceremonies performed. In the Roman Ritual the practice was followed of printing such an instruction in red (Latin, *ruber*) hence the term Rubric.

Sponsor (Godparent): One who undertakes to foster the faith of a candidate in the sacraments of Baptism and Confirmation. Such a person should be mature, living the faith and able to fulfil a spiritual role for the candidate. By custom each candidate has two sponsors, one of whom must be a Catholic.

Vernacular (meaning "home-born"): The term used to describe the native language of a country as opposed to a language of foreign origin. Following Vatican II the vernacular came to be universally used in the administration of the sacraments although the Council also insisted that the Latin language be preserved in the Latin rites.

NO. 3 DEVOTIONS

The heart of the Church's life is the celebration of the liturgy and, above all, the Eucharist. Every liturgical celebration, because it is an action of Christ the priest and of his Body, the Church, is a sacred action surpassing all others. But there are many "acts of devotion" which, although not part of the Church's sacred liturgy, are recognised by the Church as especially valuable forms of prayer. We include some of the more important of these "Devotions".

Benediction of the Blessed Sacrament: The primary purpose for reserving the Eucharist outside the celebration of Mass is for the distribution of communion to the sick. But from the custom of blessing the sick after communion

arose the practice of blessing the people by making the sign of the cross over them with the sacred host contained in a monstrance or, in simple form, in a ciborium.

Benediction must always be accompanied by at least a brief period of exposition which allows time for "readings of the word of God, hymns, prayers, and sufficient time for silent prayer". This exposition is intended to acknowledge Christ's marvellous presence in the sacrament and invites us to the spiritual union with him that is completed in sacramental communion at Mass.

If a priest or deacon is not available, a minister appointed by the bishop may place the host in the monstrance or the ciborium on the altar, but such a minister cannot give the blessing with the sacrament.

For exposition of the blessed sacrament in the monstrance, four to six candles are lighted and incense is used. Incense is a symbol of prayer: a sign of the sweet-smelling offering which rises from a heart glowing with the love of God.

Forty Hours Devotion *(Quarant Ore):* Arising from the custom of watching in prayer before the Altar of Response on Maundy Thursday, this devotion is a period of extended exposition of the blessed sacrament held with greater solemnity. "It is recommended that solemn exposition of the blessed sacrament should take place once a year in every parish, even though the period of exposition is not strictly continuous."

Rosary: A form of prayer which leads us to contemplate the mysteries of salvation. The mysteries are divided into three groups of five as follows:

The Joyful Mysteries
1. The Annunciation
2. The Visitation
3. The Nativity
4. The Presentation
5. The Finding of Jesus in the Temple

The Sorrowful Mysteries
1. The Agony in the Garden
2. The Scourging
3. The Crowning with Thorns
4. The Carrying of the Cross
5. The Crucifixion

The Glorious Mysteries
1. The Resurrection
2. The Ascension
3. The Coming of the Holy Spirit
4. The Assumption of the Virgin Mary
5. Her Coronation

To help the mind and heart attend to the contemplation of these central events of our faith each mystery is accompanied by the vocal recitation of one *Our Father,* ten *Hail Mary's* and one *Glory Be.* Thus, "the succession of Hail Mary's constitutes the warp on which is woven the contemplation of the mysteries". *(Pope Paul VI)*

The Church strongly recommends the recitation of the family Rosary. Although circumstances make such family prayer difficult "it is a characteristic of the Christian not to give in to circumstances but to overcome them". To help the recitation of the Rosary, beads are generally used.

Angelus: This prayer, recited at morning, noon and evening, provides an opportunity to pause and to contemplate the coming of God among us. It consists in the recitation of three Hail Mary's together with versicle and response and prayer as follows:

1. The Angel of the Lord declared unto Mary. *And she conceived of the Holy Spirit.* Hail Mary, etc.
2. Behold the handmaid of the Lord. *May it be done unto me according to thy Word.* Hail Mary, etc.
3. And the Word was made flesh. *And dwelt amongst us.* Hail Mary, etc.
V. Pray for us, O holy Mother of God.
R. That we may be made worthy of the promises of Christ.

Let us pray: Pour forth, we beseech you, O Lord, your grace into our hearts, that we to whom the Incarnation of Christ, your Son, was made known by the message of an angel, may by his passion and cross be brought to the glory of his resurrection, through Christ our Lord. Amen.

NO. 4 THE CHURCH BUILDING

From the time that Jesus Christ instructed his disciples to make preparations to eat the passover in "the large upper room furnished with couches" (*Luke 22:12*) his followers have set aside a special place for the celebration of the Eucharist. This church building is a sign of the Church, the Body of Christ, united in the worship of the Father. We include a short glossary of terms associated with the church building, which are here listed in alphabetical order:

Bell: At one time the bell-tower was an essential feature of every church building and was used to summon the faithful to divine service. In the Mass, a hand-bell is used to call attention to the principal parts of the Mass.

Chair: The principal "chair" in the church is the celebrant's chair from which he directs the prayer of the assembly. It is normally placed in the centre of the sanctuary facing the people.

Consecration crosses: When a church is solemnly consecrated the bishop anoints the walls in twelve different places with the oil of chrism. Each place anointed in this way is marked with a cross, and a candle-holder is placed beneath this cross. The consecration sets the seal on the church so that it can never afterwards be put to some profane use. The church building is a sign of the Church: with the "twelve apostles for its foundations, Jesus himself for its cornerstone". By custom, a church is also dedicated either to one of the divine Persons, to the Blessed Virgin or to a saint and the church thus becomes known by that title.

Images: In accordance with ancient tradition, images of Christ, Mary and the saints are venerated in churches. The principal image is the cross which "must be easily seen by the congregation and be placed either on the altar or near it".

According to legend the original "image" of Christ was that made by a woman who wiped Jesus' face with a towel as he struggled under the burden of his cross to Calvary. On the cloth was imprinted Christ's face, which became known as "vera icon", which translated from the Latin and Greek means "true picture". Over the years, "vera icon" was corrupted to "Veronica", which became the name of the woman who performed this act of charity. The legend is commemorated in the sixth station of the Stations of the Cross (*see below*).

Lectern: The lectern (or ambo) is the place from which the scripture readings and the homily are proclaimed. The Church instructs that "ordinarily, this should be a fixed pulpit and not a simple movable stand".

Sanctuary: This is the area of the church (generally raised slightly) in which the ministers carry out their functions in the celebration of the liturgy. Placed within the sanctuary area is the altar, which "should be in a central position which draws the attention of the whole congregation".

Stations of the Cross: From the earliest times pilgrims to Jerusalem have retraced our Lord's steps in his passion. At those points where special events in his journey to Calvary took place they stopped to meditate (*Latin,* statio, a standing still). From this custom sprang the construction of imitations of the "Via Dolorosa" in Jerusalem which are to be found in most parish churches around the walls. Each "station" is marked by a wooden cross to which a picture is often added. There are fourteen stations:

1. Jesus is condemned to death.
2. Jesus takes up his cross.
3. Jesus falls the first time.
4. Jesus meets his mother.
5. Simon of Cyrene helps Jesus.
6. Veronica wipes the face of Jesus.
7. Jesus falls the second time.
8. Jesus speaks to the women of Jerusalem.
9. Jesus falls the third time.
10. Jesus is stripped of his garments.
11. Jesus is nailed to the cross.
12. Jesus dies on the cross.
13. Jesus is taken from the cross.
14. Jesus is laid in the tomb.

Tabernacle: The blessed sacrament used to be reserved in a room near the sanctuary or in a cupboard in the wall of the sanctuary. In more recent times it has been reserved in a tabernacle, which must be solid and unbreakable and positioned in the church in a place "that is prominent and properly decorated". At all times a sanctuary lamp is to be kept burning as a sign that the blessed sacrament is reserved.

SECTION 3
The Law of the Church

NO. 1 THE CANON LAW

"A community without law" wrote the late Pope Paul VI, "has never been and will never be anything else than a community of the arbitrary." In the following section we take a closer look at Canon Law, the law of the Church.

What is Canon Law? Canon Law is the body of rules (from the Greek *kanon,* a rule), by which the Church provides guidelines for the faithful to help them come closer to Jesus Christ and his Body, the Church.

Where can we find the Church's law? The laws of the Church are found in a book known as the *Code of Canon Law.* A revised code came into force in 1983. New and altered laws are published in the Acta Apostolicae Sedis (Acts of the Holy See) and come into force three months after publication. The Oriental Churches have their own Code of Law.

Who makes the laws? Those who exercise authority in the Church. The Pope, as successor of St. Peter, is obviously an important legislator and issues new laws in documents known as Papal Constitutions or Apostolic Letters (Motu Proprio). Ecumenical Councils, together with the Pope, can draw up new laws in the form of decrees of the Council. Roman Congregations (the Curia), which link the various facets of the Church's life, can also issue laws binding on the faithful. Conferences of Bishops may promulgate laws binding on all who live in their territory. A local diocese, acting through the bishop or a local synod, can also draw up legislation on certain matters binding all the faithful living in the territory of the diocese. Religious Institutes, acting through their Major Superiors or Chapters, are empowered to draw up certain rules binding on their own members.

Who is obligated by Canon Law? The following are bound by the law of the Church: those who are baptised; those who have reached the age of reason; those who have attained seven years of age. A Catholic is only bound by a Church law if it is in force in the place where he or she is resident. In theory, since baptism constitutes membership of the Church, the Church has jurisdiction over all baptised persons. The Code, however, expressly exempts baptised non-Catholics from Church law in some matters. The Church, of course, recognises that by reason of faith and conscience baptised non-Catholics are not bound in most cases to observe Catholic ecclesiastical law.

What are the main features of the 1983 Code of Canon Law? Like the 1917 Code, which it replaced, the 1983 Code of Canon Law sets out to revise and renew the laws of the Church in accordance with the mission of her Divine Founder. The Code has been revised in the light of the teaching and decisions of Vatican II. The laws, then, reflect the Church's "new" understanding of herself as the People of God, with each member sharing, in his or her own measure, in the threefold priestly, prophetic and kingly office of Christ. Thus the responsibilities and the rights of the laity are emphasised, Hierarchical authority is seen less as a privilege and more as a service. More responsibility for important decisions is given to local hierarchies rather than to the central authority in the Church. The Church's concern for ecumenism is also evident.

What place has law in everyday Christian life? Church law helps us to grasp what under normal circumstances is indispensable for the common good of the Church and for our own individual salvation. But it is important to remember that Church law sets before us the *minimum* demands. The law puts before us in a codified form the minimum efforts of love required to establish order, justice, stability and freedom. But Christian love will desire to go far beyond the lower limits set by law and will constantly search for what God requires of us over and above the codified law.

NO. 2 RIGHTS AND RESPONSIBILITIES

In recent years the Catholic Church has become more aware of its role as protector and guardian of the rights of the individual and all the people in the world. In this section we examine both the rights of the individual in the Church and in the world at large.

What is the basis of human rights? The answer to this question has always fascinated the philosophers and proved to be something of a battleground in the history of human thought.

Some groups, like the Fascists in recent years, have identified *power* as the source of human rights and assert that a person's rights are those which he can impose on others. Another idea is that the rights of the individual are determined by what the *majority* in society hold them to be. Alternatively, some hold that the *state* alone can decide what a person's rights are. Such a theory is the foundation of all totalitarian states. Christianity, however, always points to the mysteries of Creation, Incarnation and Redemption as the source of human rights. As Christians we believe that every person shares in the life of God and so it follows that rights, dignity and responsibilities transcend any one culture, philosophy or political system. They are part of the mystery of God and as such can never really be fully defined or listed.

Nevertheless are there some basic human rights? The Church has always held that there are some basic rights which belong to every human being. This notion of fundamental human rights was described by Pope John XXIII in his encyclical *Pacem in Terris* (1963) as one of the major issues of the modern world.

What are these basic human rights? In the light of the Church's teaching over the last century the following can be regarded as the most important human rights: the rights to life and to housing worthy of human dignity; the right to social security; the right to respect, free enquiry, free expression, and the right to education; the right to full participation in government; the right to free exercise of one's religion and to a free choice of a state in life; the right to a fair share of material goods and full economic rights; the right to free association and assembly; the right to emigrate and immigrate; the right to active sharing in public life and to the legal protection of personal rights even against the state.

What rights does the Catholic have in the Church? It is very important to remember that the divinely established community of the Church is made up of human beings who, because of sin, can sometimes ignore justice and fail to act in charity. We have constantly to remind ourselves that baptism confers upon the Christian full membership of the Church and all the rights to secure a full share in the life of the community.

Can one list these rights? Our understanding of rights and responsibilities in the Church grows as we deepen our common understanding of the mysteries of God. An exhaustive list is for that reason impossible. Some rights are embodied in the Code of Canon Law and include the following: the right to hear the Word of God and share in the sacramental and liturgical life of the Church; freedom to exercise the apostolate and share in the Church's mission; freedom to speak, to be listened to, and to receive objective information on the pastoral needs and affairs of the Church; the right to education, the right to freedom of enquiry and expression in the sacred sciences; freedom to gather and associate together in the Church; the right to protect one's reputation and one's person, to activity in accord with the upright norm of one's conscience, to the protection of privacy; the right not to be deprived arbitrarily of any right or office in the Church.

What is the Church's role on the issue of human rights? Recent popes and numerous hierarchies around the world have challenged Catholics to show themselves as protectors of human rights and to speak in defence of those who have been deprived of them. The Church is also a prophet of human rights in that Christians must try to deepen awareness in a fast-changing world of the new

responsibilities and rights which change brings. The Church must in every way protect both the rights of the individual and the rights of the community as a whole, whether it be Church or State.

NO 3 MINISTRIES

"For the nurturing and constant growth of the People of God, Christ the Lord instituted in the Church a variety of ministries, which work for the good of the whole body." (*Lumen Gentium*) In this section we take a closer look at how each person in the Church is called to exercise a particular ministry in the Church.

What do we mean by ministry? The word ministry is derived from the Latin word meaning "to render service". Within the Church it describes the different ways in which Catholics can exercise functions within the community of the Church. Until fairly recently the word has been used in Catholic circles almost exclusively of the ordained and hierarchical ministries. The use of the word in a wider context than the activity of priests and bishops reflects a deepening vision in the Church of the service exercised by all in the name of Christ.

How many ministries are there? In a very real sense there is only one ministry – the ministry of Jesus Christ. It is Jesus Christ who reaches out to serve the world through the members of his body, the Church. To help our understanding of this mystery, however, we speak of three different types of ministry.

What are they? Ministries undertaken by the baptised; instituted ministries; ordained ministries. The first kind,

ministries undertaken by baptised Catholics, refers to any activity which is undertaken without a formal commission from the Church. One can list here the work of nurses, teachers, social workers. But we must recognise that this type of ministry is not limited to the caring professionals. What of those who work in their local parish or go about their everyday work in a spirit of Christian dedication? The second type of ministry, the instituted ministries, refers to officially recognised forms of service in the Church such as lector, catechist and acolyte. The third type, the ordained ministries, refers to the diaconate, priesthood and episcopate. These ministries are exercised by those who have received the sacrament of Holy Order.

What do we mean by "ecclesial ministry"? This is quite a common phrase these days and simply means that all forms of ministry, if they are to be true and genuine, must be exercised in the context of the *Church's* activity (Greek, *ecclesia*). If teaching, preaching, and other forms of ministry take place outside the context of the community of those who believe, they run the danger of becoming personal ventures with little real relation to the building up of the kingdom of God. For this reason the Church has always regulated and organised the various forms of ministry.

Do these different ministries have different aims? All ministry has as its ultimate aim the preaching and building up of the kingdom of God. Each baptised person is called to do this. As we have seen, however, different tasks, some officially recognised and others unheralded, are undertaken by individuals to build up the community of believers. They are gifts, St Paul tells us, "to build up the body of Christ until we become one in faith and in the knowledge of God's Son, and form that perfect man who is Christ come to full stature." (*Ephesians 4:11-13*) We are encouraged to search in prayer for the particular ministry that Jesus Christ is calling us to in the Church. Perhaps ours is the ministry of listening, of helpfulness, of meekness, or of suffering? Perhaps we are being called by God to the ordained ministry or the religious life? Only in prayer can we discover what God is asking of us and only in the Church can we truly contribute to the building of the kingdom.

NO 4 THE SACRAMENT OF BAPTISM

We have already seen that there are many hundreds of laws of the Church of varying importance and application. Some laws express Christ's direct command; some express the practical needs of church organisation. But *all* express the minimum effort of love required to establish order, justice, stability and freedom. We now include the more important of these laws and begin by looking at those which relate to the sacrament of baptism.

Who are the ordinary ministers of baptism? The ordinary ministers of baptism are bishops, priests and deacons. But in danger of death of any member of the faithful (or even any person who has the requisite intention) should baptise, preferably in the presence of a witness or witnesses. Later, a child who survives should be taken to the parish church to be received solemnly into the Catholic community.

How does one baptise in case of an emergency? Baptism is celebrated by the minister pouring water over the head of the one being baptised and saying at the same time: "I baptise you in the name of the Father, and of the Son, and of the Holy Spirit."

Are there any other ministries associated with the sacrament of baptism? All Christians share in the ministry of building up the faith of the "catechumen" (i.e. the adult preparing for baptism). In the case of the baptism of the young a special role belongs to the parents.

What is the role of the parents in the baptism of children? The parents accept the responsibility of training the child in the practice of the faith and of bringing the child up to keep God's commandments as Christ taught us, by loving God and our neighbour. This obligation is indicated clearly in the solemn celebration of baptism during which the parents publicly ask that their child be baptised; they sign their child with the sign of the cross after the celebrant; they renounce Satan and make their profession of faith; they hold the lighted candle; and they are blessed with the special prayers for mothers and fathers. If one of the parents cannot make the profession of faith (if, for example, he or she is not a Catholic) he may keep silent.

What is the role of godparents? In the baptism of infants the godparents' role is secondary. If necessary, they should be ready to help in the spiritual education of their godchild. The godparent should be: a) sufficiently mature; b) already initiated as a Christian (by baptism, confirmation and the Eucharist); c) a member of the Catholic Church. A baptised person of a non-Catholic Church may act as a Christian witness provided that the other sponsor is a Catholic.

How soon should children be baptised after birth? The Church encourages Catholic families to have their children baptised within the first few weeks after birth. This is because of Christ's teaching on the fundamental importance of baptism. If there is any danger of death the baby must be baptised immediately and anyone can baptise. You pour water over the baby, at the same time saying the words: "I baptise you in the name of the Father, and of the Son, and of the Holy Spirit."

The date of the baptism will depend partly on the mother's health, for it is important that she is present; and partly on the time needed for the preparation of the parents.

If parents have experienced some difficulties with the practice of their faith it may he helpful to allow a little longer in order to clarify their own beliefs and to rebuild a life of faith within their family.

How are adults baptised into the Catholic Church? In 1978 the Church re-introduced the "catechumenate" for adults wishing to be baptised into the Catholic Church. The "catechumen" is to be prepared for baptism over a suitable period of time but enters into a more intense period of preparation at the beginning of Lent in a ceremony of "election" or "enrolment" of names. Baptism, followed by confirmation and the Eucharist, is normally celebrated at Easter.

How is a baptised Christian of another communion received into full communion with the Catholic Church? After a suitable doctrinal and spiritual preparation the baptised Christian is received by the bishop or a priest appointed by him. In the prescribed ceremony he or she makes a profession of faith. The sacrament of baptism may not be repeated, and only if there is reasonable doubt as to the fact or validity of earlier baptism is it permissible to confer baptism conditionally.

NO 5 THE SACRAMENT OF CONFIRMATION

Through the sacrament of confirmation, those who have been born anew in baptism receive the gift of the Holy Spirit. Having received the character of this sacrament, they are "bound more intimately to the Church" and "they are more strictly obliged to spread and defend the faith both by word and by deed as true witnesses of Christ". In this section, we look at those laws which relate to the sacrament of confirmation.

Who is the ordinary minister of confirmation? The ordinary minister of confirmation is a bishop. But all priests who baptise an adult or a mature child, or receive them into full communion with the Catholic Church, may administer the sacrament. In addition, if there is danger of death any priest may confirm. It is the minister's responsibility to ensure that the reception of confirmation is properly recorded. This is done by notifying the parish where the confirmed person was baptised, where it is entered into the baptismal registry. (When a baptised Catholic is married, the record of marriage is similarly entered into the registry of baptisms.)

Are there any other ministries associated with the sacrament of confirmation? It is the responsibility of all Christians to prepare the baptised for confirmation. The initiation of children into the full sacramental life of the Church is for the most part the responsibility and concern of Christian parents. The sponsors, too, have a special ministry.

What is the role of the sponsor? The sponsor brings the candidate to receive the sacrament, presents the candidate to the minister for anointing, and later is to help the candidate to fulfil his baptismal promises faithfully under the influence of the Holy Spirit. It is desirable that the godparent at baptism, if available, also be the sponsor at confirmation. (This is a recent change of law which expresses more clearly the relationship between baptism and confirmation and also makes the responsibility of the sponsor more effective.) However, another suitable person may act as sponsor and even the parents themselves may present their children for confirmation.

What is the appropriate age for confirmation? In the early Church baptism and confirmation were usually celebrated at the same time, for most people entering the Church were adults. Today, it remains true that the age for confirmation can be the same as for baptism and this norm is applied in the following cases: a) children who have reached an age when they are able to receive instruction in the faith; b) infants and children who are in danger of death; c) all adults. In the Eastern Churches infants, too, are confirmed at the time of baptism. In the Latin Church, however, the confirming of those baptised in infancy is postponed. "For pastoral reasons ... Episcopal conferences may choose an age which seems more appropriate, so that the sacrament is conferred at a more mature age." The requirements for confirmation are a state of grace, proper instruction and the ability to renew one's baptismal promises.

What is the effect of confirmation? The effect of confirmation is the gift of the Holy Spirit. Confirmation draws us more deeply into the life of the Church. This living of the Christian life is expressed in the fulfilment of the two-fold love of God and neighbour, and in the fulfilment of the commandments of the Church.

What are the principal commandments of the Church? The principal commandments of the Church are dealt with in detail in this section, *The Law of the Church,* and are contained in the Church's Canon law. As an aid to memory, six commandments have traditionally been listed as of particular importance. These laws oblige Catholics to:

1. Assist at Mass on every Sunday and holy day of obligation, and to avoid unnecessary work on these days.
2. Fast and abstain on the days appointed.
3. Confess grave sins at least once a year.
4. Receive Holy Communion during Easter time.
5. Contribute to the support of the Church.
6. Observe the laws of the Church concerning the solemnisation of marriage.

No 6 THE EUCHARIST

We read in the Acts of the Apostles that the early Christian community "remained faithful to the teaching of the apostles, to the brotherhood, to the breaking of bread, and to the prayers." *(Acts 2:42)* Since the Eucharist, the Mass, is the focal point of the whole of our Christian life, the Church has been careful to lay down certain regulations to ensure that we also remain faithful "to the breaking of the bread". In this section we examine some of the Church's discipline more closely.

Who are the ministers of the Eucharist? The Roman Missal tells us that: "Every authentic celebration of the Eucharist is directed by the bishop, either in person or through the priests who are his helpers." It is the function of the ordained ministers, therefore, to *direct* our celebration of the Eucharist. But since this mystery stands at the centre of the Church's life everyone must take his or her own part according to his place and function in the Church. There is a variety of what are called special ministries which are exercised at any celebration of Mass, such as acolytes, readers, servers, musicians. The ordained deacon, in particular, exercises a very special ministry in the celebration of the Eucharist.

Can someone who is not a bishop or priest preside at Mass? No. It is the teaching of the Church that only the bishop or an ordained priest can preside at Mass and consecrate the species of bread and wine.

Does it matter what sort of bread or wine is used? Yes. At the Last Supper Jesus Christ specified bread and wine as the elements of this sacred meal. The Church has therefore been very concerned that the elements used in the celebration of the Mass really are bread and wine. To prevent any confusion in this matter the Church has laid down certain regulations. The bread used must be made of wheat and recent enough to rule out any possibility of corruption. Although leavened bread is valid, the Church prescribes that in the Latin rite unleavened bread be used. In this matter the priest must follow the rules of his own rite. The Church is also strict with regard to the type of wine used. For validity it must be grape wine. The priest must also mix a little water with the wine in accordance with the Oriental custom that Jesus no doubt followed.

When are we obliged to attend Mass? The faithful are obliged to attend Mass on all Sundays and feast days of obligation. This precept of sharing in the Sunday Mass is satisfied in those places where the local bishop has determined that the celebration may be anticipated the preceding evening. Feast days of obligation vary greatly from country to country. Obviously, the obligation does not apply to those who for a grave reason, such as sickness, cannot assist at Mass. In such circumstances the Church recommends spending some time in prayer, either personally or as a family.

How often is one obliged to receive Holy Communion? Since the Lateran Council of 1215 every Catholic who has reached the age of discretion has been required to receive Holy Communion at least once a year "at Easter or thereabouts". This obligation, together with the obligation of celebrating the sacrament of penance if one has committed mortal sin, make up the "Easter Duties" which, in most countries, must be undertaken between the First Sunday of Lent and Trinity Sunday. The commandment of Easter communion lays down the minimum requirement and frequent communion (at least once a week) is actively encouraged by the Church. Recent changes in law regarding the Eucharistic fast have encouraged frequent communion.

What are the regulations regarding the Eucharistic fast? In 1964 a decree from Rome laid down the following rules which apply at whatever time of day Holy Communion is received. 1. Water may be taken at any time. 2. Solid food may be taken up to one hour before Holy Communion. 3. Alcoholic drinks in moderation and other drinks, with or without food, may be taken up to one hour before Holy Communion. 4. Those who are sick and the elderly, and those who care for them, are not bound by the fasting laws. (Canon 919/3)

Are there any other regulations regarding fasting? In Britain, and in many other countries, there is an obligation to fast (one full meal and two lighter meals in the course of the day) and abstain (from flesh meat) on Ash Wednesday and Good Friday. The law of fasting obliges all Catholics except the sick between the ages of 18 and 59. The law of abstinence obliges all Catholics over the age of 14. At other times (e.g. on Fridays especially) Catholics must practise self-denial either by continuing to abstain or by any other act of self-denial (e.g. attending Mass, making the Stations, saying the Rosary, or visiting someone sick or lonely) in union with the death of our Saviour on the cross.

180

When can children receive Holy Communion? St Pius X's decree *Quam singulari* (1910) stated that children should be admitted as soon as they can distinguish between the Bread of the Eucharist and ordinary bread and be instructed at least "in the mysteries of the faith necessary for salvation" according to their capabilities. While the Church is careful that children do not approach the altar unprepared, there has been a constant tradition of not limiting reception to mere knowledge alone. The phrase "according to their capabilities" protects the rights of those who may be suffering from some learning difficulty but possess the gift of faith. Such children need very special care and instruction, but a full and perfect knowledge of Christian doctrine is not required of them.

No 7 THE SACRAMENT OF ORDERS

We have already seen that within the Church there are "ministries undertaken by the baptised", "instituted ministries" and "ordained ministries" (*The Law of the Church No. 3*). Now we look at some of the important laws regarding the "ordained ministries" of deacon, priest and bishop who share in a particular way in Christ's ministry through the sacrament of Holy Orders.

Who is the minister of the sacrament of orders? The minister of the sacrament of orders is a bishop. He alone can ordain a priest or deacon. For the ordination of a bishop, the principal consecrator must be assisted by at least two other consecrating bishops and his ordination must be approved by the Bishop of Rome.

How does the ordained minister share in a particular way in Christ's ministry? The ordained minister shares in Christ's ministry in a particular way by being set apart to preach the Gospel and to build up the Body of Christ. And so, at the ordination of a bishop, the principal consecrator questions the bishop-elect on his ministry.

"An age-old custom of the Fathers decrees that a bishop-elect is to be questioned before the people on his resolve to uphold the faith and to discharge his duties faithfully. Are you resolved as a devoted father to sustain the people of God and to guide them in the way of salvation in cooperation with the priests who share your ministry?"

How does the ordained minister express his intention to serve the people of God? The ordained minister states his intention to serve the people of God at the time of ordination in response to questions asked by the ordaining minister. In addition, the ordained minister in the Latin Church normally undertakes to live a life of celibacy. Celibacy is not demanded by the very nature of the priesthood but it is a sign of that new humanity which Christ raises up in the world through his Spirit: a humanity "not born of blood, nor of the will of flesh, nor of the will of man, but of God". (*John 1:13*) Also, it enables the minister to hold fast to Christ with undivided heart and through him, to the service of God and all people.

Are all ordained ministers bound to celibacy? All ordained ministers in the Latin Church are bound to celibacy except for deacons who are married at the time of ordination. However, in accordance with the traditional disciple of the Church, a married deacon who has lost his wife cannot enter a new marriage. In recent times married clergy from other Christian denominations have been exempted from the law of celibacy.

How do the faithful support the ordained minister? Just as the ordained minister serves the needs of the people of God, so it is a responsibility resting on every Christian to "contribute to the support of the Church". This support, in the first instance, is given by serving the Church in love of God and neighbour. It is to be expressed, too, by assisting ordained ministers both spiritually and financially. Writing on the subject of priestly virtue, Pope Paul VI explained that "all the faithful should encourage their fathers in Christ to overcome the difficulties of every sort which they meet as they fulfil their duties ... and by their devoted and warm friendship they can be of great assistance to the Church's ministers". (*Sacerdotalis Caelibatus*)

What is a Mass stipend? A Mass stipend is the customary offering given to a priest which obliges the priest to apply the fruits of the Mass for the special intention of the donor. The custom has led to abuses in the past but continues to serve as a reminder of the obligation of supporting the ordained ministers. The stipend also serves as a monetary equivalent of the early offerings of bread and wine. Customary stole fees (for the conducting of baptisms, marriages and funerals) are also offered to the minister, but the poor are not expected to make any offering if unable to do so. The minister of a sacrament may not request, directly or indirectly, any compensation for his ministry, no matter what the reason or the occasion. Nonetheless, the minister may expect to be materially supported by those whom he serves.

No 8 THE SACRAMENT OF MARRIAGE

"In marriage, let the blessings of marriage be loved: fidelity, offspring, and the sacrament." The words of St Augustine provide a framework for a deeper understanding of the Church's marriage law – a law which seeks to protect the wonderful relationship of marriage and apply the teachings of Jesus to this human reality which he has raised to the dignity of a sacrament. The following questions look at some common queries regarding the marriage laws of the Church.

How does the Church regard fidelity in marriage in today's more permissive world? The Church has tried particularly hard in recent years to deepen her understanding of the notion of fidelity by reflecting on the Scriptures and Tradition. Scripture scholars are in general agreement that on the question of fidelity the teaching of Jesus is clear and without qualification. "So then, what God has united, man must not divide ... The man who divorces his wife and marries another is guilty of adultery against her." (*Mk. 10:9-11*)

What then, does Church law say about the permanency of marriage? It is divine law that there are two essential properties or characteristics of any marriage – unity and indissolubility. In plain English the term *unity* means that one man has one wife and vice-versa. *Indissolubility* is understood by the Church to mean that every marriage is permanent and cannot be dissolved.

What is the Pauline Privilege? In 1 Corinthians 7:10-16 St Paul answers several questions regarding marriage. He asserts the teaching of Jesus on the indissolubility of marriage which he stresses "is not from me but from the Lord". He then goes on to say that in the case of an unbaptised couple, if one of the partners becomes a Christian, and "the unbelieving partner does not consent, they may separate; in these circumstances, the brother or sister is not tied". This teaching, which we refer to as the Pauline Privilege is, he says, "from me and not from the Lord". We can restate Paul's teaching today as follows: two unbaptised marry, one partner becomes a Christian and the other partner cannot accept this and so departs. If inquiries show that departure really was because of the deserted party's new faith, then by reason of the Pauline Privilege, the bishop can permit remarriage.

What is the Petrine Privilege? It is the teaching of the Church that a marriage between two Christians is indissoluble because it is sacramental. But what about the case of a marriage between a Christian and a non-Christian? Since this marriage is not sacramental in the strict sense, the Church recognises the power of the Vicar of Christ, the Pope, to dissolve such a marriage. This power we call the Petrine Privilege. There must, of course, be very serious reasons before such a power is invoked. One example would be if a party of the first marriage which ended in civil divorce now wants to become Catholic and remarry. Investigations will always be made to prove that the first marriage was non-sacramental. The Petrine Privilege is often referred to as a case of dissolution "in favour of the faith".

What does the term "convalidation of marriage" mean? In order to preserve the sanctity of marriage the Church insists that a marriage must be solemnised before a Catholic priest and two witnesses. (This law may be dispensed for a serious reason and under strictly determined conditions.) It may well happen that a couple, for one reason or another, fail to have their marriage solemnised in this way. The term "convalidation" refers to the later validation and blessing of the marriage by the Church after the couple have solemnly renewed their matrimonial consent. The restoration of such a couple to full communion with the Church is always an extremely happy event although, for obvious reasons, it is often done privately.

What is an "annulment" of marriage? An annulment is an official declaration by the Church that a particular marriage in fact and in law never existed. Annulment cases are handled by special Marriage Tribunals who work under the authority and guidance of the bishops. After intensive investigation into every aspect of the marriage in question, the Marriage Tribunal makes a decision which takes into due account the jurisprudence of the Church.

How does the Church look on divorce? Divorce is a very unfortunate fact of modern life. The Church does not see divorce as a way of ending one marriage so as to leave the way open to entering another: Christ preached the permanence of marriage. In our civil law, a divorce settlement can also be the simplest way of sorting out legal and financial problems and regulating care of and access to children. So the Church, always regretting the breakdown of a marriage and subsequent separation, accepts this side of a civil divorce as a way of regulating the civil effects of a breakdown; not as dissolving the bond of marriage. And Pope John Paul II, in his encyclical on the Family ("Familiaris Consortio", para 82-84) speaks at length on how the Church must care for those who have suffered divorce.

What is a "mixed marriage"? This is a phrase often used by Catholics of a marriage where one of the partners is not a Catholic. It is not an ideal phrase as it does not take into account the considerable difference between marriages of Catholics with baptised non-Catholic Christians and those marriages which take place between Catholics and unbaptised. Some people prefer to talk of the marriage between a Catholic and a practising Christian of another Church as an "Inter-Church marriage".

What does the Church ask of the Catholic partner in a mixed marriage? The Church has always recognised that a mixed marriage can prove to be a real obstacle to the unity of the couple. Pope Paul VI stressed this point in his Apostolic Letter on the subject (1970) when he reminded Catholics that such marriage is "by its nature an obstacle to full spiritual communion of the married partners". For this reason the Church requires of both partners to the marriage a very careful preparation. Real ecumenical understanding is vital and many hierarchies have strongly advised priests to work closely with non-Catholic ministers in preparing couples for mixed marriages. The Church particularly asks the Catholic party to a marriage to recognise the duty of preserving his or her own faith and to remember that it is never permitted to expose oneself to the danger of losing it. This is divine law and is absolute.

Is anything particularly required of the Catholic party in a mixed marriage? The Catholic party in a mixed marriage is obliged not only to remain steadfast in the faith but also to do everything in their power to see to it that the children are baptised and brought up in the Catholic Church. The promise to do so must be made orally or in writing (according to the prescriptions of the various hierarchies) by the Catholic partner before permission will be given by the bishop for the marriage to proceed in the Church. The Church recognises, of course, that as much respect must be paid to the parental rights of the non-Catholic as to those of the Catholic whose conscience must have regard to the teaching of the Church. It is essential, therefore, that a couple contemplating marriage should agree before the wedding about the baptism and education of any children they might have. The non-Catholic is *not* required to make any undertaking in this matter, formally or informally.

But it is only right and prudent that he is informed prior to the marriage of the obligations of conscience laid by divine law on his or her Catholic partner.

Does this promise have any meaning when, despite all the efforts of the Catholic, the children are baptised and educated in the faith of the non-Catholic? Yes. In a special Directory issued in 1977 the English Bishops stressed that the promise was still full of meaning as it made the following demands on the Catholic: 1. that he intends to play an active part in the Christian life of the marriage and of his family: 2. that he will do all he can in the actual circumstances of his marriage to draw the children to the Catholic faith. 3. that he will deepen his faith in continuing to study it so as to have a fruitful dialogue with his partner on matters of the faith and be able to answer the questions of his children: 4. that he will pray with his family, especially asking for the grace of unity, as our Lord would have willed it.

No 9 THE SACRAMENT OF PENANCE

In one of his letters Saint Ambrose reminded the people of 4th century Milan that the Church "possesses both water and tears: the water of baptism, the tears of penance." It is Catholic belief that because of human weakness the Lord instituted a special sacrament for the pardon of sins after baptism. We look at some of the regulations for the celebration of this sacrament.

Have there been changes in the way the sacrament is celebrated? Yes. Following a decree of the Second Vatican Council that "the rite and formulas of penance are to be revised in such a way that they may more clearly express the nature and effects of this sacrament", a new ritual for penance was issued by Pope Paul VI in 1973. There has, of course, been considerable change in the way this sacrament has been celebrated over the centuries but the Church has always retained its essential elements.

What are the essential elements? The essential element which must be present in the sinner who has been moved by the Holy Spirit to approach the sacrament is conversion to God with his whole heart. There must be present in him or her an inner conversion of heart (contrition) the marks of which are true sorrow for the sins committed and a firm intention to lead a new life. This inner conversion of heart brought about by the Holy Spirit is expressed in the following ways: confession made to the Church, due satisfaction, and amendment of life.

Who are the ministers of this sacrament? It has been the constant teaching of the Church that God grants pardon for sin in and through his Church by the ministry of bishops and priests. In exercise of this ministry of reconciliation, however, the Church requires more of the priest than the power of ordination. A priest who "hears confessions" must have received the faculty or jurisdiction to do so from the proper authorities. Any priest, however, even though he does not have the required jurisdiction may validly and lawfully absolve a penitent who is in danger of death.

How is the sacrament celebrated? The Rite of Penance (1973) prepared by the Congregation of Divine Worship lays down three ways of celebrating the sacrament of Penance. The Rite for reconciliation of individual penitents; of several penitents with individual confession and absolution; of several penitents with general confession and absolution. Individual confession and absolution is regarded as the ordinary way for the faithful to reconcile themselves with God and the Church. It is recognised, nevertheless, that "particular, occasional circumstances" may permit or require the use of general absolution for a group of penitents who have not made a previous individual confession. The use of this rite, however, is restricted by Church law and its application is left to the bishop of the diocese and his national episcopal conference.

What do we mean by the sacramental seal? This refers to the strict obligation laid upon the priest to treat as absolutely secret everything revealed by the penitent in the sacrament with a view to obtaining absolution. Canon 983 states: "The sacramental seal is inviolable. Accordingly it is absolutely wrong for a confessor in any way to betray the penitent, for any reason whatsoever, whether by word or by any other fashion." An 11th century canon declared that "if any priests usurps and makes public the secrets of Penance he shall be deposed and spend all the days of his life in pilgrimage." A priest who violates the seal today incurs, *ipso facto*, an excommunication most specially reserved to the Holy See.

How often are we obliged to approach the sacrament? Innocent III, in his presiding role at the 4th Lateran Council in 1215, promulgated the following decree: "Each member of the faith of both sexes who has reached the age of discretion must confess his grave sins at least once a year ..." The law of annual confession of grave sins still binds all Catholics today who have reached the use of reason and discretion. It must be understood that this law refers to the confession of grave sin and does not bind those, who with the grace of God, are not conscious of grave sin.

No 10 THE SACRAMENT OF ANOINTING

The Church's Introduction into the Rite of Anointing of the Sick reminds us that the sacrament prolongs the concern which the Lord himself showed for the bodily and spiritual welfare of the sick. Some of the legislation concerning this sacrament was changed in 1972 and we now include the more important of these laws relating to Anointing.

Who is the minister of the Rite of Anointing? The minister of the anointing of the sick is a bishop or priest. Viaticum (Holy Communion received in danger of death) may be given by a deacon or another minister who has been appointed by the bishop to distribute the Eucharist to the faithful.

faith and devotion, not misusing this sacrament by putting it off. All who care for the sick should be taught the meaning and purpose of anointing.

7. Anointing may be conferred upon sick people who have lost consciousness or lost the use of reason, if, as Christian believers, they would have asked for it were they in control of their faculties.

8. When a priest has been called to attend a person who is already dead, he should pray for the dead person, asking that God forgive his sins and graciously receive him into his kingdom. The priest is not to administer the sacrament of anointing. But if the priest is doubtful whether the sick person is dead, he may administer the sacrament conditionally.

How do we prepare for the sacrament of anointing? For the immediate preparation all that is required is a small table, covered with a white cloth, on which there should be a crucifix and two lighted candles. As the priest will probably also bring Holy Communion, a small bowl of water should be provided for him to wash his fingers. The family should leave the room if the sick person wishes to confess his sins, but after confession they should return to join in the prayers.

The remote preparation for the sacrament is prayer and the sick should be encouraged to pray when they are alone or with their families, friends, or those who care for them. Priests should also be ready to pray with them.

Are there other ministries associated with the sacrament of anointing? All those who help the sick share in the loving ministry of Christ, who was born to overcome the evil of suffering. The family and friends of the sick have a special share in this ministry of comfort. "If the sickness grows worse, they have the responsibility to inform the priest and by their kind words prudently to dispose the sick person for the reception of the sacraments at the proper time."

When should a Catholic be anointed? The Introduction to the Rite of Anointing regulates the celebration of the sacrament in the following way:

1. The Letter of James states that the anointing should be given to the sick to raise them up and save them. There should be special care and concern that those who are dangerously ill due to sickness or old age receive this sacrament.

A prudent or probable judgement about the seriousness of the sickness is sufficient; in such a case there is no reason for scruples, but if necessary a doctor may be consulted.

2. The sacrament may be repeated if the sick person recovers after anointing and then falls sick again or, if during the same illness, the danger becomes more serious.

3. A sick person should be anointed before surgery whenever a dangerous illness is present.

4. Old people may be anointed if they are in a weak condition although no dangerous illness is present.

5. Sick children may be anointed if they have sufficient use of reason to be comforted by this sacrament.

6. In public and private catechesis, the faithful should be encouraged to ask for the anointing and as soon as the time for the anointing comes to receive it with complete

No 11 ECUMENISM

The Church's laws reflect her deepest concerns: they express, in human language, her preoccupation for finding the most effective means of preaching the Gospel. Mindful of the Lord's prayer on the night before he died that his followers "may all be one", the Church has, where possible, regulated her life to achieve this aim. We now look at some recent changes in legislation which reflect the Church's concern for Ecumenism.

What is Ecumenism? The Decree on Ecumenism of Vatican II began with the words: "Promoting the restoration of unity among all Christians is one of the chief concerns of the Second Sacred Ecumenical Synod of the Vatican". It continued: "Discord among Christians openly contradicts the will of Christ, and causes damage to the most holy cause of proclaiming the good news to every creature." Ecumenism is the name given to the Church's "chief concern" to remove the "scandal" of disunity among Christians.

What are the principal changes in the Church's legislation as a result of her efforts to restore unity among Christians? Several changes have already been mentioned in this *Catechism* (e.g. laws regulating "mixed marriages"; laws regulating the reception of baptised Christians into full communion with the Catholic Church). The principal areas of changes in legislation relate to common prayer and worship, common study, and co-operation in the field of social and pastoral action. All these changes are founded on the recognition of the life of faith held in common among all Christians and, indeed, the further recognition of the God-given dignity and aspirations held in common by Christians and non-Christians.

What are the principal changes regulating common prayer and worship? The Church distinguishes between "prayer offered in common" and "sharing in liturgical worship". The former (ecumenical or inter-faith services) which consist of an assembly for listening to the Scriptures and for prayer are encouraged by the Church as "a very effective means of winning the grace of unity". Such prayer is especially suitable for common concerns, such as Church unity, peace in the world, public mourning. It is often appropriate that ministers of different denominations unite in leading the prayer. However, because "sharing in liturgical worship" ought to express the unity which already exists, such sharing "cannot be applied indiscriminately as a means to the re-union of Christians". Catholics are permitted to attend the liturgical worship of other denominations for such reasons of family unity, friendship and courtesy and may join in responses provided they are not at variance with the Catholic faith; but may not receive communion or actively exercise a ministry in such worship.

Is it permissible for Christians not in communion with the Catholic Church to receive Holy Communion? The Church teaches that "Celebration of the sacraments is an action of the celebrating Community, carried out within the Community, signifying the oneness in faith, worship and life of the Community. Where this unity of sacramental faith is deficient, the participation of the separated brethren with Catholics, especially in the sacraments of the Eucharist, Penance and Anointing of the Sick, is forbidden. Nevertheless, since the sacraments are both signs of unity and sources of grace the Church can, for adequate reasons, allow access to those sacraments to a separated brother or sister. This may be permitted in danger of death or in urgent need (during persecution, in prisons) if the separated brother or sister has no access to a minister of his own Communion, and spontaneously asks a Catholic priest for the sacraments – so long as he declares a faith in these sacraments in harmony with that of the Church, and is rightly disposed." (*Ecumenical Directory, n.55*)
Because of the close ties between the Catholic Church and the Eastern Orthodox Churches by reason of their possession of the priesthood and the Eucharist, sacramental sharing is permitted under specified circumstances.

May Catholics be cremated? The preference of the Church has always been for the burial of the dead in a grave or tomb. However, provided there is no danger of scandal (e.g. suspicion of denial of the resurrection of the body) cremation is approved by the Church.

Are Catholics forbidden to join the Masons and similar organisations? This question is not directly related to the Church's concern for ecumenism although Catholics were forbidden, under pain of excommunication, to join the

Freemasons as a secret order responsible for anti-Catholic activity. This prohibition stands, for membership still conflicts with the Catholic's primary allegiance to the Church in which true fellowship should first be sought.

No 12 THE ORGANISATION OF THE CHURCH
Throughout *Faith for the Future* we have frequently referred to Christ's "ordering" of his Church into an hierarchical community. This "ordering" into bishop, priest and deacon is of divine institution. We conclude this section of the *Supplement* by taking a brief look at those aspects of the Church's life which are of human origin and have developed over the centuries to promote the more effective organisation of the Church. For convenience, we list the titles alphabetically.

Apostolic Delegate: The papal representative in a country where the Holy See has no regular diplomatic representative. The Delegate keeps the Pope informed on ecclesiastical affairs in the territory assigned to him.

Archbishop: Generally the metropolitan bishop, i.e. the principal bishop in a province which comprises one or more (suffragan) dioceses.

Auxiliary: A bishop who assists the diocesan bishop in the running of the diocese. If he is appointed with the right to succeed the residential bishop at the latter's death

or retirement he is called a "coadjutor bishop".

Canon: Generally a member of the Cathedral Chapter whose primary function is to give God solemn worship in the Cathedral. "It is for the Cathedral Chapter, besides, to fulfil those roles entrusted to it by law or by the diocesan Bishop." (Canon 503)

College of Consultors: This is a diocesan body whose role is to assist in the governance of the diocese. (Canon 502 ff)

Cardinal: A member of the supreme council of the Church. A cardinal is appointed by the pope and on his death the college of cardinals is responsible for the election of a successor. In origin the cardinals were the "parish priests" of Rome and this is recognised in the contemporary practice of giving to each cardinal the care of one of the churches in Rome. Most of the cardinals have pastoral responsibility for the major dioceses around the world but some are in charge of the various sections of the Roman Curia.

Curia: An organ of government. The curia is either:

i) Diocesan: the central governing office of the diocese, generally headed by the Vicar-General and including those responsible for administration, finance and the Marriage Tribunal. It is organised not only for administering the diocese but also for carrying out the works of the apostolate. *Or:*
ii) Roman: The central administrative body of the Church which governs in so far as it is necessary in the name of the pope and with his authority for the good of the churches. The Congregations, Tribunals, Offices and Secretariats of the Curia are roughly equivalent to the ministries in a modern government and each is headed by a cardinal. The Second Vatican Council stated that "the Fathers of the Council believe it would be most advantageous if these departments would give a greater hearing to laypeople who are outstanding for their virtue, knowledge and experience. Thus they, too, will have an appropriate share in Church affairs."

Dean: Generally the head of the group of parishes in a given area.

Episcopal Conference: A kind of council in which the bishops of a given nation or territory jointly exercise their pastoral office. In Great Britain, there are two Episcopal Conferences: England & Wales and Scotland.

Episcopal Vicar: One who enjoys for a certain part of the diocese, or for a determined type of activity, or for the faithful of a determined rite, the same responsibilities as the vicar-general.

Legate: A representative of the Holy See either as a nuncio (*see below*) or for a particular occasion.

Monsignor: In origin, the title given to members of the papal household. The title remains attached to offices or distinctions ordinarily bestowed by the pope.

Nuncio: The permanent representative of the Holy See in a country and who enjoys diplomatic status as an ambassador.

Papal decorations: Honours bestowed on lay people by the pope. They are of three kinds:

i) Titles of nobility.

ii) Orders of Knighthood – of which there are six orders, the best known being the *Order of St. Gregory* given for distinguished service to the Church.

iii) Medal and Crosses. The best known of these are the cross *Pro Ecclesia et Pontifice* given for services in education, missions, etc. And the *Benemerenti* medal given "to one who deserves well".

Parish Priest: One who assists the bishop in a given area of the diocese. The parish priest is sometimes helped by an assistant or curate.

Synod of Bishops: A council of bishops which meets periodically to assist the Roman Pontiff by sharing explicitly his responsibility for the universal Church. The Synod is made up of bishops throughout the world, meets every four years, and is a new council in the Church, only being established since 1965.

Vicar Apostolic: One who governs an area of mission territory but where there is no established hierarchy. Usually a bishop, he is directly answerable to the Holy See.

Vicar-General: One appointed by the bishop to assist him in the administration of his diocese and who is empowered to act in his name in most matters except those which the bishop reserves to himself. He has the right of precedence over all other priests of the diocese. Sometimes, the vicar-general is an auxiliary bishop.